R. Gupta's®

Kerala
GENERAL KNOWLEDGE

A Complete Description of History, Geography, Flora & Fauna, Economy, Polity, Culture and many more ...

by
RPH Editorial Board

AF366955

2021
EDITION

Ramesh Publishing House, New Delhi

Published by:
O.P. Gupta *for* Ramesh Publishing House
Admin. Office:
12-H, New Daryaganj Road, Opp. Officers' Mess,
New Delhi-110002 ℡ 23261567, 23275224, 23275124

E-mail: info@rameshpublishinghouse.com
Website: www.rameshpublishinghouse.com

Showroom:
● Balaji Market, Nai Sarak, Delhi-6 ℡ 23253720, 23282525
● 4457, Nai Sarak, Delhi-6, ℡ 23918938

Book Code: R-1588

ISBN: 978-93-5012-365-2

HSN Code: 49011010

Contents

❏❏❏

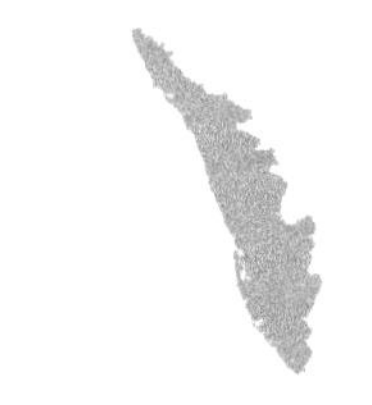

WHO'S WHO

The State Government

Governor
Arif Mohammad Khan

Pinarayi Vijayan

Council of Ministers

✦ **Pinarayi Vijayan**	Chief Minister
✦ **A.K. Balan**	Welfare of Scheduled Castes, Scheduled Tribes and Backward Classes; Law; Culture; Parliamentary Affairs
✦ **E. Chandrasekharan**	Land Revenue and Housing
✦ **K. T. Jaleel**	Higher Education and Minority Welfare
✦ **Kadakampally Surendran**	Co-operation, Tourism and Devaswoms
✦ **M. M. Mani**	Minister for Electricity
✦ **J. Mercykutty Amma**	Fisheries; Harbour Engineering; Cashew Industry
✦ **A. C. Moideen**	Local Self Governments
✦ **K. Raju**	Forests, Animal husbandry, Zoos
✦ **Ramachandran Kadannappally**	Ports; Museums; Archaeology and Archives
✦ **T. P. Ramakrishnan**	Labour and Excise
✦ **C. Raveendranath**	General Education
✦ **A. K. Saseendran**	Transport
✦ **K. K. Shailaja Teacher**	Health; Social Justice and Woman and Child Development

(v)

- ✦ **G. Sudhakaran** — Public Works; Registration
- ✦ **V. S. Sunil Kumar** — Agriculture
- ✦ **P. Thilothaman** — Food and Civil Supplies
- ✦ **T.M Thomas Isaac** — Finance; Coir
- ✦ **K. Krishnankutty** — Water Resources
- ✦ **E.P. Jayarajan** — Industries, Sports and Youth Affairs

Heads of the State Administration

Governors

Name	Tenure
Dr. B. Ramakrishna Rao	November 22, 1956 – July 1, 1960
Sri V.V. Giri	July 1,1960 – April 2, 1965
Sri Ajith Prasad Jain	April 2, 1965 – February 6, 1966
Sri Bhagwan Sahay	February 6, 1966 – May 15, 1967
Sri V. Viswanathan	May 15, 1967 – April 1, 1973
Sri N.N. Wanchoo	April 1, 1973 – October 10, 1977
Smt. Jyothi Vencatachellum	October 14, 1977 – October 27, 1982
Sri P. Ramachandran	October 27, 1982 – February 23, 1988
Smt. Ramdulari Sinha	February 23, 1988 – February 12, 1990
Sri Swaroop Singh	February 12, 1990 – December 20, 1990
Sri B. Rachaiah	December 20,1990 – November 9, 1995
Sri P. Sivasankar	November 12, 1995 – May 1, 1996
Sri Khurshid Alam Khan	May 5, 1996 – January 25, 1997
Sri Sukhdev Singh Kang	January 25, 1997 – April 18, 2002
Sri Sikander Bakht	April 18, 2002 – February 23, 2004
Sri T.N. Chaturvedi	February 25, 2004 – June 23, 2004
Sri R.L Bhatia	June 23, 2004 – July 9, 2008
Sri R.S. Gavai	July 10, 2008 – September 07, 2011
Sri M.O.H. Farook	September 8, 2011 – January 26, 2012
Dr. H.R Bhardwaj (in charge)	January 26, 2012 – March 22, 2013
Sri Nikhil Kumar	March 23, 2013 – March 10, 2014
Smt. Sheila Dikshit	March 11, 2014 – September 4, 2014
Sri. P. Sathasivam	September 5, 2014 – September 5, 2019
Sri. Arif Mohammed Khan	September 6, 2019 —

Chief Ministers

Name	Tenure
Sri E.M.S. Namboothiripad	April 5, 1957 – July 31, 1959
Sri Pattom A. Thanu Pillai	February 22, 1960 – September 26, 1962
Sri R. Sankar	September 26, 1962 – September 10, 1964
Sri E.M.S. Namboothiripad	March 6, 1967 – November 1, 1969
Sri C. Achutha Menon	November 1, 1969 – August 1, 1970
Sri C. Achutha Menon	October 4, 1970 – March 25, 1977
Sri K. Karunakaran	March 25, 1977 – April 25, 1977
Sri A.K. Antony	April 27, 1977 – October 27, 1978
Sri P.K. Vasudevan Nair	October 29, 1978 – October 7, 1979
Sri C.H. Mohammed Koya	October 12, 1979 – December 1, 1979
Sri E.K. Nayanar	January 25, 1980 – October 20, 1981
Sri K. Karunakaran	December 28, 1981 – March 17, 1982
Sri K. Karunakaran	May 24, 1982 – March 25, 1987
Sri E.K. Nayanar	March 26, 1987 – June 17, 1991
Sri K. Karunakaran	June 24, 1991 – March 16, 1995
Sri A.K. Antony	March 22, 1995 – May 9, 1996
Sri E.K. Nayanar	May 20, 1996 – May 13, 2001
Sri A.K. Antony	May 17, 2001 – August 29, 2004
Sri Oommen Chandy	August 31, 2004 – May 12, 2006
Sri V.S. Achuthanandan	May 18, 2006 – May 14, 2011
Sri Oommen Chandy	May 18, 2011 – May 19, 2016
Sri Pinarayi Vijayan	May 25, 2016 –

Speakers Since 1957

Name	Tenure
Sri R. Sankaranarayanan Thampi	April 27, 1957 – July 31, 1959
Sri K.M. Seethi Sahib	March 12, 1960 – April 17, 1961
Sri C.H. Mohammed Koya	June 9, 1961 – November 10, 1961
Sri Alexander Parambithara	December 13,1961 – September 10,1964
Sri D. Damodaran Potti	March 15, 1967 – October 21, 1970
Sri K. Moideenkutty Haji	October 22, 1970 – May 8, 1975
Sri T.S. John	February 17, 1976 – March 25, 1977
Sri Chakkeeri Ahmedkutty	March 28, 1977 – February 14, 1980
Sri A.P. Kurian	February 15, 1980 – February 1, 1982
Sri A.C. Jose	February 3, 1982 – June 23, 1982

Name	Tenure
Sri Vakkom B. Purushothaman	June 24, 1982 – December 28, 1984
Sri V.M. Sudheeran	March 8, 1985 – March 27, 1987
Sri Varkala Radhakrishnan	March 30, 1987 – June 28, 1991
Sri P.P. Thankachan	July 1, 1991 – May 3, 1995
Sri Therambil Ramakrishnan	June 27, 1995 – May 28, 1996
Sri M. Vijayakumar	May 30, 1996 – June 4, 2001
Sri Vakkom Purushothaman	June 6, 2001 – September 4, 2004
Sri Therambil Ramakrishnan	September 16, 2004 – May 24, 2006
Sri K. Radhakrishnan	May 25, 2006 – May 31, 2011
Sri G. Karthikeyan	June 02, 2011 – March 07, 2015
Sri N. Sakthan	March 12, 2015 – May 2016
Sri P. Sreeramakrishnan	May 2016 —

Deputy Speakers Since 1957

Name	Tenure
Smt. K.O. Aysha Bai	May 6, 1957 – July 31, 1959
Smt. A. Nabisath Beevi	March 15, 1960 – September 10, 1964
Sri. M.P. Mohammed Jafferkhan	March 20, 1967 – June 26, 1970
Sri. R.S. Unni	October 30, 1970 – March 22, 1977
Sri. P.K. Gopalakrishnan	July 6, 1977 – October 23, 1979
Sri. M.J. Zakaria	February 21, 1980 – February 1, 1982
Sri. K.M. Hamsakunju	June 30, 1982 – October 7, 1986
Sri. Korambayil Ahammed Haji	October 20, 1986 – March 25, 1987
Smt. Bhargavi Thankappan	April 2, 1987 – April 5, 1991
Sri. K. Narayana Kurup	July 19, 1991 – May 14, 1996
Sri. C.A. Kurian	July 17, 1996 – May 16, 2001
Sri. N Sundaran Nadar	July 4, 2001 – May 12, 2006
Sri. Jose Baby	June 20, 2006 – May 14, 2011
Sri N. Sakthan	June 28, 2011 – March 10, 2015
Sri. Palode Ravi	December 02, 2015 – May 2016
Sri. V. Sasi	May 2016 —

CURRENT AFFAIRS

ASCEND 2020 HELD IN KOCHI

A two day Global Investors Meet—ASCEND 2020 was held in Kochi, Kerala at Lulu Bolgatty International Convention Centre, Grand Hyatt, from January 9-10, 2020. The meet was inaugurated by the Chief Minister of Kerala Shri Pinarayi Vijayan and was organised by states Department of Industries. Totally ₹ 1 lakh crore worth investment proposals were received. Addressing ASCEND 2020, Chief Minister Pinarayi Vijayan said that a proposal to subsidise a part of the wage commitment of newly-set up industries for the first five years in under consideration. He said workers in the newly-established institutions would get a monthly wage subsidy for first five years. This benefit will be available only to those units which provide ESI and PF benefits to workers. Women employees will get at least ₹ 2,000 more than their men counterparts under the proposed scheme. Besides, the bar on women factory workers being put on night shift would be lifted. It will be the responsibility of the employer to ensure their safe transport an stay during the night. Observing that the government has amended several regulations to help investors, Vijayan said many more such measures are on the anvil to enable a fast, transparent and corruption-free investment regime in the state. He said for investments worth at least ₹ 250 crore or projects that give direct employment to at least 1,000 persons, the government would relax the 15-acre ceiling on holding land. This would encourage private industrial estates. Another investor-friendly step announced by the CM is that the government would relax rules that regulate roadside construction depending upon the width of the road. As of now, on the side of roads having a width of eight metres, only structures of up to 18,000 square feet are allowed. This would be relaxed to enable real estate projects.

KERALA EXTENDS MATERNITY LEAVE BENEFITS

On October 17, 2019 the Kerala govt, as a first in the nation has planned to extend maternity leave benefits to teachers and other staff of private educational institutions, including the people working in the unaided sector. This extension of maternity leave under the Maternity Benefit Act was approved by the Central govt and when once amended, Kerala would be the first state to provide maternity benefits in the private educational sector. According to the law, employees can avail 26 weeks' maternity leave with salary and in addition, the employer should provide ₹ 1000 as medical allowance. It is an Act to protect the employment of women during the time of her maternity entitles her of a 'maternity benefit' which is full paid absence from work – to take care for her child.

1

KERALA : AT A GLANCE

Kerala is a small coastal State, situated in the southwest peninsular part of India. It lies between latitudes 8°18'N and 12°48'N and between longitudes 74°52'E and 77°22'E. It has an area of 38863 sq. km which represents only 1.18 per cent of the total area of India. But it supports a population of 3,34,06,061 which is 2.47 per cent of the total population of the Country (Census 2011). The disproportion between its area and population is reflected in the density which in 2011 was 860 persons to per sq. km. This is the third highest density among the States of the Union, higher density being registered only by the State of Bihar (1106) and West Bengal (1028).

When India became free, Kerala was made up of two princely states, Travancore and Cochin. Malabar was under the direct administration of the British. One of the first steps taken by independent India was to amalgamate small states so as to make them viable administrative units. In pursuance of this policy the Travancore and Cochin states were integrated to form Travancore-Cochin State on July 1, 1949. But Malabar remained as part of the Madras Province. Under the States Re-organization Act of 1956, Travancore-Cochin State and Malabar were united to form the State of Kerala on November 1, 1956.

Kerala at a glance (as per Census of 2011)	
Area	38863 sq. km
Language	Malayalam
Population	3,34,06,061
Males	1,60,27,412
Females	1,73,78,649

KERALA: IMPORTANT FACTS

Date of Formation	—	November 1, 1956
Location	—	South West tip of the India's main land/North latitude between 8°18' and 12°48'; East longitude between 74°52' and 77°22'
Capital	—	Thiruvananthapuram
Area	—	38,863 Sq. Km.
Principal Language	—	Malayalam
Currency	—	Indian Rupee
State Festival	—	Onam
State Animal	—	Elephant
State Bird	—	Hornbill
State Flower	—	Kanikonna
State Tree	—	Coconut Tree
State Food	—	Rice
Neighbouring States/UTs	—	Tamil Nadu, Karnataka and Lakshadweep
Demography Population (2011)	—	3,34,06,061
Male (2011)	—	1,60,27,412
Female (2011)	—	1,73,78,649
Sex Ratio		
(Females per 1000 males)	—	1,084
Population Density (2011)	—	860/sq. km
Urban Population (2011)	—	1,59,34,926
Rural Population (2011)	—	1,74,71,135
Decadal Growth Rate (2011)	—	4.9%
Child Population (0-6 years)		
Total (2011)	—	34,72,955
Rural Child Population (2011)	—	18,23,664
Urban Child Population (2011)	—	16,49,291
Scheduled Caste Population		
(In million)	—	3.03
Scheduled Tribe Population		
(in Million)	—	0.48
Maternal Morality Ratio 2001-03		
(SRS 2007)	—	110

Crude Birth Rate (2011)	—	14.8%
Crude Death Rate (2011)	—	7%
Total Fertility Rate (NFHS-111)	—	1.9
Infant Mortality Rate (2011)	—	13
Life expectancy	—	71
Male Life Expectancy	—	71
Female Life Expectancy	—	73.62
Per capita Income	—	1,36,811
Total Literate	—	2,81,35,824
Male Literate	—	1,37,04,903
Female Literate	—	1,44,30,921
Literacy Rate (%)	—	94.0
Male Literacy Rate (%)	—	96.1
Female Literacy Rate (%)	—	92.1
Development Blocks	—	152
Districts	—	14
Revenue Divisions	—	21
Sub-Districts	—	75
Villages	—	1664
No. of Towns	—	520
Grama Panchayats	—	941
District Panchayats	—	14
Assembly Seats	—	140+ 1 Anglo-Indian Nominee
Lok Sabha Seats	—	20
Rajya Sabha Seats	—	9
Municipalities	—	87
Municipal Corporations	—	6
Cantonments	—	1 (Kannur)
No. of Urban Agglomerations	—	19
Township	—	1 (Guruvayoor)
Legislative Constituencies	—	140
Educational Districts	—	41
Sub Educational Districts	—	163
Universities	—	14

Other Information

Seat of High Court	Kochi (Ernakulam)
Highest Populated District	Malappuram
Lowest Populated District	Wayanad
Largest District	Palakkad
Smallest District	Alappuzha
Longest River	Periyar
Highest Peak	Anamudi
Largest Lake	Vembanad Lake
National Highways	11 (1781.57 km)
Road Length	2,05,545 km
Railway Route	1,588 km
Airports	3 (Thiruvananthapuram, Kochi and Kozhicode)
Regional Passport Offices	4 (Thiruvananthapuram, Kochi, Kozhicode and Malappuram)
Annual Rainfall	3,428 mm (2006)
Major Religions	Hinduism, Islam and Christianity
Number of Rivers	44
Number of Navigable Rivers	41
Total Length of inland water ways	1,687 km

District-wise Area

District	Area (sq. km)
1. Thiruvananthapuram (Trivendrum)	2192
2. Kollam (Quilon)	2491
3. Alappuzha (Alleppey)	1414
4. Pathanamthitta	2637
5. Kottayam	2208
6. Idukki	4358
7. Ernakulam	3068
8. Thrissur (Trichur)	3032
9. Palakkad (Palghat)	4480
10. Malappuram	3550
11. Kozhikode (Calicut)	2344
12. Wayanad	2131
13. Kannur (Cannanore)	2966
14. Kasargode	1992

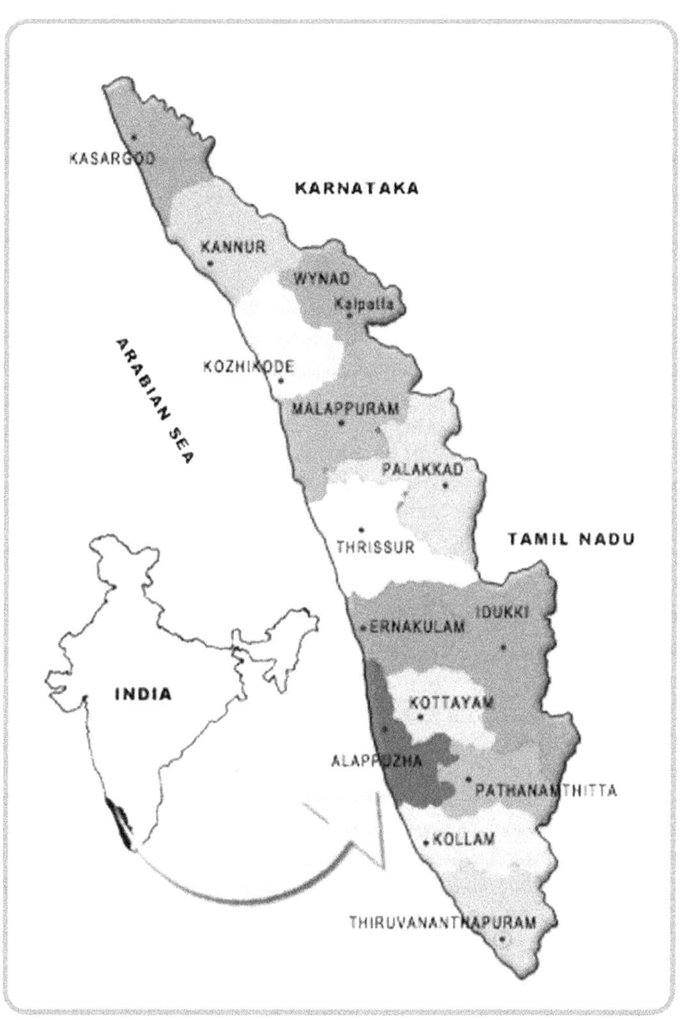
KASARGOD
KARNATAKA
KANNUR
WYNAD
Kalpatta
ARABIAN SEA
KOZHIKODE
MALAPPURAM
PALAKKAD
THRISSUR
TAMIL NADU
IDUKKI
ERNAKULAM
INDIA
KOTTAYAM
ALAPPUZHA
PATHANAMTHITTA
KOLLAM
THIRUVANANTHAPURAM

KERALA : HISTORY TIMELINE

AD

52	—	St. Thomas Mission to Kerala.
68	—	Jews migrated to Kerala.
630	—	Huang Tsang in Kerala.
788	—	Birth of Sankaracharya.
820	—	Death of Sankaracharya.
825	—	Beginning of Malayalam Era.
851	—	Sulaiman in Kerala.
1292	—	Italian traveller Marcopolo reached Kerala.
1295	—	Kozhikode city was established.
1342-1347	—	African traveller Ibn Batuta reached Kerala.
1440	—	Nicholo Conti in Kerala.
1498	—	Vasco da Gama reached Calicut.
1504	—	War of Cranganore (Kodungallor) between Cochin and Kozhikode.
1505	—	First Portuguese Viceroy De Almeida reached Kochi.
1510	—	War between the Portuguese and the Zamorin at Kozhikode.
1573	—	Printing Press started functioning in Kochi and Vypinkotta.
1616	—	Captain William Keeling reached Kerala.
1663	—	Capture of Kochi by the Dutch.
1694	—	Thalassery Factory established.
1695	—	Anjengo (Anchu Thengu) Factory established.
1721	—	Attingal Revolt.
1729	—	Marthanda Varma becomes king of Travancore.
1731	—	Sree Padmanabha Swami Temple was rebuilt by Marthanda Varma.
1741	—	Battle of Kulachal—Marthanda Varma defeated the Dutch.
1750	—	Thrippadidhanam.
1755	—	Last Mamamkom festival at Tirunavaya.
1766	—	Haidar Ali invades Malabar Kingdoms.

1772	—	*Samkshepa Vedartham*, the first book in Malayalam was published.
1792	—	Treaty of Sreerangapatanam.
1797	—	Revolution of Pazhassi.
1805	—	Death of Pazhassi Raja.
1809	—	Kundara Proclamation of Velu Thampi.
1809	—	Velu Thampi commits suicide.
1812	—	Kurichiya revolt against the British.
1831	—	First census taken in Travancore.
1834	—	English education started by Swatithirunal in Travancore.
1847	—	*Rajyasamacharam* the first newspaper in Malayalam, published.
1855	—	Birth of Sree Narayana Guru.
1865	—	Pandarappatta Proclamation.
1891	—	The first Legislative Assembly in Travancore formed. Malayali Memorial.
1895–96	—	Ezhava Memorial.
1904	—	Sreemulam Praja Sabha was established.
1920	—	Gandhiji's first visit to Kerala.
1920-21	—	Malabar Rebellion.
1921	—	First All Kerala Congress Political Meeting was held at Ottapalam, under the leadership of T. Prakasam.
1924	—	Vaikom Satyagraha.
1928	—	Death of Sree Narayana Guru.
1930	—	Salt Satyagraha.
1931	—	Guruvayur Satyagraha.
1932	—	Nivarthana Agitation.
1934	—	Split in the congress. Rise of the Leftists and Rightists.
1935	—	Sri P. Krishna Pillai and Sri E.M.S. Namboothiripad jointly formed the Communist Party in Malabar.
1936	—	Temple Entry Proclamation, allowing the lower castes (untouchables) to enter temple.
1937	—	Travancore University established (in 1957 it is re-named Kerala University).
1940	—	The first hydroelectric project of Kerala was started at Pallivasal.
1941	—	Kayyur Samaram.
1946	—	Punnapra Vayalar Revolt.
1948	—	The first Ministry in Travancore assumes charge with Sri Pattom Thanu Pillai as Chief Minister.
1949	—	Integration of Travancore and Kochi.
1952	—	Consequent to the General Election of December 1951, a new ministry headed by Sri A.J. John assumes charge.

1954	—	General Election in Travancore-Cochin. P.S.P. Ministry headed by Sri Pattom Thanu Pillai and supported by the Congress, sworn in.
1954	—	Mahi was united with Indian Union.
1956	—	Formation of the Kerala State (November 1).
1957	—	General Election. The first Communist Ministry headed by Sri E.M.Sankaran Namboothiripad assumes power.
1959	—	Beginning of the Liberation Movement. Kerala put under President's rule.
1960	—	Sri V.V. Giri appointed Governor of Kerala.
1961	—	Kerala Postal Circle established.
1963	—	Land Reforms Act enacted in Kerala.
1965	—	First Jnanapith Award was given to G. Sankara Kurup.
1968	—	Municipal Elections all over Kerala. Kozhikode University established.
1969	—	Resignation of the EMS Ministry. Sri C. Achutha Menon sworn in as Chief Minister.
1970	—	Death of Sri Mannathu Padmanabhan. Death of Sri Pattom Thanu Pillai.
1972	—	Formation of Idukki District.
1974	—	Death of former Union Defence Minister Sri V.K. Krishna Menon.
1976	—	Prime Minister Smt. Indira Gandhi inaugurates the Railway Broad Gauge Line between Ernakulam and Trivandrum.
1979	—	President's rule in Kerala for the fifth time.
1980	—	The first ship built in Cochin shipyard, Rani Padmini launched.
	—	Formation of Wayanad District.
1981	—	Punalur Liquor tragedy.
	—	Pottekkad wins the 1980 Jnanapith award for his work *Oru Desathinte Katha.*
1984	—	Kasargode, the 14th district of Kerala comes into existence.
1986	—	Pope John Paul II visits Kerala.
1989	—	The first literate town in India—Kottayam.
1990	—	Ernakulam declared the first fully-literate district of India.
	—	Smt. Padma Ramachandran becomes the first woman to be appointed as the Chief Secretary of Kerala.
1991	—	Kerala declared the first fully-literate state in the country.
	—	Sree Chithira Thirunal Balarama Varma, former Maharaja of Travancore passes away.
1992	—	Alleppey—Kayamkulam railway line inaugurated.
1996	—	Right Livelihood award given to Kerala Sastra Sahitya Parishad.
1997	—	K.R. Narayanan becomes the President of India.

1998	—	E.M.S. (First Chief Minister of Kerala) passes away.
1999	—	Kayamkulam Thermal Project commissioned.
2000	—	International status given to the Nedumbassery airport in Ernakulam.
2001	—	A.K. Antony sworn in as the Chief Minister of Kerala.
	—	UNESCO accepted Kudiyattom as a most valued art form of humanity.
	—	Government banned the use of Endo sulphan as it is injurious to health of people.
	—	First Malayalam audio novel 'Ithanente Peru' written by Sakkariya published.
2002	—	Sikandar Bakht becomes Kerala Governor
	—	First Malayalam Playback singer, Sarojini, dies.
	—	Kumarakom boat tragedy.
	—	Kerala becomes India's first child-friendly state.
	—	Jeevan TV becomes first Malayalam channel to telecast English news.
	—	Dr. Kamala Surayya is selected for the Ezhuthachan Award.
2003	—	Kerala's first Coast-Guard station is started at Vizhinjam.
	—	Vellanadu Panchayat in Trivandrum becomes the country's first fully-computerised Panchayat.
	—	Global Investors Meet (GIM) in Cochin inaugurated by the Prime Minister A.B.Vajpayee.
	—	Communal Riots in Maradu.
	—	The state's first heart transplant successfully done in the Medical Trust Hospital (Ernakulam).
2004	—	Kerala government decides to start Jalanidhi Project.
	—	Kerala Governor Sikandar Bakht dies.
	—	Anamudi forest area is proclaimed a National Park.
	—	Kerala wins the 59th Santhosh Trophy defeating Punjab.
	—	Tsunami brings disaster to Kerala coastal villages.
2005	—	Kerala Government bans online lottery.
	—	Kerala Legislature's first woman Deputy Speaker K.O. Ayisha Beevi dies.
	—	Retired High Court Judge T.K. Chandrasekharadas is appointed the Ombudsman.
	—	Famous writer and cartoonist O.V. Vijayan dies.
2006	—	Justice V.K. Bali is appointed the Chief Justice of Kerala High Court.
	—	Famous literary critic and writer Prof. M. Krishnan Nair dies.
	—	P. Kamal Kutty is appointed the Chief Election Commissioner.
	—	Muttathu Varkey Award 2006 is given to Kamala Surayya.
	—	K. Radhakrishnan sworn in as the speaker of 12 Kerala Legislative Assembly.

	—	Justice N. Dinakar is appointed the state Human Rights Commission Chairman.
2007	—	Thiruvananthapuram district declared Child Beggar-Free Zone.
	—	Disaster Management Authority formed Chief Minister as Chairman and Minister for Revenue as Vice Chairman.
	—	State government declared Vallamkali (Boat race) as sport event.
	—	Silent Valley National Park declared as buffer zone.
2008	—	Chief Minister V.S. Achuthanandan inaugurated the Ramakkalmedu Windmill Project.
	—	Government decided to setting up of country's first aqua park for ornamental fish production and marketing at Kadungalloor, near Aluva.
	—	Government decided to celebrate October 13 as State Sports Day.
2009	—	A Rs. 9.56 crore inland container terminal under public and private participation was inaugurated in Kottayam.
2010	—	First Architecture College of Kerala opened.
2011	—	Malappuram (Kerala) Off-campus of the Aligarh Muslim University (AMU) starts functioning.
	—	Kerala High Court okeyed opening of first Indian-Islamic bank in the state.
2012	—	Prime Minister Manmohan Singh inaugurated Kochi Metro Rail on September 13.
2013	—	Kerala cabinet ratified the Kerala Abkari Act Amendment Ordinance 2013 which envisages raising the age for buying and selling liquor from 18 to 21.
	—	Government decided to establish a New Action Force to deal with the threat of Maoists.
2014	—	Kerala government dilutes liquor policy.
2015	—	Kerala achieved 100 per cent mobile density.
2016	—	President Pranab Mukherjee declared Kerala as the first digital state of the country; Pinarayi Vijayan sworn-in as new CM on May 25, 2016.
2017	—	Kerala government proposes stray Dog Zoos; PM Narendra Modi inaugurates Kochi Metro.

❏❏❏

3

HISTORY

Pre-Historic Kerala

Kerala is believed to have originated by the withdrawal of sea, when Parasurama threw his axe from Gokarnam to Kanyakumary. Kalidasa's *Raghuvamsam* mentions about Kerala. Parasurama divided Kerala into 64 villages and donated them to Brahmins. Famous Rock-cut caves in the Ambukuthi hills in the Wayanad district is known as *Edakkal Caves*. The pre-historic people of Kerala were belonged to the *Negrito race* and *Proto Australoids*. From 3000 BC onwards Kerala had trade relations by sea with the Indus Valley people. Early inhabitants of Kerala belonged to the last phase of *Middle Stone Age*. Writings in the Edakkal Caves belonged to the Dravida Brahmi script. *Chathanparambu* near Farrokh is a famous pre-historic site in the Malabar region.

The first recorded background of Kerala seems inside the inscriptions in the Mauryan Emperor, Ashoka (269-232 B.C.). In these inscriptions, Ashoka refers to 4 independent kingdoms that lay for the south of his empire. These were the kingdoms in the Cholas, the Pandyas, the Keralaputras and the Satiyaputras. Amongst them, the Keralaputras or the Cheras, as they had been known as, reigned in excess of Malabar, Cochin and North Travancore—all part of present-day Kerala. They managed to preserve their independence for the reason that they had been on very good terms using the Terrific Maurya. Otherwise, Ashoka, who was a fantastic empire builder, would certainly have attempted to bring these kingdoms beneath his tutelage. The four South Indian Kingdoms prolonged a hand of friendship in direction of the Mauryas. It was actually Hobson's choice for them, possessing currently skilled the Mauryan onslaught during the reign of Ashoka's predecessor, Bindusara (297-272 B.C.).

The Sangam Age

The Sangam Age refers on the period during which Sangam literature was composed. Sangam literally signifies academy and these terrific functions in Tamil had been published within the initial 4 centuries from the Christian era. Tradition has it that the initial three academies met at Madurai and were attended by kings and poets. Having said that, the literature composed in the 1st Sangam is no longer extant.

Tolkappiyam: The earliest do the job on Tamil grammar, was composed during the 2nd Sangam.

Ettutogai: The 3rd Sangam created an exceptional collection of Tamil literature recognized as Ettutogai ("Eight Anthologies"). These anthologies give us a comprehensive description from the political, social and financial disorders of that period.

The Chera Kingdom

The Sangam Age witnessed 3 political powers ruling the region which now constitutes the State of Kerala. These were the Ays within the south, the Cheras in Central Kerala and Ezhimalas to north. The Ays established a kingdom which in its halcyon days, prolonged from Tiruvalla within the north to Nagercoil inside the south. Antiran, Titiyam and Atiyan had been the most prominent of the Ay rulers.

The Ezhimalas as well ruled through an intensive area that covers the current Kannur and Wayanad districts of North Kerala. Nevertheless, the Cheras had been probably the most conspicuous from the dynasties and founded a powerful kingdom in Kerala.

The first Chera ruler was Perumchottu Utiyan Cheralatan—a modern on the excellent Chola, King Karikalan. Right after suffering a humiliating defeat on the hands of Chola ruler on the battle of Venni, he committed suicide.

His son, Imayavaramban Nedum Cheralatan, another Chera ruler, succeeded him. During his lengthy rule of 58 years, Imayavaramban Nedum Cheralatan consolidated the Chera Dynasty and extended its frontiers. He inflicted a crushing defeat on his sworn enemies, the Kadambas of Banavasi. Imayavaramban's reign is of unique significance on the improvement of artwork and literature. Kannanar was his poet laureate.

Having said that, the greatest Chera King was Kadalpirakottiya Vel Kelu Kuttuvan, who is also identified using the mythical hero in the Silappadigaram (The Jewelled Anklet). Silappadigaram is 1 of 3 terrific Tamil epics of Sangam Age. The other two are Manimegalai and Sivaga-Sindamani. The wonderful Tamil poet, Paranar, refers to his military exploits which includes his well-known victory at Mogur Mannan and Kongar. Kuttuvan was the proponent in the Patni (spouse) cult. The cult emphasised the utter devotion of a wife in direction of her husband. He devoted a temple at Vanchi to Kannagi (the female protagonist of Silappadigaram), as well as the current Kurumba Bhagavati Temple at Kodungallor (Cranganore) is modelled on it. Kannagi's devotion in the direction of her husband was legendary.

Though the Cheras had their capital at Vanchi in the interior, they had the famous harbour towns of Tyndis and Muziris on the Arabian Sea coast for trade. They seemed to have attracted a good deal of Roman trade. There are vivid descriptions in Sangham literature of Yavana ships coming to Muziris, laden with gold and waiting for pepper, the black gold of the Romans, at some distance from the shore. The hoards of Roman gold coins unearthed from Kottayam and Eyyal in Kerala authenticity to such statements. There were a number of other minor chieftains who flourished in different parts of Kerala.

Trade

Contact with the Mauryan empire gave the first impulse for the transformation of tribal policy into civilized polity. The stimulus of overseas trade provided by the Roman empire in the first three centuries of the Christian era triggered off the next phase of development in Tamilakam.

The geographical advantages, *i.e.*, the abundance of pepper and other spices, the navigability of the rivers connecting the high mountains with the seas and the discovery of favourable trade winds which carried sailing ships directly from the Arabian coast to Kerala in less than forty days, combined to produce a veritable boom in Kerala's foreign trade. The harbours of Naura near Kannur, Tyndis near Quilandy, Muziris near Kodungallor and Bacare near Alappuzha owed their existence primarily to the Roman trade. Roman contact with Kerala might have given rise to small colonies of Jews and Syrian Christians in the chief harbour towns of Kerala. The Jews of Kochi believe that their ancestors came to the west coast of India as refugees following the destruction of Jerusalem in the first century AD.

Brahmin Settlement

The fourth and fifth centuries witnessed the decline and fall of the western Roman empire. A shriveling of the Roman sea trade followed, leading in its turn, to a decline of the harbour towns like Tyndis and Muziris. Further, political incursions from the north into Tamilakam took place. The traditions of Namboothiris (Kerala Brahmins) recorded in the Keralolpatti chronicle refer to Mayurvarman, the Kadamba king, as their patron during the period after Parasurama. A Kadamba record of the 5th century at the Edakkal cave in Wayanad bears testimony to the Kadamba presence in Kerala.

The last phase of the Sangam age coincided with a silent revolution that was brewing within the social system in Kerala. By about the 8th century, a chain of thirty-two Brahmin settlements had come up, which eventually paved the way for the social, cultural and political separation of Kerala from the Tamil country, in due course. These colonies were capable of producing a great philosopher, Sankaracharya.

Sri Sankara was born in the village of Kaladi in central Kerala. He was an intellectual giant of the 9th century, who saved the Hindu orthodoxy through the synthesis of cults and who can well be ranked with St. Thomas of Acquinas in clarity of thought and understanding. He was a product of the post Sangam, new Aryan settlements of Kerala, who were far removed from the cradle-land of the Indo-Gangetic civilization.

The whole of Kerala came to be covered by a network of temple centered Brahmin settlements. Under their control, these settlements had a large extend of land, number of tenants and the entailing privileges. With more advanced techniques of cultivation, socio-political organization and a strong sense of solidarity, the Brahmins gradually formed the elite of the society. They succeeded in raising a feudal fighting class and ordered the caste system with numerous graduations of upper, intermediate and lower classes. In due course, the consolidation of these settlements and the establishments of their ascendancy gradually led to the evolution of a new Malayalee language and a new Malayalee culture, the separate identity of Kerala was in the making.

The 2nd Chera Empire

Just following the eclipse on the Kalbhras, the Second Chera Empire created its appearance in the annals of Kerala historical past. Mahodyapuram (modern Kodungalur) was its funds. It was founded by Kulasekhara Alvar (A.D. 800–820), one from the 12 Alvars. Alvars were Tamil saints who composed and sang hymns in praise of Vishnu (The Preserver in the Hindu Holy Trinity of Creator-Preserver-Destroyer). They had been exponents of Bhakti (devotional) cult in South India. The Alvars gave a fantastic impetus to the Bhakti cult in South India between the seventh plus the 10th centuries. Kulasekhara Alvar was a scholar along with a fantastic patron with the arts. He composed five dramas—the Perumal Tirumozhi in Tamil, and Mukundamala, Tapatisamvarna, Subhadradhamala and Vichchinnabhiseka—all in Sanskrit, which testify to his scholarship.

Rajasekhara Varman (A.D. 820–44)

He succeeded Kulasekhara Alvar. He founded the 'Kollam Era' of Kerala, which started inside A.D. 825. He is also reputed to get issued the Vazhappali Inscription, the 1st epigraphical file with the Chera Kingdom. Rajasekhara Varman was followed by Sthanu Ravi Varman (A.D. 844–55), a modern with the Chola King, Aditya I (A.D. 870-906).

The Tillaisthanam Inscription signifies that he was on pleasant terms with the Chola monarch. His reign witnessed a flourishing trade between Kerala and China. This is borne out by the Arab merchant Sulaiman who visited India in 851. His 1st enjoy was astronomy and Sankaranarayana, who composed the astronomical operate Sankaranarayaniyam, adorned his court.

After Rajasekhara's death, hostilities broke out between the Cheras and the Cholas, which continued until the disintegration in the Chera Kingdom. The Pandyas of the Madurai also concerned on their own within the conflict.

Rama Varma Kulasekhara (A.D. 1090–1102) was the last from the Chera Kings. He shifted his capital to Quilon when the Cholas sacked Mahodyapuram during his reign.

The Medieval Kingdoms

The period after the dissolution of the Second Chera Empire of the Kulasekharas witnessed the rise of several small kingdoms in Kerala. The important ones are Venad (Travancore), the Perumpadappu Swarupam (Cochin), the Nediyirippu Swarupam of the Zamorins of Calicut. The minor principalities are Desinganad, Attingal, Karunagappally, Karthikappally, Kayamkulam, Purakkad, Pantalam, Tekkumkur, Vadakkumkur, Punjar, Karappuram, Anchi Kaimals, Edappally, Parur, Alangad, Cranganore, Airur, Talappilly, Valluvanad, Palghat, Kollengode, Kavalappara, Parappanad, Kurumpranad, Kottayam, Cannanore, Nileswaram and Kumbla.

The Venad Kingdom

Following the fall of Kulasekharas, Venad emerged as an independent power. The kingdom reached its zenith under Udaya Marthanda Varma (1175–1195) and Ravi Varma Kulasekhara (1299–1314). An effective ruler, Udaya Marthanda Varma was the architect of a brilliant administrative method for temples. The copper plates, which he issued during his rule, and which had been referred to as the Kollur Madham Plates and the Tiruvambadi Inscription of 1183, testify to this fact.

Ravi Varma Kulasekhara was the most crucial ruler from the dynasty. He was a brave and active warrior. He brought peace and order towards the strife-torn Pandya Empire, following Malik Kafur, lieutenant of the Delhi Sultan, Ala-ud-din Khilji (1296–1315), ravaged it. His reign saw the improvement of art and understanding. A scholar and musician himself, he patronised intellectuals and poets throughout his tenure. The Sanskrit drama Pradyumnabhyudayam is ascribed to him. Trade and commerce also flourished throughout his rule and Quilon became a well-known centre of company and enterprise.

Following the death of Ravi Varma Kulasekhara, the historical past with the Venad Kingdom is not of special curiosity. The kingdom lingered on till the centre with the 18th century just before it disintegrated.

Cochin

Nothing much is known about the Cochin royal house (Perumpadappu Swarupam) until the arrival of the Portuguese in the fifteenth century. The Cochin ruler claims to be a descendant of the Kulasekharas. The only important ruler of Cochin was Saktan Tampuran (1790–1805) who introduced the system of central administration with the advice of the British Resident Colonel Munro.

Emergence of Calicut

Throughout the medieval period, Calicut rose to prominence from the ashes of mighty Kulasekhara Empire, within the northern component of Kerala. The Zamorins (actually Lord in the Sea) were the hereditary rulers of Calicut who traced their lineage towards the old Perumal dynasty of Kerala. Calicut emerged as a key seaport throughout the reign on the Zamorins.

Trade with foreigners such as the Chinese and Arabs was the principal source of revenue for that Zamorins. However it was the Arabs who managed to determine stronger trade links with the rulers of Calicut. Artwork and culture flourished under the Zamorins who were wonderful patrons of literature.

Accounts of travellers like Ibn Batuta (1342-47), Ma Huan, the Chinese scholar, Abdur Razzak (1443), Nicolo Conti (1444) and Athanasius Nikitin (1468-74) corroborate this fact. Not content using the dimension of their kingdom, the Zamorins set about expanding its boundaries. The powerful Zamorins conquered Beypore, Parappanad, Vettat, Kurumpranad, Nilambur, Manjeri, Malappuram, Kottakal and Ponnai. By the 15th century, clashes in between Cochin and Calicut became more and more regular. The reigning Zamorin emerged since the undisputed monarch on the North Malabar region, extending up to Pantalayani Kollam.

Post Chera Period

The post Chera period witnessed a gradual decadence of the Namboothiris, until by about the 16th century, they put of their affairs in the hands of their Nair secretaries. A Namboothiri— Nair alliance came into being.

Another feature of this period was the widening gulf between the Namboothiri—Nair upper class and the Thiyya—Pulaya lower class. In order to accommodate the class differences properly, the four—fold caste system came to be sub-divided with infinite gradations, based on real occupation, habitat and political influence. New dimensions were invented and added on to the scale of unapproachability and unperceivability.

With increasing rigidity of caste, the worst sufferers were the *Parayar, Pulayar, Cheramar*, etc. They were attached to plots of cultivable land and unceremoniously exchanged along with the plots without any right to family or children. This feudal society, however, was prosperous and complacent. With agricultural and commercial prosperity on the increase, festivals like *Onam* and *Vishu*, which began as mere sectarian religious observances, acquired the character of popular celebrations. They were fixed up at a time when the tenants had to pay their feudal dues to the owners of land. The enthusiasm of the tenants transformed *Onam*, a *Vaishnava* sacred day commemorating the Vamana incarnation, into a harvest festival.

At this point of time, feudal society was blissfully ignorant of the Afghan, Pathan and Mongol invasions which uprooted ancient Hindu society in most parts of India beyond the Sahya, the great sentinel of Kerala. This coastal area had, along the rest of Tamilakam, remained outside the big empires in the past. This time also, it escaped the catastrophe of Alauddin Khilji's campaign, which pushed southward straight to Rameshwaram.

Portuguese

The arrival of Vasco-da-Gama at Calicut in 1498, was a landmark occasion within the annals of background. At that time, Kerala was inside the throes of political turmoil. Although the Portuguese did not appreciate cordial relations using the Zamorin, they succeeded in procuring some buying and selling amenities at Quilon and Cannanore. But the Portuguese were intent on stopping the Arabs from buying and selling with India.

Hostilities in between Cochin and Calicut had been exacerbated due to the fact the Raja of Cochin acted as a prepared supporter from the Portuguese. Nevertheless, the Zamorin faced a crushing defeat on the fingers of the Portuguese when they laid siege on Cochin.

Gama was sent to India by Portuguese king Dom Manuel. Gama was received at Calicut by the Zamorin. Gama left Calicut and reached Cannanore at the invitation of Kolathiri Raja. Vasco-da-Gama reached Kerala in a ship called St. Gabriel. Gama returned to Lisbon in 1499. Gama's second visit was in 1502. Gama reached Kerala for the third time in 1524 and died here on 29 December, 1524 and was cremated at the St. Francis Church at Fort Cochin. Later his mortal remains were brought back to Lisbon, Portugal. The second expedition of the Portuguese to Kerala was led by Pedro Alvarez Cabral. He reached Cochin on 24 December, 1500. Francisco Almeida was the first Viceroy of the Portuguese in the East. He was appointed in 1505 AD. Albuquerque is regarded as the greatest of the Portuguese statesmen who came to the East. Kunjali Marakkar opposed the Portuguese. Kunjali Marakkars were the traditional naval commanders of Calicut Zamorin. Kunjalis were four in number. Kutti Ali was the first Kunjali. The policy of Kunjali was 'Hit and run policy'. Fourth and last Kunjali was Muhammed Kunjali. He adopted the titles 'King of the Moors' and 'Lord of the Indian Seas'. In 1600, the Kunjali IV was captured by the Zamorin and he was executed by the Portuguese at Goa. The Portuguese power in India declined by the coming of the English. The bungalow type of building was introduced in Kerala by the Portuguese. The Portuguese introduced in India a number of new agricultural products such as the Cashewnuts, Tobacco, Custardapple, Guava, Pineapple and Pappaya. The Chavittunatakam, the Christian counterpart of the Hindu Kathakali was also introduced by the Portuguese. The Synod of Diamper (Udayamperur) to reform Kerala Church was conducted by the Portuguese (1599). The 'Oath of the Coonan Cross' against the appointment of Latin Bishop was in 1653. First European fort built in India was the Fort Manual at Cochin by Albuquerque.

The Portuguese had a strong influence on the educational and cultural existence in the persons of Kerala. The introduction on the printing press in Kerala can be counted as one of their greatest achievements. Nonetheless, religious intolerance and bigotry marked their rule, resulting in strife and disharmony among the nearby populace. This period also saw the revival in the Bhakti movement.

The Dutch

The Dutch East India Company, formed in 1592, sent Admiral Van der Hagen to India in 1603; the admiral entered into a commercial and political treaty with the Zamorin of Calicut who wanted to expel the Portuguese from Kerala. In 1662, the Dutch captured Cranganore from the Portuguese and in 1663 they captured the Fort of Cochin and installed their partisan as King of Cochin. In 1664 they acquired monopoly of pepper trade in

Cannanore. In 1613, the Dutch brought the state of Cochin under their effective political control. The Mysore invasions of Hyder Ali and the coming of the British spelled the doom of Dutch power in Kerala. In 1795, a British force under Major Petrie from Calicut marched against Cochin and forced the surrender of the Dutch fort of Cochin. Marthanda Varma (1729–1758) of Travancore also crippled the Dutch power in a series of encounters, especially in the battle of Koiachel. The Dutch sued for peace, withdrew from Kerala, and left for the East Indies.

Like the Portuguese, the Dutch also introduced new agricultural products and scientific techniques of cultivation. They improved the agricultural economy of Kerala; they cultivated coconut, rice and indigo on extensive scale. They are most remembered for the celebrated botanical work on the medicinal value of Kerala plants, *Hortus Malabaricus.*

Most important contribution of Dutch to Kerala is the monumental work, *Horthus Malabaricus.* It was compiled under the patronage of Admiral Van Rheede. Carmelite Monk Mathavus, three Gowda Saraswath Brahmins, Ranga Bhat, Appu Bhat and Vinayaka Bhat and an Ezhava Physician Itti Achuttan were associated with its compilation. The work was published from Amsterdam (Holland) between 1678 and 1703.

Rise of Travancore

Travancore or Venad occupied centre stage in the political arena of Kerala around 18th century, during its two illustrious rulers, Marthanda Varma (1729–58) and Rama Varma, popularly known as Dharma Raja (1758–98). In his lifetime, Marthanda Varma efficiently annexed the territories below the Dutch. An important innovation introduced by Marthanda Varma was the framing of the annual budget called "Pativukanakku". Marthanda Varma is known as the maker of modern Travancore. The Chief Minister of Travancore was known as Dalawa. Ramayyan Dalawa was Diwan of Marthanda Varma. Marthanda Varma was born in the year 1705 and came to the throne in 1729. Marthanda Varma dedicated the kingdom to Sri Padmanabha of Trivandrum (Thrippadidhanam) on Wednesday, January 3, 1750 (Makaram 5, 725 KE). Thereafter the Travancore Rajas came to be known as Padmanabhadasas. The "Bhadradeepam" and "Murajapam" in the Padmanabha Swami Temple was also started by Marthanda Varma. Recognized as the Maker of Modern Travancore, Marthanda's tenure is really a exceptional period inside the history of Kerala.

Rama Varma ascended the throne and ably completed the job of administration. Two distinguished ministers, Ayyappan Marthanda Pillai and Raja Kesava Das assisted him in administering the kingdom. Rama Varma had to bear the brunt of Haider Ali and Tipu Sultan's invasion.

Travancore was lucky sufficient to become governed by many enlightened administrators like Velu Thampi, Rani Gouri Lakshmi Bai (1810–15), Gouri Parvati Bai (1815–29), Swati Tirunal (1829–47), Ayilyam Tirunal (1860–80), Sri Mulam Tirunal (1885–1924) who did a lot to determine science, art and culture flourish in Travancore.

Raja Kesava Das was the first Chief Minister of Travancore who assumed the title Diwan. Raja Kesava Das was respectfully referred to as "Valia Diwanji". Vizhinjam was developed into a small port by Raja Kesava Das. Alleppey was also developed into a town and port by Raja Kesava Das. The Chalai Bazar, the completion of the Gopuram of Sri Padmanabha Swami temple were also done by Raja Kesava Das. The name "Raja Kesava Das" was given to him by the Governor General Lord Mornington (original name Kesavapillai). Kunjan Nambiar and Unnayi Warrier were the famous poets in the court of Dharma Raja. It was Dharma Raja who shifted the capital of Travancore from Padmanabhapuram to Trivandrum. People respectfully called him "Kizhvan Raja" because when he died he was 74 years old.

Mysore Invades Kerala

Haider Ali, the ruler of Mysore, turned his consideration in direction of Kerala after subduing Bednore in 1763. The regions of Kolathiri, Kottayam, Kadathanad, Kurumbranad and Calicut came under the dominion of Haider Ali. Again in 1773, Haider Ali laid siege on Kerala and conquered Trichur following restoring his authority in Malabar. Haider's son, Tipu Sultan ascended the throne in 1782. Continuing inside the footsteps of his illustrious father, Tipu managed to annex the whole South Malabar in 1783. Nonetheless, it was only in 1790 that he succeeded in breaching the Travancore Line.

But the beginning in the Third Mysore War spelt catastrophe for Tipu as, one right after yet another, most of the kingdoms below Tipu surrendered on the British forces. With the signing in the Treaty of Sreerangapatanam in 1792, the final blow was dealt to Tipu's reign. Based on the terms from the treaty, Tipu had to hand in excess of Malabar on the British.

Socio-Religious Reform Movement

From 1812 until almost the close of the century, though political life was characterized by inactivity and society presented an outward calmness, subversive forces were forming and developing. This current of social transformation gradually led Kerala into the mainstream of political struggle for freedom and responsible government in the 20th century.The important outcome of this ferment was the awakening of the masses especially the lower orders in the Hindu society, against social injustice and evils. This awakening found articulation in Kerala towards the last quarter of the 19th century. A number of socio-religious reform movements, which were also the earliest democratic mass movements in Kerala, took shape. On the whole, these movements were peaceful and non-violent, though there was an undercurrent of militancy in them. These movements were of the utmost significance, because Kerala had, for centuries, tolerated the caste system in its most oppressive form. The rigid caste system and irrational caste taboos existed in such a heinous way that the lower orders were not only 'untouchable' but "unapproachable" as well. In Malabar, despite the advent of direct British rule and the resultant separation of the caste system from the administrative machinery, social status and economic competence of the individual was still determined by his position in the caste hierarchy. In the princely states of Kochi and Travancore, the hold of the caste system was even more suffocating. Until the 20th century, governmental positions were denied to lower castes and non-Hindus.

One of the most important social reform movements was spearheaded by Sri Narayana Guru, the great Hindu saint and social reformer. The Guru was born in 1856 in the Ezhava Community which had a status far below that of the Namboothiris. He fearlessly criticized and campaigned against the rigours of the caste system, the Brahmin hegemony and the numerous social disabilities of the Ezhavas and other lower castes. Soon Sri Narayana Guru became the rallying point for the Ezhavas and Thiyyas to unite and organize. The Sri Narayana Dharma Paripalana Yogam (SNDP), literally the society for the propagation of moral teaching of Sri Narayana came into being 15th May 1903. Within a short period, the Guru and Yogam drew towards them a brilliant band of dedicated workers, including the poet Kumaran Asan, whose efforts constitute an eloquent testimony to what a community, submitted to centuries of tyranny, can do and achieve through unity, realism and organism. Sri Narayana was, however, no sectarian philosopher and leader. A programme of action founded upon such sublime humanism and social purpose was not destined to remain confined to one caste only; it soon became the philosophy of Hindu reformation, encompassing all castes, including the Brahmin.The Nairs also felt the need for reform. Throughout the medieval period and until well into the 19th century, the Nairs had a pre-eminent role in Kerala. By the middle of the 19th century, however, this dominance started waning. Institutions like the sambandam (non-legal marriage) and the matrilineal joint family system which had ensured the strength of the Nair community earlier, now became productive of many evils; the system of non-legal marriage produced immorality and vices, while the joint family set-up stifled individual initiative and enterprise. The impact of the market economy, the disappearance of traditional military training, the absorption of new values through the new system of education, the self-consciousness being generated among the lower castes and their cry for equality and privileges—all these factors brought about a decline of Nair dominance. The sense of decline gave an impetus to the spirit of reform that expressed itself in the work of religious men like Chattambi Swamikal, in literature, on the press and platform and later in legislative enactments in respect of marriage, inheritance, property rights, etc. Ultimately, the movements crystallized in the foundation of the Nair Service Society, in 1914.The impulse to change was not confined to the Ezhavas and other untouchables and the Nairs only. As a matter of fact in varying degrees, it affected every caste in Hindu society as well as the Christians and the Muslims.

Vaikom Satyagraha

A movement had set on foot to demand admission of the certain sections of the people, the so called "unapproachables" banned from approach into the public roads adjacent to the famous temple at Vaikom. Conservative opposition was trotted out with obstinate determination. The feeding of Brahmins inside the temple was regarded as an important offering to the deity, and uninterrupted custom was pleaded by those who opposed the movement.

It was contended that if the 'Avarnas' were allowed to come into the approach roads the temple priests would be polluted and the temple consequently defiled. The forward section resolved to try the methods of 'Satyagraha' and several individuals, a large number of whom being Nayars and other caste Hindus, organised a "Jatha" to lay their grievance before Maharani Sethu Lakshmi Bai, the Regent of Travancore.

A resolution was moved in the Legislative Council demanding the opening of the temple roads to the 'Avarna' Hindus. But it was thrown out by a majority of twenty-two against twenty-one votes. A little after this Mahatma Gandhi visited Vaikom in 1924, interviewed several orthodox Brahmins and others, and explained the movement as one which was calculated to remove social injustice and to advance the cause of humanity. Public opinion in the state was so favourable that the government threw open the approach roads to the 'Avarnas'. "I call it a bed-rock of freedom", said Mahatma Gandhi, "because the settlement is a document between the people and the state constituting a big step in the direction of liberty in one respect at least". The course of events in Vaikom led to similar attempts in Sucheendram in Hindu society as well as the Christians and the Muslims.

Guruvayur Satyagraha

The famous Guruvayur Satyagraha is a memorable episode in the history of the national movement. With the blessings of Mahatma Gandhi the Kerala Provincial Congress Committee decided to begin Satyagraha before the famous temple at Guruvayur with effect from 1st November, 1931. It was a movement for temple entry and abolition of untouchability.

The Satyagraha began accordingly under the leadership of Sri K. Kelappan. Among the Kerala leaders other than Kelappan were Mannath Padmanabhan, A.K. Gopalan and N.P. Damodaran.

Guruvayur began to attract the attention of all India. There were certain untoward incidents during the early period of the Satyagraha. They served to heighten the tension in the minds of the people who were in sympathy with the movement. After the movement had run its course for about ten months, Kelappan entered on a fast before the temple on September, 21, 1932. The fast electrified the atmosphere. On October 2, 1932 Kelappan broke his fast in response to Gandhiji's wishes. Thereafter a referendum was held among the Hindus to find out their views on the question of temple entry. More than 77 per cent of the Hindus expressed themselves in favour of temple entry. The Guruvayur temple was thrown open to Harijans only in 1946. Though the Satyagraha did not immediately result in the opening of the Guruvayur temple to all Hindus, the movement helped to create a strong public opinion in the country in favour of temple entry and abolition of untouchability.

Temple Entry Proclamation

In Travancore, the movements for the mitigation of the severities of caste, if not its total abolition, have been popular. The teachings of Sri Narayana Guru gave a momentum to the forces which were generated by the extension of western education among the masses and the tolerant policy pursued by the state in recognising the legitimate claims of the backward communities.The promulgation of the Temple Entry Proclamation was a reform of far-reaching importance, not only to the teeming millions of Travancore but a momentous act of emancipation and hope to the whole of India. The Proclamation runs as follows:-

"Profoundly convinced of the truth and validity of our religion, believing that it is based on divine guidance and on all-comprehending toleration, knowing that in its practice it has through out the centuries, adapted itself to the needs of changing times, solicitous that none of our Hindu subjects should, by reason of birth or caste of community, be denied the consolations and the solace of the Hindu faith." 'Avarnas', to find out the extent of the demand for reforms, to ascertain the attitude of the Savarna castes, to examine the question in the light of the Hindu scriptures and formulate proposals as to the lines on which the reform might be effected. The committee expressed their considered opinion that a Parishad of learned persons, well versed in the theory and practice of Hinduism, should be summoned, and that the reform might be effected by the ruler with their approval. They also suggested certain methods by which the rigour of the custom excluding the Avarnas from the temple

IMPORTANT YEARS	
Attingal Rebellion	1721
Kulachal Battle	1741
Kundara Proclamation	1809
Kurichiyar Rebellion	1812
Channar Lahala	1859
Malayali Memorial (Travancore)	1891
Ezhava Memorial	1896
Mopla Rebellion, Wagon Tragedy	1921
Vaikom Satyagraha	1924
Civil Disobedience Movement	1930
Guruvayur Satyagraha	1931
Nivarthana Agitation	1932
Temple Entry Proclamation	1936
State Congress Movement	1938
Kayyur Rebellion	1941
Punnapra Vayalar Rebellion	1946
Formation of Kerala State	1956
Liberation Movement	1959

might be softened. But the Maharaja did not believe in half measures. With an outlook which no Indian monarch had been able to entertain for a couple of thousands of conservative years. His Highness the Maharaja Sree Chitra Thirunal affixed the Sign Manual to the momentous Proclamation. It was on the eve of the Maharaja's birthday in (1936 AD) that the edict was promulgated. The Proclamation was received throughout India with delight and admiration. It was welcomed by the whole civilised world. To the Hindus it was matter of pride and fresh hope. The repercussions of the Proclamation were so great that the Christians and Muslims were equally warm in giving it a hearty reception. Dr. C.P. Ramaswami Iyer referred to the day of the Proclamation as a unique occasion in the history of India and specially of Hinduism. Gandhiji expressed the hope that "all other Hindu Princes will follow the noble example set by this far-off ancient Hindu State." The Prime Minister of Madras described the Proclamation as the "greatest religious reform in India after the time of Ashoka". The Maharaja gave the biggest charity that any ruler could give to his subjects in opening the doors to every class and creed.

The Growth of British Power in Kerala

First Englishman who came to Kerala was perhaps Master Ralph Fitch. He is known as "Pioneer Englishman". In 1616, Captain William Keeling arrived in Calicut with three ships which brought Sir Thomas Roe on his embassy to the court of Jahangir. British merchants exported pepper to England for the first time from Cochin in 1626. First English factory in

Kerala was set up at Vizhinjam. In 1695, the English constructed the Anjengo fort with the permission of Attingal Rani. Construction was started in 1684. The Attingal Outbreak was on 15 April, 1721. It was between the natives and the British traders. 140 Englishmen were massacred by the natives. The event occurred near Anjengo. Attingal Revolt was the first organised revolt against the English in Kerala. In April 1723, a formal treaty was concluded between the English East India Company and the king of Travancore. It was the first treaty negotiated by the English East India Company with an Indian State. This was a treaty of friendship. By 1800 Cochin came under the control of the English East India Company. By the treaty concluded in 1795 Travancore accepted the Supremacy of the Company. Col. Macaulay was appointed as the first British Resident in Travancore. The treaty of 1805 which was negotiated by Velu Thampi Dalawa resulted in the loss of the political freedom of Travancore.

Against the Regime

The East India Company ruled the Indian territories by organising them as provinces. Malabar, which was under the Bombay Presidency till 1800, was later brought under the Madras Presidency. The British followed anti people policies in Malabar. The Company declared that both the rulers and their subjects should be under its control. The people were required to pay the high taxes under pain of stringent action. This led to anti-British feelings everywhere in Malabar. When new officers were appointed to collect taxes, disputes began to surface. Kerala Varma Pazhassi Raja was a ruler who questioned the British usurpation of the right to collect taxes and the removal of royal power. The revolt staged under his leadership was very difficult for the British to deal with. To begin with, Pazhassi Raja was among those who helped the British in collecting taxes and other things. But when he realised the real intention of the Company, he led a revolt against them. Kerala Varma knew very well that it was difficult for him fight the well equipped army of the British. He expected that in the feud among the members of the royal family the Company should stand by him. But he was disappointed. It was in this context that he mobilised his forces against the Company.

Opposition Escalates

Following the friendly relations with the British and the conclusion of treaties with them, Kochi and Travancore accepted their suzerainty. Against the attempts to intervene in the internal affairs of Travancore Divan Velu Thampi took an independant position. The Divan opposed the move of the Company to appropriate huge amounts from the royal treasury. This even cost him his Divanship. Thereupon he attempted to resist the British by strengthening anti-British feelings among the people. The Kundara Proclamation of 1809 was part of this move. In Kochi, too Paliath Achan raised the banner of revolt against British hegemony. The Kurichia revolt of Vayanad was a reaction against the revenue reforms introduced by the British. The Kurichias used to pay tax in kind. But the British declared that tax would be collected only in cash. This caused resentment among them. Those who were in arrears of tax were punished by the British by confiscating their properties, household utensils, ransacking their huts, eviction from land, etc. With this, a spontaneous resistance against the British was thrown up. It developed into an open rebellion. The Kurichia revolt was a popular resistance against British domination.

Before the establishment of British rule the villages were more or less self-sufficient. The essential articles for day-to-day life and clothes were produced within the respective villages. Those things which could not be produced within were brought from outside. With the beginning of British rule the indigenous production of goods began to decline. British products were imported in their place.

The British took away raw materials necessary for the industries of England at cheap prices. The English products were imposed on the natives at high prices. Roads and bridges and rail roads were constructed for enabling the easy transportation of army and commodities. British products were available aplenty in every village. As a result, the rural economy was in ruins. Many families were reduced to starvation. Land became a ground for the British capitalists to make enormous profit.

The establishment of monopoly in trade by the East India Company made the life of the people miserable. Trade on salt, tobacco, timber, spices, etc. came under the control of the Company. The prices of these products shot up. As a result, the poor people were thrown to great misery.

By making the teak wood industry of Malabar a monopoly of the Company, the timber workers and traders began to suffer. The Company tried to increase their income by imposing taxes irrespective of the size or quality of the houses.

Land Revenue

The land laws introduced by the British brought many hardship to the people.

- Land revenue was collected in cash
- Land revenue was increased many times
- Actual peasants were denied ownership of land
- Landlords got rights over all land
- Landlords were granted more rights and powers

When prices of products increased, landlords would evict old tenants whom they did not like. They would assign that land to tenants who were ready to pay higher rents. Each landlord levied many exactions from tenants over and above the rent. The plight of the tenants was made even more miserable by practices like "polichezhuthu".

The peasants had to put obey whatever the lord and his manager commanded. Or else, they had to suffer severe consequences. The peasants and leaseholders lived in utter fear of the landlords.

The peasants were harassed to the maximum by the British government, landlords, police and judiciary. Resenting this, peasants protested. Their ire turned against the lords and the officials who assisted them. This turned into organised revolts. The Government imposed mass fines not only on those who resisted but on entire villages. This resulted in furthering the resentment.

Peasant Uprisings of Malabar

The revolts against the British in Malabar were the culmination of the protests of the Mappila tenants, agricultural labourers, artisans, petty traders, etc. over a period of time. The involvement of the ordinary people in this struggle was noteworthy. A sizeable number of the peasants of Eranad and Valluvanad taluks of Malabar were Mappila Muslims. It was they who participated in these struggles. Hence these uprisings were called 'Mappila uprisings' by the British.

During the time of Mysorean invasion the chieftains and landlords of Malabar fled to Travancore for asylum. The land owned by them was distributed among the Mappila tenants.They enjoyed the land after paying tax. After Malabar came under the British, the landlords who had gone to Travancore returned. The British recovered land from the Mappilas and gave it back to the landlords. The landlords were allowed to collect revenue from the tenants.

The British realised that they could carry on imperialist exploitation only with the support of the landlords and chieftains.

The British calculated that if they were able to gain the support of the natives by winning over the landlords and chieftains, they could continue their rule for a long time. The landlords in their turn thought that they could remain influential in their locality collecting rents as they wished so long as they did not question the authority of the company.

The landlords harassed the peasants by imposing excessive rent. This was the result of the British-landlord alliance. Most Mappila peasants were small scale peasants and agricultural labourers. The imposition of heavy rent sowed the seed of anger in them. The British and the landlords nursed a special enmity to the Mappila tenants and agricultural labourers on the plea that they were the aides of Tipu. This ended up in revolts. As those who revolted were Mappilas and those against whom the revolts were directed were Hindu landlords and officers who supported them, the British represented these peasant revolts as communal riots. The British employed the policy of divide and rule even in this context. The landlords and others assisted the British in their despicable acts of suppressing the revolt by creating a communal rift and increasing hatred in society.

Plantation Crops

Cultivation of cash crops in the place of paddy became widespread in many areas. Crops linked to industry had a greater spread. The heavily forested High Ranges were opened up for cash crops and plantation crops. To begin with, huge plantations under the ownership of the British came up. Gradually, migrations began from the plains. Migrations spread to the High Ranges first and then to the forested areas of Malabar. Most immigrants became owners of large estates. Thus, the valleys of Kerala became the production ground of cash crops.

KNOW THE FACTS

- *Famous Rock-cut caves in the Ambukuthi hills in the Wayanad district is known as Edakkal Caves.*
- *Writings in the Edakkal Caves belonged to the Dravida Brahmi script.*
- *Avvayar was the most famous poetess of the Sangam period.*
- *Utiyam Cheralatham of first Chera Empire had the title 'Vanavarampan'.*
- *Paliyam Copper Plate (925 AD) of Vikramaditya Varaguna mentions about the Ay rulers.*
- *Kollam Era was started in AD 825 (August 15) (Chingam 1) by Rajashekhara Varman Kulasekhara.*
- *Kollam Era is also known as Malayalam Era.*
- *Kulasekhara Alwar wrote Perumal Tirumozhi in Tamil and Mukundamala in Sanskrit.*
- *The famous "hundred years war" between the Cholas and Cheras began during the reign Bhaskara Ravi Varman I.*
- *Sankaracharya (788 - 80 AD) the great Advaita philosopher was an younger contemporary of Kulasekhara Alvar.*
- *Sankaracharya was a Namboothiri Brahmin born at Kaladi on the banks of river Periyar.*
- *Bhakti movement became prominent under the Kulasekharas.*
- *Assyrians and Babylonians were the first to have trade relations with ancient Kerala.*
- *Italian (Venetian) traveller Marcopolo reached Kerala in 1292 (13th Century).*
- *Muziris, Tyndis, Barace and Nelcynade were the famous sea ports in ancient Kerala.*
- *African Traveller (Morocco), Ibn Batuta reached Kerala during 1342-1347.*
- *Nicholo Conti reached Kerala in 1440.*

☞ *Christianity was introduced in Kerala in the first century AD (52 AD) by St. Thomas.*

☞ *Islam was introduced to Kerala probably in 644 AD by Malik Ibn Dinar. He founded the Cheraman Mosque at Kodungallur.*

☞ *One and only Muslim ruling dynasty in Kerala was the Arakkal Dynasty. It had its centre at Kannur. If the ruler of this dynasty, is a male he is known as Ali Raja and a female is known as Arakkal Beevi.*

☞ *Vasco da Gama reached at Kappad near Calicut on 20 May 1498. He was sent to India by Portuguese king Dom Manuel.*

☞ *Vasco da Gama was received at Calicut by the Zamorin.*

☞ *Vasco da Gama reached Kerala for the third time in 1524 and died here on 29 December 1524 and was cremated at the St. Francis Church at Fort Cochin. Later his mortal remains were brought back to Lisbon, Portugal.*

☞ *The Chavittunatakam, the Christian counterpart of the Hindu Kathakali was also introduced by the Portuguese.*

☞ *First European fort built in India was the Fort Manual at Cochin by Albuquerque.*

☞ *Dutch Admiral Steven Van Der Hagen was the first Dutch Admiral to reach Kerala (Calicut).*

☞ *In the famous battle fought at Colachel (10 Aug. 1741) the forces of Marthanda Varma defeated the Dutch and captured D'Lannoy, who later became the 'Valiakappitham' of Marthanda Varma's army.*

TEST YOUR SELF

1. Early inhabitants of Kerala belonged to the last phase of ....
   A. Middle Stone Age
   B. Early Stone Age
   C. Iron Age
   D. Copper Age

2. The first recorded history of Kerala seems inside the inscriptions of ....
   A. Bindusara
   B. Ashoka
   C. Pulkesin I
   D. Raj Raja I

3. Which among the following is correct?
   A. Ays — North Kerala
   B. Cheras — Central Kerala
   C. Ezhimalas — South Kerala
   D. All of these

4. Kannur and Wayanad districts were ruled by ....
   A. Ezhimalas
   B. Ays
   C. Cheras
   D. None of these

5. Kannanar was a poet laureate of ....
   A. Utiyam Cheralatam
   B. Nedum Cheralatam
   C. Kuttuvam
   D. None of these

6. Which among the following was a famous harbour town of Cheras?
   A. Vanchi
   B. Tyndis
   C. Muziris
   D. Both B and C

7. Who founded the 'Kollam Era' of Kerala?
   A. Rejasekhara Varman   B. Sthanu Ravi Varman
   C. Aditya-I   D. Kulasekhara Alvar

8. Vasco-da-Gama arrived Calicut in ....
   A. 1502   B. 1498
   C. 1458   D. 1707

9. In which year Mahatma Gandhi visited Vaikom?
   A. 1928   B. 1932
   C. 1924   D. 1918

10. Attingal Rebellion was broke out in ....
   A. 1721   B. 1728
   C. 1815   D. 1803

ANSWERS

1	2	3	4	5	6	7	8	9	10
A	B	B	A	B	D	A	B	C	A

❏❏❏

EMERGENCE OF NATIONALISM

The last decades of the 19th century saw the emergence of nationalism in India. The Indian National Congress was established in 1885 and it soon became the spearhead of the Indian Nationalist Movement. These developments did not go unnoticed in Kerala. A conference was held at Kozhikode in 1904 under the auspices of the Congress and in 1908, a District Congress Committee was formed in Malabar. Beyond this, there was no political activity worth the name in Malabar.

Malayalee Memorial

In Travancore, political agitation began with the Nairs who found their dominance on the decline and resented the monopolization of higher officers by the Tamil Brahmins inducted from outside. Their appetite for political participation was whetted with the formation of the Travancore Legislative Council in 1888—the first ever legislative started in an Indian State. The Malayali Memorial, a memorandum bearing the signatures of over 10,000 people, including a sprinkling of Ezhavas, Christians and Muslims, was submitted to the Maharaja in 1891. It was really a Nair plea for privileges and positions. This was soon followed by an Ezhava Memorial (1896), submitted with over 13,000 signatures pleading for extension of civic rights, Government jobs, etc. to the lower castes.

Both the memoranda came to naught. But in the historical perspective, the impact was considerable as they laid the bases for the constitutional style of political agitation in Travancore.

Political activity in Kerala received a new impetus with the outbreak of the First World War and the spread of the Home Rule Movement. Home Rule leagues sprouted in different places in Malabar and the activities of Congress men received enthusiastic encouragement from the people. In 1916 and 1917, the annual meetings of the District Congress Committee were held with great fanfare under the name of the Malabar District Political

Conference. Resolutions were adopted at these conferences, demanding self-government for India and the release of political prisoners. In Travancore and Cochin also, political activities were taken up under the aegis of the Congress. Congress Committees were started in Thiruvananthapuram and Ernakulam. In 1920, the following resolutions adopted at the Nagpur Session of the Indian National Congress to organise Provincial Congress Committees on a linguistic basis, a Kerala Provincial Congress Committee was formed integrating Congress activities in the three territorial divisions of Kerala. The first All-Kerala Political Conference held at Ottappalam in April 1921 was attended by delegates from Malabar, Cochin and Travancore. In a sense, this was the herald of the movement for a united Kerala which—became a reality, 35 years later.

Malabar Rebellion

The Non-co-operation movement was in full swing during this period of time. It was particularly strong in Malabar, where the Moppilas were agitated over the Khilafat issue. The Gandhian movement had a tremendous impact in Kerala, with large numbers joining the Satyagraha campaign. Gandhiji visited Malabar in 1921, giving a further impetus to the movement. Khilafat Committees sprang up in large numbers and the fraternity between the Hindus and Muslims, through the work in Congress-Khilafat Committees, was a truly remarkable feature of the Non-co-operation movement in Kerala, in its early stages.

The speed with which the Khilafat agitation spread, especially in the Eranad and Valluvanad taluks, created alarm in official circles. A perplexed officialdom clamped down prohibitory orders in the two taluks.

Meetings were banned and many people were arrested in the name of law and order. A tragic episode then ensued, namely the Moppila Rebellion or the Malabar Rebellion of 1921. Police attempted to arrest the secretary of the Khilafat Committee of Pokottur in Eranad on a charge of having stolen a pistol. A crowd of 2000 Moppilas from the neighbourhood foiled the attempt. The next day, a police party in search of Khilafat rebels entered the famous Mambaram mosque at Tirurangadi. They seized some records and arrested a few Khilafat volunteers. A rumour spread that the mosque was desecrated. Hundreds of rustic Moppilas converged on Tirurangadi and besieged the local police station. The police opened fire. The mob reacted in a mad fury. Violence spread and engulfed Eranad and Valluvanad taluks and neighbouring areas for over two months. Congress leaders tried in vain to check the violence. Towards the later stages of the rebellion, owing to unfounded rumour of Hindus having helped the police or sought police help, there were instances of atrocities perpetrated on Hindus. This marred the relations between the two communities. Meanwhile British and Gurkha regiments were rushed to the area. Martial law was clamped. A series of repressive measures followed and by November, the rebellion was practically crushed. Relief operations in the ravaged areas,

FIRST MINISTRY OF KERALA (1957)	
1. E.M.S. Namboothiripad	Chief Minister
2. C. Achutha Menon	Finance
3. T.V. Thomas	Transport
4. K.C. George	Food, Forest
5. K.P. Gopalan	Industry
6. T.A. Majeed	P.W.D
7. P.K.Chathan	Local Self Government
8. Joseph Mundassery	Education, Cooperation
9. K.R. Gauri	Land Tax, Excise
10. V.R. Krishna Ayyar	Law, Electricity
11. Dr. A.R. Menon	Health

undertaken mostly by voluntary agencies which received help and funds from Gandhiji, lasted for over six months.

Wagon Tragedy

The epilogue (in the sense that it came to be known only later) was the "Wagon Tragedy" in which 61 of the 70 Moppila prisoners packed in a closed railway goods wagon and carried to Coimbatore jails, died of suffocation on November 10, 1921. In the wake of the suppression of the Malabar Rebellion and until almost the end of the decade, struggle purely for political freedom was on a low key. This lull was largely because of the brisk activity on the social front. The emphasis was on constructive programmes in which all people could join together and work irrespective of political views or affiliation. The cry for social equality was particularly strong. This was the background of the famous Satyagraha at Vaikom Temple (1924) to be followed up later at the Guruvayur Temple in 1931. Both of them exemplified the immense potentialities of Satyagraha as an instrument of social change and both were started with the blessings of Gandhiji.

Civil Disobedience

The second phase of the Civil Disobedience movement, started by Gandhiji with his famous Salt March in March 1930, found enthusiastic response from all parts of Kerala. In several places, particularly at Payyannur and Kozhikode, salt laws were broken and hundreds of agitators courted arrest. A Youth League was formed in Travancore which was able to enlist the dedicated services of quite a good number of spiritual and radical minded young men who later became the prop of the Travancore State Congress.

In the wake of the Civil Disobedience Movement, a parallel movement for responsible Government had begun in Travancore and Kochi. In Travancore, the Nivartana (abstention) movement began as a protest against the inadequacy of the constitutional reforms of 1932.

The Ezhavas, the Christians and the Muslims apprehended that the new reforms, owing to the provisions for restricted franchise on the basis of possession of property and other qualifications, would secure for them far less number of seats in the enlarged legislature than the Nairs.

They therefore demanded that the seats be apportioned on the basis of population strength. The Government, however, did not view their demands favourably.

The abstentionists then organized a Joint Political Congress to exhort the voters to abstain from voting. Since the three communities together formed about 70 per cent of the population, their agitation had the characteristics of a mass movement. The Government at first adopted a repressive policy but later yielded to the demands of the abstentionists to some extent. In the election held in 1937, most of the candidates fielded by the Joint Political Congress were elected.

The Left Movements

An important feature of the freedom movement in Kerala in the 1920's and 1930's was the increasing involvement of peasants and workers. This was to release a tremendous mass force into the mainstream of the national movement, giving it a new momentum and a social content. The peasant and labour movements of the 1930's were to a great extent the cause as well as the consequence of the emergence of a powerful left wing in politics. In 1934, the left nationalists joined together and organized the Congress Socialist Party.

A powerful factor that helped the growth of the left movement was the support it received from the radical section of the nationalist Muslims in Malabar. Left groups started functioning in several parts of Malabar and soon the Kerala Provincial Congress Committee was dominated by them.

The leftists preferred to remain organizationally within the Congress and call themselves socialists. Thus both the left and right groups joined together in order to ensure the success of the Congress candidates in the election of 1936 in Malabar. But the rift came into the open with the outbreak of the Second World War, the resignation of the Congress ministries in the provinces and the starting of individual Satyagraha. The left-dominated KPCC, contrary to directive of the Congress, observed. The left met in secret enclave at Pinarayi and in December 1939, the Communist Party was born.

Responsible Government

The struggle for responsible Government had been launched in Travancore and Cochin by 1938-39. The struggle in Cochin was far less in intensity than that in Travancore because the rulers of Cochin adopted on the whole, a lenient policy of political concessions which averted violent clashes. In June 1938, a diarchial form of Government was established allowing popular ministers to control some departments.

The end of the Quit India Movement saw Malabar returning to elections and a constitutional Government. Administratively Malabar was a district of Madras Province at the time of independence.

Rise of Travancore State Congress

The Haripura session of the Indian National Congress in February 1938 resolved that while the Congress committees functioning in the Indian states should not engage themselves in parliamentary activity or direct action in the name of the Congress independent organisations may be encouraged to carry on internal struggles in these states. Gandhi's view was that the demand made by the people of princely states for responsible government was just and proper. For that purpose they should organise themselves into a movement. The active involvement of Congress in this regard would be a hinderance to achieve their aim. It was under such circumstances that a meeting of prominent leaders was held in the office room of A. Narayana Pillai, a lawyer at Pulimoodu, Trivandrum in February 1938 with C.V. Kunjuraman on the chair and it was resolved to launch the Travancore State Congress with Pattom Thanu Pillai, an outstanding lawyer and public figure of Trivandrum as its first president. The committee of Indian National Congress was formally dissolved.

The Travancore State Congress started an active campaign for the achievement of responsible government in Travancore. The Dewan Sir C.P. Ramaswamy Ayyar adopted all possible measures to break up the new organisation. The Dewan tried to create communal discord by pointing out that it was a Christian dominated body. The Dewan sponsored another organisation called the Travancore National Congress in which leaders of Nair Service Society took an active part. However this policy of divide and rule on the part of Sir C.P. Ramaswamy Ayyar failed to yield dividends.

The Dewan Sir C.P. Ramaswamy Ayyar resorted to manifold measures of repression. Meetings and demonstrations were banned and A. Narayana Pillai was arrested on a charge of sedition. Leaders like K.P. Nilakanta Pillai, Anne Mascrene and M.R. Madhava Warrier were manhandled. None of these measures could dishearten the people who had rallied under the banner of the State Congress. The Dewan soon started a reign of terror to suppress the State Congress. In these circumstances, the State Congress presented a memorandum to the Maharaja impressing upon him the imperative need for the early grant of responsible government and also bringing to his notice the repressive policies of his Dewan and the vagaries of his administration. The Dewan retaliated by declaring State Congress and its ally, All Travancore Youth League, as disloyal and subversive bodies. He cancelled the licences of Malayala Manorama and Kerala Kaumudi which published news relating to the activities of State Congress. On 26 August, 1938, the State Congress started a widespread Civil Disobedience Movement. The 1938 State Congress struggle, a struggle that was far more extensive than the 1921 Malabar movement; for, while the latter was confined to certain Taluks of Malabar, the 1938 Travancore movement embraced the whole state of Travancore. The State Congress leaders like Pattom Thanu Pillai and T.M. Varghese were arrested in Trivandrum and this was followed by the arrest of other leaders elsewhere in the state. The State Congress decided to hold a massive demonstration under the leadership of Accamma Cherian on the birthday of the Maharaja on 12 November, 1938. Having realised the gravity of the situation the government announced the withdrawal of the ban on the State Congress and the unconditional release of its leaders.

Though the ban on the State Congress and on meetings and processions had been withdrawn, the organisation was not in a position to pursue its normal political activities in the face of the arrests and other repressive measures which still continued unabated. The State Congress therefore concentrated its attention to strengthen its organisational framework. A delegation of State Congress leaders met Mahatma Gandhi and apprised him of the situation. C.P. Ramaswamy Ayyar had by now made it a condition of withdrawing the earlier memorandum which contained personal allegations against him. For an amicable settlement Gandhi advised the leaders to withdraw the memorandum in order to demonstrate that their action was not motivated by any personal malice. The senior leaders accepted Gandhi's advice but the younger elements disapproved this action and left the Congress and strengthened the ranks of the Youth League. Some of the activists with communist leanings formed themselves into a radical group within the league with P. Krishna Pillai as the moving spirit.

During the Quit India Movement of 1942, the prominent State Congress leaders were behind the prison, bars. The radical wing of the Youth League comprised of the Communists, had decided to cooperate with the government in its war efforts following the entry of the USSR in the Second World War. At the end of the war C.P. Ramaswamy Ayyar announced constitutional reforms based on universal adult suffrage with an irremovable executive. The State Congress rejected the scheme on the ground that it only sought to perpetuate the autocratic rule of the Dewan. The catchy slogan 'American Model Arabikkadalil' (American model in the Arabian sea) which rent the air in those days gave clear expression to the feelings of popular disapproval of the proposed scheme of reform. The leadership and the sacrifices of Pattom Thanu Pillai, C. Kesavan, T.M. Varghese, Accamma Cherian, A.J. John, Mamman Mappila, C.V. Kunjuraman, R. Sugathan, R. Sankar, P.T. Chacko, Anne Mascrene, Ponnara Sreedhar, P. Krishna Pillai, A.K. Gopalan, K. Damodaran, Sreekantan Nair and so on made the campaign of the State Congress for responsible government remarkable.

Rise of the Cochin State Praja Mandal

For the establishment of responsible government in Cochin a new political organisation was formed by N. Neelakantan Iyer, V.R. Krishnan Ezhuthachan and C. Achutha Menon in 1940. It was organised by a group of young men who stood for the establishment of responsible government on the basis of universal adult franchise. On 26 January, 1941 a new political organisation called the Cochin State Praja Mandal came into existence under the presidentship of V.R. Krishnan Ezhuthachan. It consisted mainly of Congressmen who had left the Cochin Congress in the wake of the latter's acceptance of dyarchy. It was resolved that the first session of the Praja Mandal be held at Irinjalakuda in January 1942. A.F.W. Dixon, the then Dewan of Cochin, banned the session but the leaders decided to go ahead with their plans for holding it. The government could not prevent the strength of the Praja Mandal through arrest and other repressive methods. During the Quit India Movement of 1942, the Praja Mandal organised several meetings and demonstrations in different parts of Cochin State. This helped to boost its prestige as a political party. In the election of 1945 to Cochin legislature 12 candidates of Praja Mandal got elected. The Praja Mandal members functioned as the opposition bloc in the Cochin Legislative Council. In July, 1946, the annual conference of the Praja Mandal met at Ernakulam and decided to start a statewide agitation for the achievement of responsible government in Cochin. The Praja Mandal members decided to boycott the session of the legislature which scheduled to meet on 29 July, 1946. The Praja Mandal organised hartals, public meetings and processions throughout Cochin and introduced a vote of no-confidence on the ministers in the legislature. When the vote of no-confidence motion got majority, the Maharaja decided to transfer all departments except law and finance into the hands of the popular ministers responsible to the legislature. The reserved subjects were to be administered by the Dewan. With the support of the progressive party and socialist party the Praja Mandal organised a coalition government on 9 September, 1946 under the leadership of Panampilly Govinda Menon. On 14 August, 1947 the departments of law and finance were transferred from the Dewan. As a protest the Dewan resigned and thus Dewanship came to an end in Cochin. Meanwhile the Praja Mandal became an organ of the Indian National Congress and in the subsequent election it won a majority in the legislature. The new government under Ikkanda Warrier came into being on 20 September, 1948. By this time, the Government of India with Sardar Vallabhbhai Patel as the head of states ministry, had initiated steps at the national level for the integration of the Indian native princely states with the union of India. During the period of Ikkanda Warrier ministry, on 1 July, 1949, the integration of Cochin with Travancore took place with the hearty cooperation of its ruler. The new United State of Travancore and Cochin was to have its capital at Trivandrum and the High Court at Ernakulam.

The Maharaja of Cochin having retired in favour of Sri Chitra Tirunal, the Maharaja of Travancore, the latter was to become the head of the united state of Travancore and Cochin with the title of Rajpramukh. The covenant of integration was signed by the two rulers in the last week of May 1949. It was made clear that the Rajpramukh would have no hereditary claim to this office. The Legislative Assembly of the new state was to consist of all the members of the Representative Body of Travancore and the Legislative Assembly of Cochin at the time of integration. The Rajpramukh was to function as a constitutional head. The members of the outgoing ministries in the two states constituted the new ministry of Travancore Cochin with T.K. Narayana Pillai who headed the Travancore Ministry at the time as the Prime Minister. The new head of state and members of his Cabinet were sworn in on 1 July 1949. The event marked the end of monarchy and the beginning of democratic rule in the history of Kerala.

The Movement for a United (Aikya) Kerala

The movement for a united (Aikya) Kerala gathered momentum with the attainment of independence. The first concrete step in this direction was taken on July 1, 1949. Following the national policy of integration, the State of Kochi and Travancore were merged into Travancore-Kochi State under a Rajpramukh.

The next step came with the reorganization of States on a linguistic basis in the light of the report of the States Reorganization Commission. It was decided to add Malabar district and the Kasargode taluk of south Canara district to Travancore-Kochi and to separate the Tamil-speaking southern region of old Travancore from Travancore-Kochi for inclusion in Madras State. On November 1, 1956, the new State of Kerala was formally inaugurated. The land of Parasurama thus regained its identity with the unity of the land of Bharatha.

The first elected government was headed by T.K. Narayana Pillai. The internal dissensions within the ruling Congress Party led to the formation of a new ministry in 1951 under C. Kesavan whose chief-ministership lasted only a few months. After the Nair and Ezhava chief ministers, came the Christian Chief Minister A.J. John. He could stay in office only for about two years simply because Congress Legislators from the Tamil speaking Kanyakumari District withdrew their support and demanded the merger of Kanyakumari with the Tamil-speaking Madras State. The John-ministry was succeeded by the Praja-Socialist-Party ministry of the former chief minister Pattern Thanu Pillai March 1954.

The Tamil agitation in the South took a violent turn when police opened fire on violent demonstrators killing seven people. As a result, the PSP ministry was voted out of office and replaced in February 1955 by a Congress ministry headed by Panampilly Govinda Menon. This Cabinet fell in March 1956 due to internal discussions within the ruling party, which resulted in the imposition of President's Rule in the state—the state was ruled directly by the President of India through the Governor. It was during the President's Rule that the states of the Indian Union were reorganized on linguistic basis.

Under the States Reorganization Act, four Tamil-speaking southern Taluks were separated from Kerala and ceded to Madras. The District of Malabar and the Kasargode Taluk of South Canara District were added to Travancore-Cochin to constitute the new State of Kerala. The united Kerala came into existence on November 1, 1956 with a governor as titular head of the state; the princely Rajapramukh was forced to retire.

With the general elections of 1957, the Communist Party of India came to power with E.M.S. Namboothiripad as Chief Minister. There was widespread opposition to the rule of the Communists, which came to be known as Liberation Struggle (*Vimochana Samararm*). Fifteen persons were killed by the police, and law and order broke down. The President of India dismissed the Communist Ministry and imposed President's Rule on the state on July 31, 1959 according to Constitutional provisions. After fresh elections in February a non-Communist coalition government of the Congress, PSP, and Muslim League took over administration with Pattom Thanu Pillai as Chief Minister. In 1962, R. Shankar became Chief Minister after Pattom was appointed Governor of Punjab. In September 1964, the Shankar Ministry was voted out of power, and Kerala was again placed under President's Rule. Meanwhile the Congress Party was split into Indian National Congress and Kerala Congress (a Christian Party); the Communist Party also was split into two: The Communist Party Marxist (CPM) and the Communist Party of India (CPI).

In the General Election of 1967, the United Leftist Front won 117 out of 133 seats and the Marxist leader E.M.S. Namboothiripad (CPM) became Chief Minister. However, in October 1969, the E.M.S. Ministry fell and the CPI leader C. Achutha Menon was sworn in as Chief Minister on November 1, 1969. But in August 1970, the Menon Ministry resigned and Kerala was placed once again under President's Rule—The General Election of September 1970, a Communist (CPI) Government with the support of Congress Party and Kerala Congress Party assumed office, and Achuta Menon continued as Chief Minister till 1977. After the April 1977 elections, the Congress Party, the leadership of A.K. Antony, formed a new coalition government, which was soon followed by the CPI ministry of Nayanar. The Muslim League was also able to have Muhammad Koya made Chief Minister for a few weeks before President's Rule was again imposed on Kerala. After the 1982 elections, a non-Communist coalition ministry has taken over state administration with K. Karunakaran as Chief Minister.

KNOW THE FACTS

☞ *An important innovation introduced by Marthanda Varma was the framing of the annual budget called "Pativukanakku".*

☞ *Marthanda Varma is the known as the maker of modern Travancore.*

☞ *First English factory in Kerala was set up at Vizhinjam.*

☞ *Attingal Revolt was the first organised revolt against the English in Kerala.*

☞ *In April 1723 a formal treaty was concluded between the English East India Company and the king of Travancore. It was the first treaty negotiated by the English East India Company with an Indian State. This was a treaty of friendship.*

☞ *The reign of Swathi Thirunal (1829-1847) was a Golden Age in the history of Travancore.*

☞ *First census of the state was conducted in 1836 by Swathi Thirunal.*

☞ *Ayilyam Thirunal was also the first Raja of Travancore to receive the title 'Maharaja' from the British crown.*

☞ *Sri Mulam Tirunal formulated a Legislative Council in 1888. This was the first Legislative Council in an Indian State.*

☞ *The Malabar Rebellion was in 1921.*

☞ *One of the tragic episodes of the Malabar Rebellion was the 'Wagon Tragedy' in which 61 of 90 Moppilas carried as prisoners in a closed railway goods wagon from Tirur, to Coimbatore on November 10, 1921 died of suffocation.*

☞ *The agitation known as Nivarthana (Abstention) Movement was started as a protest against the constitutional reforms of 1932.*

☞ *On July 1, 1949 the State of Travancore-Cochin came into existence. The Maharaja of Travancore became the Rajapramukh of the New State.*

☞ *The state of Kerala formally came into existence on November 1, 1956.*

☞ *The first general elections to the Kerala state Legislature were held in February and March 1957.*

TEST YOUR SELF

1. When did Vaikom Satyagraha took place in Kerala?
   A. 1923   B. 1924   C. 1925   D. 1926

2. Who among the following is the only person from Kerala to become President of Indian National Congress?
   A. C. Sankaran Nair   B. G.P. Pillai
   C. K. Madhavan Nair   D. Gopala Menon

3. During which year princely states of Travancore and Cochin merged?
   A. 1951   B. 1950   C. 1949   D. 1960

4. Which was the main centre of Salt Satyagraha in Kerala?
   A. Malabar   B. Cochin
   C. Travancore   D. None of these

5. When the State of Kerala came into existence?
   A. 1 November 1956   B. 1 November 1955
   C. 11 November 1956   D. 1 December 1956

6. When did Malabar Mutiny took place in Kerala?
   A. 1921   B. 1922   C. 1931   D. 1932

7. In which year the First All Kerala Political Conference was held?
   A. 1920   B. 1921   C. 1922   D. 1923

8. Who was the editor of 'Madras Standard' during unindependent India in Kerala?
   A. G.P. Pillai   B. C. Sankaran Nair
   C. K. Madhvan Nair   D.   Gopala Menon

9. Name the leader from Kerala who became the General Secretary of Indian National Congress twice.
   A. C. Sankaran Nair   B. K Madhavan Nair
   C. Veluthampy Dalava   D. G.P. Pillai

10. Moppilas Revolt took place in which state during British period?
    A. Kerala   B. Tamil Nadu
    C. Karnataka   D. Andhra Pradesh

ANSWERS

1	2	3	4	5	6	7	8	9	10
B	A	C	A	A	A	B	A	D	A

□□□

5

PHYSIOGRAPHIC
FEATURES OF KERALA

Kerala is a small state, tucked away in the south-west corner of India. It represents only 1.18 per cent of the total area of India but has 2.47% of the total population of the country. It is separated from the rest of the peninsula by natural geographic boundaries.

Geologically, the State can be divided into 4 major distinct zones.

The classifications are:

1. Crystalliny rock consisting of representative of the Archaean group (oldest rock group).

2. Residual laterite formed by the decomposition *in situ* of the Archaean crystallines.

3. The Warkalli formations—lignite bearing sedimentary beds with a laterite capping.

4. Recent formations consisting of alluvial, marine and lacustrine deposits. The backwater tracts come in this zone.

The Archaean group of crystalline rocks consists to:

1. **Dharwar Formations:** These are found only in the Malabar region. They are represented by ferrugenous quartzites, mica and talc schists and are found exposed in south-eastern portions of Wayanad. Quartz beds and haematite bands are seen lying with the gneisses in south Malabar.

2. **Champion Gneiss:** This is seen in the south and south-east of Wayanad and gold bearing quartz veins occur in the gneisses.

3. **Peninsular Gneiss:** This is one of the most wide spread rock types found in Kerala. In Malabar, the gneiss surrounding the Dharwar formation is seen to be highly decomposed. In south Malabar, the gneisses are more fine grained and are well laminated. In the Cochin area, the most extensive rocks are the gneisses and resemble those of south Malabar. In the Travancore

44

area, gneisses belonging to the peninsular suite occur neat the northern most regions. They are made up of quartz, orthoclase and mica.

4. **Charnockite:** This occurs very widely in the State. In the Malabar region, large exposures of charnockite are seen in south Wayanad. This is the chief rock type in the Cochin area. The quartz of this rock is colourless or grey but not blue as in the case elsewhere. A good portion of the Western Ghats is made up of Charnockite. The charnockites of the Travancore area are mostly well foliated and show typical gneisses structure.

5. **Closepet Granite:** Archaean intrusives of post charnockite age are found in two places in the Kalpetta hills and Sultanbathery. These are younger in age than the gneisses.

Kerala may be divided into three geographical regions:

1. Highland,   2. Midland,   3. Lowland.

The highlands slope down from the Western Ghats, which rise to an average height of 900 m, with a number of peaks over 1,800 m in height. This is the area of major plantations like tea, coffee, rubber, cardamom and other species.

The 'Western Ghats' with their rich primeval forests having a high degree of rainfall, form the eastern boundary and extend from the north to Kanyakumari in the south. The entire western border is caressed by the Arabian sea. Between these natural boundaries lies the narrow strip of land extending from Kasarkode in the north to Parasala in the south.

The 'Western Ghats', which form the eastern ramparts of the State rise from very low altitudes of a few hundred metres up to about 2,000 metres on an average. The 'Anamudi' peak in the high ranges of Kottayam district rises to a height of 3,000 metres and represents the highest point in India, south of Himalayas. 'Agastyakutam' the southern most peak in the Ghats, is 2,044 metres. 'Ezhimala' is a rugged hill jutting into the sea in startling isolation on the Kannur coast. Ghats are served as an effective rampart. The range has many passes which have allowed a controlled interaction between Kerala, and the lands lying beyond the mountains. The 'Peranbadi Ghat' provides access to Coorg, the 'Periyar Ghat' to the Nilgiri district. The Palghat pass, 32 km broad, has played a bigger role in the alarums and excursions of history. In south, the Bodinaikannur pass connects Devikulam and Munnar in Kerala with the Madurai district of Tamil Nadu. Other passes linking Kerala with Tamil Nadu are Thevaram, the Kambam, the Kumili and the Aramboly.

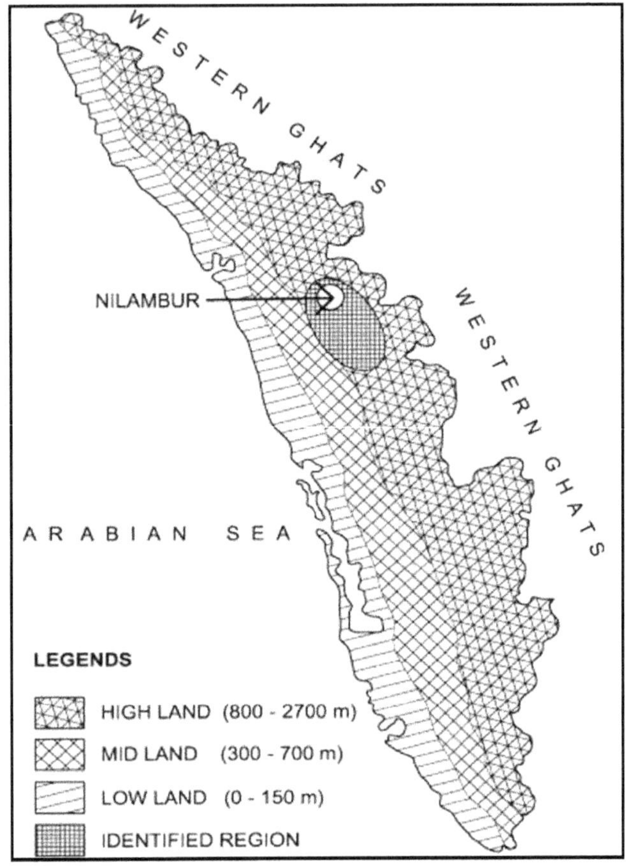

Physiographic units, altitudes and areas

Unit	Altitude (m)	Area (km²)	Area(%)
Highland	> 75 m	18653.5	48.00
Midland	7.5–75	16231.2	41.76
Lowland	0–7.5	3979.3	10.24

The hills and mountains of the Western Ghats at the eastern boundary of the State, which have an average elevation of 1 km, provide orographic lifting for the south-west monsoon winds, resulting in heavy precipitation over their slopes and very good rainfall over the midlands and lowlands.

Kerala is an elongated coastal State lied along a 590 kilometres sun-drenched coastline of the Arabian sea, banked inland by the mountain-rimmed border of the craggy Western Ghats. In between the high Western Ghats on the east and the Arabian sea on the west, this narrow green patch of land lies in the north-south direction. The width of the State varies from 35 to 120 km; with an average of about 65 km. Even within this small width, the topography and physical characteristics change distinctly from the east to west.

KNOW THE FACTS

☞ *Kerala accounts for only 1.18 per cent of India's total land area but in population accounts for only 2.47 per cent of country's total population.*

☞ *Kerala can be divided into three geographical regions namely—1. Highland, 2. Midland and 3. Lowland.*

☞ *The 'Western Ghats' form the eastern boundary and extend from the north to Kanyakumari in the south.*

☞ *The 'Anamudi' peak in the high ranges of Kottayam district rises to a height of 3,000 metres and represents the highest point in India, south of Himalayas.*

☞ *The Bodinaikannur pass connects Devikulam and Munnar in Kerala with the Madurai district of Tamil Nadu.*

TEST YOUR SELF

1. Palghat Pass joins
   A. Coimbatore with Kochi
   B. Coimbatore with Palakkad
   C. Kochi wtih Ernakulam
   D. Madurai with Ernakulam

2. Major portion of Western Ghats is located in which state?
   A. Kerala
   B. Karnataka
   C. Maharashtra
   D. Tamil Nadu

3. Western Ghats does not fall in which state?
   A. Goa
   B. Andhra Pradesh
   C. Kerala
   D. Tamil Nadu

4. Which of the following Passes lies in Kerala?
   A. Palakkad
   B. Borghat
   C. Thalghat
   D. None of these

5. Kerala shares its borders with
   A. Karnataka, Andhra Pradesh, Tamil Nadu
   B. Karnataka, Tamil Nadu
   C. Karnataka, Andhra Pradesh
   D. Karnataka, Tamil Nadu, Arabian Sea

6. What is the percentage of area of Kerala to the total area of India?
   A. 1.03%
   B. 2.03%
   C. 2%
   D. 3%

7. Western Ghats are which type of mountains?
   A. Folded
   B. Relict
   C. Block
   D. Volcanic

8. Which of the following Passes lies in Western Ghats?
   A. Palghat
   B. Borghat
   C. Thalghat
   D. All of the above

9. Which is the highest peak of Kerala?
   A. Agasthyamalai
   B. Kotamalai
   C. Anaimudi
   D. Doda Beta

10. Which of the following Passes join Tamil Nadu and Kerala?
    A. Thalghat
    B. Borghat
    C. Palghat
    D. None of the above

ANSWERS

1	2	3	4	5	6	7	8	9	10
A	D	B	A	D	A	C	D	C	C

❏❏❏

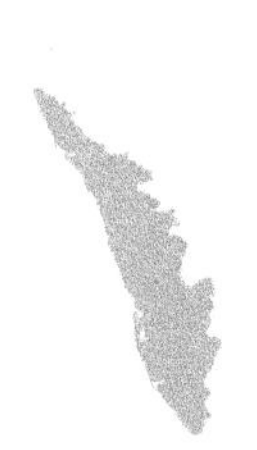

6

DRAINAGE

There are 44 rivers in Kerala with the length of main stream exceeding 15 km. Out of these 44 rivers, 41 originate from the Western Ghats region on the east of the state and flow westward to join the Lakshadweep sea. The remaining three rivers (Kabbini, Bhavani and Pambar) originate from the Western Ghats and flow towards the east and finally join the Bay of Bengal, after flowing through the neighbouring states. Here is some brief detail about some of the major rivers of Kerala.

Achankovil

The Achankovil (or Achenkovil) is a small river in Kerala, formed towards the southern tip of the peninsula from the streams of the Rishimala river, Pasukidamettu river and the Ramakkalteri river. This river joins the Pamba river at Veeyapuram in the Alappuzha district of Kerala in South India. Achankovil is also the name of the forest area, which is the catchment area for this river, and of a small town situated in the Achankovil forest area.

Mahe

Mahé river is also known as Mayyazhipuzha. It flows through the state of Kerala and the coastal exclave of Mahé in Pondicherry (Puducherry). Finally it flows to the Arabian Sea. The river passes through the villages of Naripetta, Vanimel, Iyyancode, Iringanoor, Tripangathur, Peringalam, Edachery, Kacheri, Eramala, Kariyad, Olavilam, Kunnumakkara, Azhiyoor and Mahé. The northern boundary of Mahé town is defined by the river. The influence on the economy of the region traversed by the river is very little. The river has been used for inland navigation and transportation of articles from interior villages to Mahe and back, in olden days. The government of Puducherry has planned to build a fishing harbour at the estuary of the river. To enhance tourist potential of Mahe a riverside Walkway, originating from the Water Sports Complex at Manjakkal, Mahe, on the banks of the river stretching out to the backwater of the Fishing Harbour is also being built by the government of Puducherry.

Bharathapuzha

The Bharathapuzha (Indian river), also known as Nila, and the Nile of Kerala is the second-longest river in Kerala, after the Periyar river. The word "Nila" indicates the culture more than just a river. Nila has groomed the culture and life of south Malabar part of Kerala. For the first 40 km or so, the Bharathapuzha follows an almost northerly course till Pollachi. At Parli both Kannadipuzha and Kalpathipuzha merge and flow as Bharathapuzha and follows a westerly course until it empties into the Arabian Sea at Ponnani. Thootha river merges with Nila at Pallippuram. As Thootha river is rich in water, after its merger, Nila becomes thicker in flow. The river is not navigable along most of its course except the small stretch where it joins the sea. Bharathapuzha basin is the largest among all the river basins in Kerala. Though Bharathapuzha has a large basin, the water flow is relatively less compared to other long rivers in Kerala because a large portion of the basin is located in the comparatively drier regions (Tamil Nadu and Palakkad Gap). The construction of a number of dams after independence has also reduced the river flow. In fact in the summer months, there is almost no flow in most parts of the river. The Bharathapuzha is the lifeline of many cities and villages and is the lifeline of Kerala's cultural map.

Challakudy

It is the 4th longest river in Kerala. Challakudy river is the one of very few rivers of Kerala, which is having relics of riparian vegetation in substantial level. Challakudy river is the richest river in fish diversity perhaps in India. The riparian forests of the Challakudy river have revealed the existence of a thick riparian vegetation of more than 10 metres width for a distance of 10.5 km downstream from Peringalkuth, covering an area of 58.5 hectares. Out of this, 26.4 hectares lie within the Vazachal area, including three large islands densely covered by riparian forests. The riparian forests of the area have been found to be characterised by the presence of typical riparian species of plants, in addition to evergreen and semi-evergreen species. Out of the 319 species of flowering plants identified from the study area, 24 are endemic species of the Western Ghats and 10 are rare and endangered. Moreover, the Challakudy river is known for its diversity, as it contains 85 species of fresh water fishes out of the 152 species known from Kerala. Among these, 35 are endemic species of the Western

Ghats and nine are considered to be endangered. The famous waterfalls, Athirappilly Falls and Vazhachal Falls, are situated on this river. For irrigation purposes Thumboormoozhy dam is constructed across this river. It merges with the Periyar river near Puthanvelikkara, adjacent to Manjali, North Paravur in Ernakulam district. The Parambikulam dam has been built on the Parambikulam river, one of its four tributaries.

Tirur

Tirur river begins in the Tirur taluk village of Athvanad in the Malappuram district of the state of Kerala in south India and flows south-west to Thiruvnavaya and then north-west to Elamkulam where it turns south-west, joining the Bharathapuzha river which flows into the Arabian Sea near the coastal town of Ponnani. It is known for its beautiful mangroves and its many varieties of fishes and birds. This river is navigable and forms part of west coast water transport system.

Korapuzha

Korapuzha also known as Elathur river is a short river. It is formed by the confluence of two streams, Agalapuzha and Punnoorpuzha which originate in the mountains of Wayanad district. The Korapuzha empties into the Arabian sea at Elathur. The river and its main tributaries become tidal as they near the Arabian sea. There is heavy boat traffic over the last 25 km of its course. It forms part of the West Coast Inland Navigation System. The Korapuzha is generally considered as the cordon sanitaire between the North Malabar and South Malabar in the erstwhile district of Malabar.

Karamana

The river flows 68 km westward and merges into the Arabian Sea at Thiruvallom-Karumam area near Kovalam. The river gets its name from Karamana, a suburb of Trivandrum city, through which it flows. The Karamana river has the distinction of having two dams on it despite its relatively short length. These are the Peppara dam meant for irrigation on the upper reach of the river, and the Aruvikkara dam, meant for irrigation as well as drinking water supply to the city of Trivandrum. The Karamana river has several bridges across it. The largest is at Karamana itself, where the NH-47 crosses it. Other important bridges are at Thrikkunnapuram, Mangattu Kadavu, Kundamon Kadavu, Vellaikadavu, Aruvikkara (on the dam), Maruthoor Kadavu, Aryanad and a low bridge near Malamukal. The latter makes the river unusable for navigation. Some of the bridges provide spectacular views of the river.

Manimala

It is an important water way of Central Travancore. Rising in the hills of Kottayam-Idukki ranges, the river flows through the midland plains and joins with Pamba and Manimala junction. The river offers a beautiful view at this spot and flows swiftly striking against the many rocks in the river.

Meenachil

It flows through Poonjar, Teekoy, Erattupetta, Palai, Ettumanoor and Kottayam before emptying itself into the Vembanad Lake at Kumarakom, the famous tourist place of Kerala. The Meenachil river is formed by several streams originating from the Western Ghats. The river has 47 sub watersheds and 114 micro watersheds. Meenachil river is the holy river in Kottayam district. It is also called Gauna Nadi, Kavanar and Valanjar. The name Meenachil comes from Goddess Meenakshi of Madurai, the deity of the ruling Karthas of Meenachil. Meenakshi became Meenachi and later Meenachil. The Kerala State Electricity Board has constructed two tunnels near Wagamon to divert the water from the Meenachil to the Idukki Dam. One is from the Vazhikkadavu check dam to Karinthiri and the other from Koottiyar to Kappakkanam. The Kerala Government has accorded high priority to the implementation of the Meenachil river Valley Project. The project aims at diverting excess water from the Moovattupuzha river into the Meenachil river basin by constructing a tunnel from Arakkulam to Melukavau.

Mogral

It gets its name from Mogral, a coastal village on its northern banks. The river empties into the Arabian Sea in Mogral Puthur. After flowing in a north-westerly direction through Bettipadi and Muliyar, it is joined by another stream rising from the northern part of Karadka Reserve Forest. From Yedhir, the river takes a meandering course and flows through the fairly flat regions of Madhur and Patla. Toward the end of its course, it forms a long stretch of backwaters several kilometres long.

Chandragiri

Chandragiri, also known by the name Payaswini, is a river in Kasargode district of Kerala state. On the banks of this river is 17th century Chandragiri fort. This river is considered as the traditional boundary between Tulu Nadu and Malayalam regions of Kerala. The river originates in a village called Koinadu of Kodagu district in Karnataka State. It flows in a north-westerly direction through Sullia taluk of Dakshina Kannada district. In Sullia taluk, it is the major water source for domestic and agricultural purposes. It then flows west to Kasargode district of Kerala state to join the Arabian sea.

Muvattupuzha

Muvattupuzha is a municipality in Ernakulam district in Kerala. The name is made up of three Malayalam words: 'Moonu', which stands for 'three', 'aaru'—small river, and 'puzha', which also means river. 'Aaru' is a word that is usually used for rivers in the southern half of Kerala, while the term 'puzha' is used in the northern parts. The three rivers in this case are the Kothamangalam river or Kothayaar, Kaliyar and Thodupuzhayaar, which merge to form a single river. Thus it is called centre point of confluence of three rivers or Thriveni Sangamam in Malayalam. It is situated on midland regions with planes and hills scattered all around especially on the Southern and Eastern side.

Important River Basins of Kerala

Name of River Basin	Length (km)	Catchment Area (sq. km)
Periyar	244	5398
Bharathapuzha	209	6186
Pamba	176	2235
Chaliyar	169	4765
Challakudy	130	1704
Achenkovil	129	1484
Muvattupuzha	121	2004
Kallada	121	1919
Valapattanam	110	1867
Chandragiri	105	1538

Pamba

Pamba river is the third longest river in Kerala and the longest river in the erstwhile princely state of Travancore. Sabarimala temple dedicated to Lord Ayyappa is located on the banks of the river Pamba. River Pamba is considered as the Dakshina Ganga due to its association with Kerala's largest pilgrim centre–Sabarimala. It flows through Ranni, Ayroor, Pathanamthitta, Kozhenchery, Chengannur, Kuttanad and Ambalappuzha taluks and finally empties into the Vembanad Lake. Kuttanad, an important rice cultivating area in Kerala gets the irrigation water from the Pamba river. The Pamba basin is bounded on the east by the Western Ghats. The river shares its northern boundary with the Manimala river basin, while it shares the southern boundary with the Achankovil river basin.

Periyar

The Periyar river is the longest river in the state of Kerala, India, with a length of 244 km. The Periyar is known as The Lifeline of Kerala; it is one of the few perennial rivers in the region and provides drinking water for several major towns. The Idukki Dam on the Periyar generates a significant proportion of Kerala's electrical power. It flows north through Periyar National Park into Periyar Lake, a 55 km² artificial reservoir created in 1895 by the construction of a dam across the river. Water is diverted from the lake into the Vaigai river in Tamil Nadu via a tunnel through the Western Ghats. From the lake, the river flows north-west through the village of Neeleswaram into Vembanad Lake and out to the Arabian sea coast. Its largest tributaries are the Muthirapuzha river, the Mullayar river, the Cheruthoni river, the Perinjankutti river and the Edamala river. Through the Periyar Lake dam and tunnel, the river serves as the major water source for five drought-prone districts in the state of Tamil Nadu, including Theni, Madurai and Ramanathapuram.

Valapattanam

Valapattanam river is the largest river in the Kannur district, located in the state of Kerala.

Other Rivers of Kerala

Anjarakandy	Tellichery	Ayroor	Vamanapuram
Mamom	Bhavani	Ithikkara	Kabbini
Kadalundi	Karuvannurm	Keecheri	Puzhakkal
Kuppam	Kuttiyadi	Neyyar	Nileswar
Kariangode	Kavvayi	Pallikkal	Kallada
Pambar	Peruvamba	Ramapuram	Chittari

Backwaters

In addition to the rivers, Kerala has a continuous chain of lagoons and backwaters that run parallel to the sea-coast and receive water from the numerous streams and rivers of the land. They facilitate almost through communication between the northern and southern parts of Kerala. The most important lakes in North Kerala are Kumbla, Kalnad, Bekal, Kavvai etc. The place of pride among the Kerala backwaters goes to the ever blue Vembanad lake which stretches from Alleppey to Cochin and is 52 miles long. It covers an area of 79 sq. miles. The famous pilgrim centre of Vaikom is situated on the banks of this lake. The Vembanad Lake has taken its name from the ancient kingdom of Vempolinad which split itself into the principalities of Vadakkumkur and Tekkumkur sometime about 1200 A.D. The chief lakes in South Kerala are the Kayamkulam lake

(19 miles) and the Ashtamudi lake (10 miles) each of which covers an area of 20 sq miles. The Sasthamcotta Lake in the Quilon district is the one and only major fresh-water lake in Kerala. It is surrounded by high hills on three sides and a one-mile long earthen bund on the fourth. The area of the lake is 1.44 sq. miles. On its banks is situated a famous Sastha temple fabled to have been founded by Sri Rama. There are also a few important places called *Azhis* on the Kerala coast where the backwaters establish permanent communication with the sea. The Chief *Azhis* in the state are those of Azhikkal (Valapattanam), Chettuvai, Cranganore, Cochin, Nindakara etc.

KNOW THE FACTS

- *There are 44 rivers in Kerala, 41 of them originate from the Western Ghats region on the east and flow westward to join the Lakshadweep sea while in remaining three flow towards the east to join Bay of Bengal.*
- *Mahé river flows through the state of Kerala and the coastal exclave of Mahé in Puducherry.*
- *The Bharathapuzha (Indian river), is also known as Nila, and the Nile of Kerala.*
- *Thootha river merges with Nila at Pallippuram.*
- *Bharathapuzha basin is the largest among all the river basins in Kerala.*
- *Challakudy river is the richest river in fish diversity perhaps in India.*
- *The famous waterfalls, Athirappilly Falls and Vazhachal Falls, are situated on river Challakudy.*
- *Tirur river is known for its beautiful mangroves. This river is navigable and forms part of west coast water transport system.*
- *Korapuzha is formed by the confluence of two streams, Agalapuzha and Punnoorpuzha which originate in the mountains of Wayanad district.*
- *Sabarimala temple dedicated to Lord Ayyappa is located on the banks of the river Pamba.*
- *The Pamba basin is bounded on the east by the Western Ghats.*
- *The Periyar river is the longest river in the state of Kerala.*
- *The Periyar is known as The Lifeline of Kerala.*
- *The Idukki Dam on the Periyar generates a significant proportion of Kerala's electrical power.*
- *Vembanad lake which stretches from Alleppey to Cochin is 52 miles long.*

TEST YOUR SELF

1. Which is the longest river of Kerala?
   A. Bharathapuzha
   B. Periyar
   C. Pamba
   D. Chalakudy

2. Solayar HEP is located on which river?
   A. Pamba
   B. Chaliyar
   C. Periyar
   D. Chalakudy

3. Which of the following is the smallest river of Kerala?
   A. Kallai
   B. Ramapuram
   C. Ayiroor
   D. Bangra Manjeswara

4. One of the largest irrigation project 'Pazhassi Project' is situated on which river?
   A. Valapattanam
   B. Kalladayar
   C. Cholakudy
   D. Chandragiri

5. Sabirigiri Hydro-Electric Project (HEP) is located on which river?
   A. Periyar
   B. Pamba
   C. Chalakudy
   D. Chaliyar

6. Out of the following rivers, which river does not flow eastward?
   A. Mahi
   B. Samba
   C. Kabani
   D. Bhavani

7. Which is the largest lake of Kerala?
   A. Asthmundi
   B. Vembanand
   C. Vembanattu
   D. Sasthamkotta

8. Aranmula Boat Race event took place on which river?
   A. Pamba
   B. Periyar
   C. Bharathapuzha
   D. Mahi

9. Which of the following is the second largest lake in Kerala?
   A. Vembanand
   B. Sasthamkotta
   C. Asthmundi
   D. Veeranpuzha

10. The Idukki Dam which generates a significant proportion of Kerala's electrical power is situated on which river?
    A. Periyar
    B. Pamba
    C. Chandragiri
    D. Challakudy

Answers

1	2	3	4	5	6	7	8	9	10
B	D	D	A	B	A	B	A	C	A

❑❑❑

7

CLIMATE OF KERALA

The climate of Kerala, is tropical monsoon with seasonally excessive rainfall and hot summer except over Thiruvananthapuram district, where the climate is tropical savana with seasonally dry and hot summer weather. The year may be divided into four seasons. The period March to the end of May is the hot season. This is followed by South-west Monsoon season that continues till the beginning of October. From October to December is the Northeast Monsoon season and the two months January and February winter season. The climate is pleasant from September to February. Summer months March to May is uncomfortable due to high temperature and humidity. The State is extremely humid due to the existence of Arabian Sea in the west of it.

The seasonal variation of atmospheric pressure over the State takes place in a systematic manner with maximum pressures during January and minimum pressures during May-June. The pressure gradient over the State generally remains weak except during late summer and in the monsoon season. The annual range of pressure is less than 5 mb. The total diurnal range of pressure increases from the coast to the inland regions and this is also within about 5 mb. The maximum in the diurnal range of pressure is seen in the month of February when clouding is almost minimum. June and July with maximum clouding have the minimum diurnal range. In all the seasons, the pressure gradients over the State is in the east-west direction. The pressure decreases from west to east except during the period from about middle of October to beginning of March, when reverse gradient prevails.

Day temperatures are more or less uniform over the plains throughout the year except during monsoon months when these temperatures drop down by about 3 to 5°C. Both day and night temperatures are lower over the plateau and at high level stations than over the plain. Day temperatures of coastal places are less than those of interior places. March-April are the hottest months with a mean maximum temperature of about 33°C.

Mean maximum temperature is minimum in the month of July when the State receives plenty of rainfall and the sky is heavily clouded. The mean maximum temperature for the entire State in July is 28.5°C, varying from about 28°C in the north to about 29°C in the south. The night temperature is minimum in January when clouding is also minimum. For the State as whole, the mean minimum temperature is about 22.5°C in January, varying from 22°C in the north to 22.6°C in the south. At hilly stations, the values are much lower.

Over the entire Indian subcontinent the moisture content of the atmosphere is minimum during the winter months and maximum during the summer monsoon months. The annual variations over Kerala are less than over north India. At the coastal stations of Kerala the monthly mean relative humidity at the surface is the order of 75% in the morning during the winter months and increases to about 90% in the monsoon months.

The total annual rainfall in the State varies from about 4500 mm over the northern parts to about 2000 mm in the southern parts. The south-west monsoon, locally known as 'Edavapathi', (June-September) is the principal rainy season. During this season, the State receives about 73% of its annual rainfall.

Winter Season

In Kerala, the winter season starts when the north-east monsoons ends. That is from the month of November till the middle of February. During this time, the temperature is less but it does not have much difference with the other seasons. The temperature remains cool constantly throughout the year in the highlands but the winter temperatures falls below 10°C. It is during this winter season that we receive some of the lowest amount of rainfall.

Summer Season

The temperature starts to increase with the end of February which indicates the beginning of summer in Kerala. The characteristics of summer in Kerala are relatively higher temperature, less rainfall and humid weather. The other Indian states have a temperature of about 40°C, whereas in Kerala it is comparatively cool and pleasant. It is mainly because of the presence of the Western ghats that prevents the northern wind from entering the state. The Arabian sea gives a cool breeze which helps to make the temperature moderate. Another important feature of this season is the arrival of rain which is accompanied by thunder and lightening. The summer season extends from March till May or the beginning of June. It ends with the beginning of monsoon.

South-West Monsoon

The rainy season in Kerala is the south-west monsoon. In Malayalam, this season is called as Edavapathi which means in the middle of the Malayalam month Edavam. It is called so because the rain starts by the middle of this month that is the end of May or early June. The following two months have torrential rain. As Kerala lies on the windward side of the Western Ghats and is the first state to get hit by the monsoon winds, this state receives heavy rainfall. It is the monsoon that provides almost 85% of the rains. The slopes of the Western Ghats receive the highest amount of rain. The rivers get flooded by the monsoons. This season continues till the end of September.

North-East Monsoon

The north-east monsoon is also known as the Retreating Monsoon or the Reverse monsoons. This hits Kerala when the south-west monsoon winds take their return. These rains are called as Thulavarsham in Malayalam because it rains during the Malayalam month Thulam. It comes in the month October and November and at times continues up to December. The main feature of this season is heavy rains during afternoon together with lightening and thunder. The days are usually warm and humid without much variation in temperature.

KNOW THE FACTS

- *The State is extremely humid due to the existence of Arabian Sea in the west of it.*
- *The seasonal variation of atmospheric pressure over the State takes place in a systematic manner with maximum pressures during January and minimum pressures during May-June.*
- *The maximum in the diurnal range of pressure is seen in the month of February.*
- *Day temperatures are more or less uniform over the plains throughout the year except during monsoon months.*
- *Both day and night temperatures are lower over the plateau and at high level stations than over the plain.*
- *The total annual rainfall in the State varies from about 4500 mm over the northern parts to about 2000 mm in the southern parts.*
- *The south-west monsoon, locally known as 'Edavapathi', (June-September) is the principal rainy season.*
- *The slopes of the Western Ghats receive the highest amount of rain.*
- *The north-east monsoon hits Kerala when the south-west monsoon winds take their return.*
- *Rains during North-east monsoon are called as Thulavarsham in Malayalam.*

TEST YOUR SELF

1. Kerala lies close to ....
A. North Pole   B. South Pole
C. Equator   D. None of these

2. Western Ghats lie in which part of Kerala?
A. East   B. West
C. North   D. South

3. Kerala is bestowed with a pleasant and equable climate throughout the year because of ....
A. nearness to the sea   B. presence of Western ghats
C. low altitude   D. Both A and B

4. Kerala receives highest rainfall during ....
A. South-West monsoon   B. North-East monsoon
C. Cyclones   D. None of these

5. Peerumedu received highest rainfall in Kerala is located in which district?
A. Kannur   B. Idukki   C. Kasaragode   D. Thrissur

6. Kerala receives average rainfall during summer is ....
A. 105 mm   B. 120 mm   C. 135 mm   D. 182 mm

7. *Edavappathi* is the local name of which of the following seasons?
A. Summer season   B. Winter season
C. South-West monsoon season   D. North-East monsoon season

8. Which types of rains is called *Thulavarsam*?
A. Cyclonic rains   B. North-East monsoon rains
C. South-West monsoon rains   D. None of these

9. Atmospheric pressure in Kerala is highest during ....
A. May   B. December
C. January   D. April

10. The maximum in the diurnal range of pressure is seen in the month of ....
A. April   B. May   C. September   D. February

ANSWERS

1	2	3	4	5	6	7	8	9	10
C	A	D	A	B	C	C	B	C	D

❑❑❑

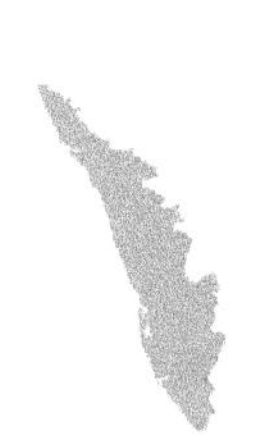

8

<u>SOILS</u>

The soils of the State can broadly be classified into sandy, alluvial, laterite, red, black, peaty, and forest-hill soils. The sandy soils occur as a narrow belt all along the coast. Varying in texture from sandy loams to pure sand, they are highly porous with low retentive capacity. The alluvial soils are transported soils and cover almost the entire tract of Kuttanad and the Kole lands of Trichur and Mukundapuram taluks. Heavy in textures they are generally well supplied with organic matter, nitrogen and potash but are deficient in phosphate and lime. Laterite soils are, by far, the most important group found in Kerala and cover the largest area. They are formed by the weathering of acidic rocks under alternate wet and dry tropical conditions. These are generally developed in regions of heavy rainfall and high temperature. Porous and well drained, their capacity for retaining water and fertilizers is somewhat poor. Laterite soils are usually of low fertility. Those found in the hills are gritty and shallow, but in the plains it is deeper, finer texture containing fair quantity of organic matter and deficient in phosphate, potash and lime. Though laterite soils are of low natural fertility they respond well to cultivation and judicious application of fertilizers.

In some parts of Kerala, where rainfall is only less than 2000 mm, the soils have not developed into true laterites. There is an accumulation of iron and aluminium in these soils and they show many of the properties of laterites. Peaty or Kari soils occur in the taluks of Ponnai, Kanayannur, Vaikom, Chertala, Ambalapuzha and Kuttanad. These are clayey soils with poor aeration and drainage. They are characterized by a deep black colour, high content of organic matter and very strong acidity. The failure of crops in Kari lands is largely due to the production of free sulphuric acid. Due to annual inundation with salt water, there is considerable accumulation of soluble alkali salts in these soils which further complicate their fertility problems. On the whole, these soils are noted for their poor fertility and low yields of crops.

Forest-hill soils are formed in about 26% of the area of the State. They are characterised by a surface layer of organic matter derived from forest growths. These soils are rich in nitrogen but extremely poor in bases due to heavy leaching. When the forest are cleared, these soils gradually undergo laterisation. Plantation crops such as tea, cardamom, and rubber are extensively grown on cleared forest soils. In Chittur and Palakkad taluks, black soils are also found covering a small area. These soils are neutral or slightly alkaline in reaction. Cotton is the main crop growing on these soils.

Morphological Classification of Soils

In general, the soils of Kerala are acidic, kaolintic and gravelly with low CEC (Cation Exchange Capacity), low water holding capacity and high phosphate fixing capacity. On the basis of the morphological features and physico-chemical properties, the soils of the State have been classified into red loam, laterite, coastal alluvium, riverine alluvium, Onattukara alluvium, brown hydromorphic, saline hydromorphic, Kuttanad alluvium, black soil and forest loam.

Red Loam

Red loams of Kerala are localized in occurrence and are found mostly in the southern parts of Thiruvananthapuram district. These soils occur in catenary sequence along with laterites and are found mainly as deposits by colluviation in foothills and small hillocks. The soils have red colour, which has been attributed to the presence of haematite or anhydrous ferric oxides. The rapid permeability of the surface soils also has been responsible for the characteristic development of these loamy soils, which are very deep and homogeneous without much expression of horizons. They are not fertile due to low organic matter content as well as low essential plant nutrients.

Laterite Soil

Laterite of Kerala is typical kaolinitic weathering products of gneissic and granitic rocks developed under humid tropical conditions. Heavy rainfall and high temperature prevalent in the State are conducive to the process of laterisation. The surface soil, which is reddish brown to yellowish red, is mostly gravelly loam to gravelly clay loam in texture. The profiles have well-developed B-horizon with abundant ferruginous and quartz gravels. The plinthite is characterized by a compact vesicular mass below the B-horizon, composed essentially of a mixture of hydrated oxides of iron and aluminium. Laterites are in generally poor in nitrogen, phosphorus and potassium and are low in the bases. They have poor water-holding capacity, CEC and high phosphorus fixing capacity with low organic matter content. They are generally acidic with pH ranging from 4.5 to 6.2.

They cover about 65% of the total area of the State, occupying a major portion of the midland and mid-upland regions and are the most extensive of the soil groups found in Kerala.

Coastal Alluvium

As it has been developed from recent marine deposits Sand is the chief constituent of this type of soil. Soil profile surface is not well developed. They show incipient development.

These soils are seen in the coastal tracts along the west as a narrow belt with an average width of about 10 km. The texture is dominated by sand fraction. The horizon is usually thin and the surface textures observed are loamy sand and sandy loam. It has very rapid permeability. These soils are of low fertility level.

Riverine Alluvium

This soil occurs throughout the state cutting across the extensive laterite soils. They are important in Kollam taluk. This type of soil, developed along river valley, occurs mostly along the banks of rivers and their tributaries. They are very deep soils which surface texture ranging from sandy loam to clay loam. Horizon differentiation is not well expressed. They are moderately supplied with organic matter, nitrogen and potassium. They are acidic and poor in phosphorus and lime.

Onattukara Alluvium

They occur as marine deposits extending to the interior up to the lateritic belt. These soils are confined to the Onattukara region comprising the Karunagapally, Karthikapally and Mavelikara taluks of Kollam and Alappuzha districts. The soils are, in general, coarse textured with immature profiles. These soils have very rapid permeability. In low-lying areas, the water table is high and drainage is a problem. Addition of sufficient organic matter and irrigation facilities improve the water holding capacity. Coconut, Paddy and Tapioca are the major products derived from these soils. They are acidic in reaction and are extremely deficient in all the major plant nutrients.

Brown Hydromorphic

They have been formed as a result of transportation and sedimentation of material from adjacent hill slopes and also through deposition by rivers.

Presence of Lateritic and gravel suggest that these are formed by the action of gravity. Hydromorphic soils, as a group, occur extensively in the State. These soils are mostly confined to valley bottoms of undulating topography in the midland and to low lying areas of coastal strip. These are also found in areas of wetland. The soil is deep brown in colour. Compositionally it ranges between sandy loam to clay. Drainage is the major problem of this kind of soil.

Saline Hydromorphic

These soils are usually seen within the coastal tracts of the districts of Ernakulam, Alappuzha, Thrissur and Kannur. These soils are in general brownish and deep. The profile show wide variation in texture, as is common in most of the alluvial soils. This soil is imperfectly drained. In these soils one crop of Paddy is cultivated during August-December.

Kuttanad Alluvium

The Kuttanad region covering about 875 km^2 is a unique agricultural area in the world. A good portion of this area lies 1–2 m below MSL and is submerged for major parts of the year. The area is susceptible to seasonal ingress of saline water as a result of tidal inflow from the sea. During the monsoons, the rivers and rivulets pour fresh water into the area. As the north-east monsoon recedes, seawater again enters the Vembanad Lake and the whole area becomes saline. Hence, the soils of Kuttanad area are faced with the serious problems of hydrology floods, acidity and salinity. Consequent on the construction of the Thanneermukkam bund, salinity hazards have been considerably reduced. The soils of Kuttanad form the typical waterlogged soils and are entirely different from normal well-drained soils in their morphological, chemical and physical characteristics.

Black Soils

These soils are dark, low in organic matter, calcareous, neutral to moderately alkaline and high in clay content. Black soils are restricted in their occurrence to Chittur taluk of Palakkad district. They are found to occur in patches and are considered as extension of the black cotton soils observed in the adjacent Coimbatore district of Tamil Nadu.

Forest Loam

They are the products of weathering of crystalline rocks under forest cover. They generally show wide variation in depth and are dark reddish brown to black, with loam to silty loam texture. They have immature profiles with shallow soils, followed by gneissic parent material in various stages of weathering. In areas with lesser canopy cover, signs of laterisation have been observed in the profiles. In denuded areas, leaching and deposition of humus in the lower layers are observed. They are found in the eastern parts of the State.

Land Use Pattern

Kerala has a diverse land use and cropping pattern. The land reforms introduced in the State brought in radical and comprehensive institutional changes leading to drastic transformation in the land holding pattern. This has resulted in shift in the land use pattern. Agriculture is the dominant land use type of the State.

Land use Pattern in Kerala

Sl. No.	Land Use	Area in '000 ha	Percentage
1.	Total Geographical Area	3,886	
2.	Reporting area for land utilization	3,886	100
3.	Forests	1,082	27.83
4.	Not available for cultivation	525	13.50
5.	Permanent pastures and other grazing lands	0	0
6.	Land under Misc. Tree crops and groves	3	0.07
7.	Culturable wasteland	97	2.49
8.	Fallow lands other than current fallows	56	1.44
9.	Current fallows	77	1.97
10.	Net area sown	2,048	52.70

Source: Landuse statistics, Ministry of Agriculture, GOI, 2012-13.

KNOW THE FACTS

☞ *The sandy soils occur as a narrow belt all along the coast and are highly porous with low retentive capacity.*

☞ *The alluvial soils are transported soils and cover almost the entire tract of Kuttanad and the Kole lands of Trichur and Mukundapuram taluks.*

☞ *Laterite soils are, the most important group found in Kerala and cover the largest area. These are generally developed in regions of heavy rainfall and high temperature.*

☞ *Peaty or Kari soils occur in the taluks of Ponnai, Kanayannur, Vaikom, Chertala, Ambalapuzha and Kuttanad. These are clayey soils with poor aeration and drainage.*

☞ *Forest-hill soils are formed in about 26% of the area of the State. These soils are rich in nitrogen but extremely poor in bases due to heavy leaching.*

☞ *Plantation crops such as tea, cardamom, and rubber are extensively grown on cleared forest soils.*

☞ *Red loams of Kerala are localized in occurrence and are found mostly in the southern parts of Thiruvananthapuram district.*

☞ *Black soils are restricted in their occurrence to Chittur taluk of Palakkad district.*

TEST YOUR SELF

1. Which soils are most suitable for cotton cultivation?
   A. Red Loams
   B. Coastal Alluvium
   C. Black Soils
   D. Laterite Soils

2. Which soils cover the maximum area of the state?
   A. Black Soils
   B. Coastal Alluvium
   C. Red Loams
   D. Laterite Soils

3. Red Loams of Kerala are localized in occurrence and are found mostly in southern part of ....
   A. Thrissur
   B. Kannur
   C. Thiruvananthapuram
   D. Wayanad

4. Saline Hydromorphic Soils are not usually seen in ....
   A. Ernakulam
   B. Alappuzha
   C. Thrissur
   D. Wayanad

5. Which soils are formed by the action of gravity?
   A. Brown Hydromorphic
   B. Saline Hydromorphic
   C. Kuttanad Alluvium
   D. Forest Loams

6. Which among the following soils are found in the eastern parts of the state?
   A. Black Soils
   B. Forest Loams
   C. Saline Hydromorphic
   D. Laterite Soils

7. Out of total geographical area, net sown area in Kerala is ....
   A. 48 per cent
   B. 28 per cent
   C. 53 per cent
   D. 43 per cent

8. Black soils are mainly found in ....
   A. Wayanad   B. Thrissur   C. Palakkad   D. Kannur

9. Which soils are acidic and poor in phosphorus and lime?
   A. Riverine Alluvium
   B. Onattukara Alluvium
   C. Coastal Alluvium
   D. Red Loams

10. Which soils are the products of weathering of crystalline rocks?
    A. Saline Hydromorphic
    B. Kuttanad Alluvium
    C. Black Soils
    D. Forest Loams

ANSWERS

1	2	3	4	5	6	7	8	9	10
C	D	C	D	A	B	C	C	A	D

FORESTS AND WILDLIFE

The forests in the State come under the broad category of tropical forests and form the western extremity of the Indo-Malayan rain forest formation. On account of the variation in precipitation, temperature, altitude, etc., the forests in Kerala are characterised by extreme floristic diversity. The major types of forests in Kerala are:

1. Evergreen and semi-evergreen forests,
2. Moist deciduous forests,
3. Dry deciduous forests and
4. Montane sub-tropical and temperate forests.

In addition to these natural types, extensive areas have been converted into man-made forests.

In Kerala, forests fall in two biogeographic provinces of Western Ghats and the western coast, and are rich in biodiversity and vital for environmental protection and considered to be a repository of rare and endangered flora and fauna.

Evergreen and Semi-evergreen Forests

The tropical evergreen and semi-evergreen forests are chiefly found in Thenmala, Achankovil-Kakki belt, Periyar, Sholayar, Attappady, Silent Valley, New Amarambalam and Wayanad. The total area of the evergeen forests has been estimated as 4750 sq. km.

Typically an evergreen and semi-evergreen forest has a multi-storeyed structure with the dominants reaching a height of 40 metres or even higher. Important species that occur in the top canopy are *Acrocarpus fraxinifolius, Antiaris toxicaria, Calophyllum spp, Cullenia exarillata, Dichopsis ellipticum, Dipterocarpus indicus, Hopea parviflora, Mesua ferrea,* etc.

On account of the heavy shade, the forest floor is devoid of undergrowth and is usually covered with a thick layer of leaf litter at various stages of decomposition. By improving the physical qualities, particularly the porosity of the soil, the leaf litter plays an important role in regulating the surface run off. The semi-evergreen forests occur as a transitional zone between the moist deciduous and the evergreen forests. Micro climatic factors, especially the availability of moisture during summer has led to the existence of semi-evergreen patches along stream banks and protected valleys.

Moist Deciduous Forests

Moist deciduous forests are less inaccessible, and their proximity to habitations makes them extremely vulnerable to the various anthropic disturbances. Moist deciduous forests form a closed high forest in which the dominant species are deciduous. From the point of view of wood production, these forests play an important role. Important timber species are *Tectona grandis, Dalbergia latifolia, Pterocarpous marsupium, Artocarpus hirsuta, Adina cordifolia, Xylia xylocarpa, Lagerstroemia lanceolatea, Grewia tilifolia, Bombax ceiba*, etc. Another economically important constituent in the moist deciduous forest is Bamboos. On account of the unsystematic exploitation coupled with the luke warm approach to extending the area by artificial regeneration, the bamboo resources in the State is getting depleted at a very rapid rate.

Dry Deciduous Forests

The dry deciduous forests are seen in the rain shadow region of the Western Ghats and extend over an area of about 170 sq. km. As far as floristic diversity is concerned this is an inferior type. Important species found are *Santalum album, Anogeissus spp.* and Bamboos.

Montane Temperate Forests

The climatic conditions at higher elevation in the Western Ghats have helped the formation of montane wet temperate forests or what are popularly known as Sholas. They usually occur in protected valleys of the hills and form a thick mass of tangled growth. Although they are not commercially valuable, especially from the point of timber production, ecologically they play an important role, more specifically in the hydrological cycle. Between the Shola patches there are extensive grasslands. Vast stretches of these grasslands have been converted into plantations.

Man-made Forests

Kerala is a pioneer in raising man-made forests. By 1978 the total area of plantations under the control of the Forest Department was about 1350 sq. km. In addition, the Kerala Forest Development Corporation has also planted extensive areas with Eucalyptus. Although several species have been raised, teak continues to be the most important species. At the beginning of 1978, teak covered an area of about 68,500 ha or more than half of the area under plantations. Other species raised in mixture with teak are *Bombax ceiba, Ailanthus triphysa, Euodia lunaankenda,* etc. Due to the poor performance of these species, in effect most of these plantations contain only teak.

Forest Cover

The pressure on India's forests is very high because of high population. The rapid growth in the economy of the country in the last one decade has put additional demands on forest for infrastructure development. Forest plays an important role in the country's ecological stability and economic development. The national forest policy in India, since 1952 has set a goal of bringing one-third area of the country under forest cover. India aims at maintaining a minimum of 33% of country's geographical area under forest and tree cover.

District-wise Forest Cover of Kerala (Area in km²)

District	Geographical Area	2015 Assessment				Per cent of GA
		Very Dense Forest	Mod. Forest	Open Forest	Total	
Alappuzha	1,414	0	45	67	112	7.92
Ernakulam	2,407	12	282	412	706	29.33
Idukki	5,019	349	2,081	1,340	3,770	75.11
Kannur	2,966	21	346	971	1,338	45.11
Kasargode	1,992	0	306	551	857	43.02
Kollam	2,491	99	671	632	1,402	56.28
Kottayam	2,203	12	530	341	883	40.08
Kozhikode	2,344	30	316	706	1,052	44.88
Malappuram	3,549	142	417	916	1,475	41.56
Palakkad	4,480	317	677	767	1,761	39.31
Pathanamthitta	2,641	158	1,202	382	1,742	65.96
Thiruvananthapuram	2,193	60	718	539	1,317	60.05
Thrissur	3,033	181	454	490	1,125	37.09
Wayanad	2,131	142	1,256	301	1,699	79.73
Grand Total	**38,863**	**1,523**	**9,301**	**8,415**	**19,239**	**49.50**

Wildlife

At present, there are 17 Wildlife Sanctuaries (including three Bird Sanctuaries) and six National Parks in Kerala, covering a total area of 2,346.33 km². Parts of two Biosphere Reserves, namely Nilgiri Biosphere

Reserve with an extent of 1455.40 km^2 and the newly proposed Agasthiyavanam Biosphere Reserve with an area of 1701 km^2 in Kerala are also protected areas within the State to preserve the forests and biodiversity. Including Biosphere Reserves, a total area of about 5,502.78 km^2 is under the protected area network, which comes to about 14 per cent of the geographic area of Kerala.

Project Tiger

Project Tiger programme was launched during 1973 to conserve the wild populations of the species in the country. The programme is spread over different States of which 777 km^2 is in Kerala. It was launched in the State in Thekkady Wildlife Sanctuary during 1978 to preserve Tiger and its prey base and the habitat. The programme is successful and recent wildlife census shows that the number of tigers in the State has increased substantially.

Project Elephant

Project Elephant was launched in 1991 aimed at conservation of elephant through protection and management of their habitat range. The elephant reserves identified in Kerala include Wayanad, Nilambur, Animudi and Periyar.

National Parks and Wildlife Sanctuaries in Kerala

Name (District in Brackets)	Year of Notification	Area Sq. Km	Importat Animals and Plants
NATIONAL PARKS			
Eravikulam (Idukki)	1972 1978 (N.P.)	97	Nilgiri Tahr (Ibex), Nilgiri Pine Marten, High elevation shola birds
Silent Valley (Palakkad)	1984	89.52 + 148 (added in 2007 as buffer zone)	Lion Tailed Macaque, Tiger, Lesser carnivores
SANCTUARIES			
Periyar Tiger Reserve (Idukki)	1950 350 sq. Km. notified in 1982 as National Park	777.54+148 (added in 2007, actual transfer 2012)	Tiger, Lion Tailed Macaque, Black Panther, Elephant, smaller mammals
Peechi-Vazhani Wildlife (Thrissur)	1958	125	Tiger, Leopard, Sloth Bear, Elephant, Sambar, Barking Deer, Bonnet Macaque, Nilgiri langur, Slender Loris, Porcupine

Neyyar Wildlife (Thiruvananthapuram)	1958	128	Ibex, Lion Tailed Macaque, Elephant, Nilgiri Langur, Crocodile, Shola birds. More than 150 endemics.
Parambikulam Wildlife (Palakkad) Tiger Reserve	1973 Notified as TR in Dec. 2009	274 Core of Tiger Reserve 390.88 Buffer zone 252.77 from 2009	Nilgiri Tahr, Lion Tailed Macaque, Tiger, Gaur, Elephant, Nilgiri Marten, Mouse Deer, Hornbill, King Cobra, Cane Turtle, Malabar Gaint Squirrel, Sloth Bear, Drongos, Bee-eaters, Treepies
Wayanad Wildlife (Wayanad)	1973	344	Elephant, Tiger, Gaur, Panther, Sambar, Spotted Deer, Barking Deer, Wild Boar, Sloth Bear, Nilgiri Langur, Bonnet Macaque, Common Otter, Malabar Giant Squirrel
Idukki Wildlife (Idduki)	1976	77.6	Elephant, Sambar
Peppara Wildlife (Thiruvananthapuram)	1983	53	Lion Tailed Macaque, Elephant, Shola birds
Thattekkad Wildlife (Idukki)	1983	25.14	Ceylon Frogmouth, Bourdillon's Long eared Indian Nightjar, Peninsular Bay owl, Crimson throated barbet, Malabar hornbill, Malabar shama, Greyheaded fising eagle, Malabar trogon, Leopard, Sloth Bear
Chinnar Wildlife (Idukki)	1984	90.44	Nilgiri Tahr, Elephant, Panther, Dry habitat species of animals & birds, Rhododendron, Neelakurinji and other shola species
Chimmony Wildlife (Thrissur)	1984	90	Elephant, Tiger
Aralam Wildlife (Kannur)	1984	55	Gaur, Sambar, Nilgiri Langur
Chenduruny Wildlife (Kollam)	1984	100.32	Tiger, Lion Tailed Macaque, Shola birds & lesser predators.
Kurinjimala (Idukki)	2006	32 (approx.)	Strobilanthes kunthiana (neelakurinji plant) and other shola species
Mangalavanam Bird Sanctuary (Ernakulam)	2004	0.0274	Birds

Choolannur Pea Fowl (Thrissur & Palakkad)	2007	3.42	Pea fowl
Malabar Wildlife (Kozhikode)	2009 (intention notified)	74.22	Brown Palm Civet, Tiger, Kerala laughing thrush, Wayanad laughing thrush, Musheer (fish), King cobra, butterflies

OTHER NATIONAL PARKS

Anamudi Shola National Park (Idukki)	2003	7.5	Shola Species
Mathikettan Shola National Park (Idukki)	2003	12.82	Shola Species
Pambadum Shola National Park (Idukki)	2003	1.32	Shola Species, Tiger
Periyar National Park	1982	350	

COMMUNITY RESERVE

Kadalundi-Vallikunnu (Mallappuram)	2008	1.5	Birds (terns, gulls, herons, sandpipers, whimbrels etc) Mangroves, crabs, mussels

In Kerala there are six National Parks, three bird sanctuaries, 14 sancturies, and one community reserve.

KNOW THE FACTS

☞ *The tropical evergreen and semi-evergreen forests are chiefly found in Thenmala, Achankovil-Kakki belt, Periyar, Sholayar, Attappady, Silent Valley, New Amarambalam and Wayanad.*

☞ *The dry deciduous forests are seen in the rain shadow region of the Western Ghats.*

☞ *The climatic conditions at higher elevation in the Western Ghats have helped the formation of montane wet temperate forests, popularly known as Sholas which usually occur in protected valleys of the hills and form a thick mass of tangled growth.*

☞ *There are 17 Wildlife Sanctuaries (including three Bird Sanctuaries) and five National Parks in Kerala.*

☞ *Project Tiger programme was launched in the State in Thekkady Wildlife Sanctuary during 1978 to preserve Tiger and its prey base and the habitat.*

☞ *Project Elephant was launched in 1991 aimed at conservation of elephant through protection and management of their habitat range.*

☞ *The elephant reserves identified in Kerala include Wayanad, Nilambur, Animudi and Periyar.*

TEST YOUR SELF

1. Which of the following is first Biosphere Reserve of India?
   A. Nilgiri Biosphere Reserve
   B. Sunderbans Biosphere Reserve
   C. Nanda Devi Biosphere Reserve
   D. Simlipal Biosphere Reserve

2. Which district of Kerala has the largest area under forest cover?
   A. Alappuzha   B. Kollam
   C. Kannur   D. Idukki

3. Which one of the following is the first Wildlife Sanctuary of Kerala?
   A. Periyar Wildlife Sanctuary   B. Peppara Wildlife Sanctuary
   C. Neyyar Wildlife Sanctuary   D. Aralam Wildlife Sanctuary

4. Which one out of the following is a Bird Sanctuary?
   A. Mangalavanam   B. Aralam
   C. Chimmony   D. Chinnar

5. Kerala has how many National Parks?
   A. 5   B. 6   C. 4   D. 9

6. In which year government of Kerala has banned clear felling of natural forest?
   A. 1981   B. 1982   C. 1983   D. 1984

7. Which type of forest has maximum expansion in Kerala?
   A. Tropical dry decidous forest   B. Tropical moist decidous forest
   C. Tropical wet evergreen forest   D. Mountain sub-tropical forest

8. During which year Nilgiri Biosphere Reserve was established in Kerala?
   A. 1980   B. 1986   C. 1990   D. 1985

9. 'Tiger Project' was launched in which year in the state?
   A. 1973   B. 1975   C. 1978   D. 1980

10. Which is the biggest National Park of Kerala?
    A. Eravikulam National Park   B. Silent Valley National Park
    C. Pampadam Sola   D. Anamudi Sola

ANSWERS

1	2	3	4	5	6	7	8	9	10
A	D	A	A	B	C	C	B	C	A

❑❑❑

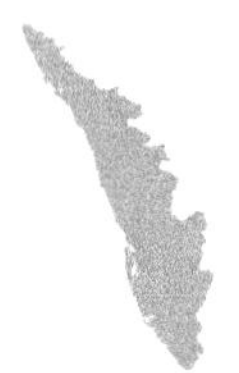

10

AGRICULTURE

ood grain production in country has reached a record value of 252.02 million tons in 2014–15. Production of rice alone was to the tune of 105.48 million tons in 2014–15. The estimated production of rice for the country is 104.32 million tons in 2015–16. Kerala State which had a low base in food production is facing serious challenges in retaining even this meager area. Kerala agricultural economy is undergoing structural transformation from the mid seventies by switching over a large proportion of its traditional crop area which was devoted to subsistence crops like rice and tapioca to more remunerative crops like banana and other plantations.

Land use Pattern

The total geographical area is classified according to thirteen different uses of land. The cultivated area of the state comes to around 67.6 per cent of the total geographical area. Within this, the Net Sown Area accounts for 52 per cent and 16.83 per cent of the cultivated area is sown more than once. More than one-fourth of the area is under forest cover and 11.18 per cent of the area is put to non-agricultural use. On the other hand, there was a 4 per cent increase in the area put to non-agricultural uses and a 7 per cent increase in the land under fallow.

However, if the total area is further regrouped into two major categories: 'land that is available for cultivation' (including net sown area, cultivable waste, current fallow, fallow other than current fallow and land under miscellaneous tree crops) and 'land not available for cultivation' (which includes land put to non-agricultural use, barren and uncultivable land and permanent pastures and other grazing land besides forest area). In that case it can be seen that land that is available for cultivation comes to 57.9 per cent of the total geographical area. The current Net Sown Area is 52 per cent of the total geographical area. Thus most of the land that is available for cultivation is already under cultivation. Hence the scope of bringing more area under cultivation is marginal and increase in agriculture production can be achieved mainly through increasing the productivity of crops.

Cropping Pattern

Cropping pattern in Kerala is dominated by cash crops. Food crops comprising of rice, tapioca and pulses accounted for just 10.21 per cent of the total cultivated area in 2015-16 while cash crops (cashew, rubber, pepper, coconut, cardamom, tea and coffee) constituted 62.8 per cent of the total cultivated area. Plantation crops like rubber, coffee, tea and cardamom accounted for 26.8 per cent of the total cultivated area. Coconut has the largest area under crop cover (30 per cent) followed by rubber (20.9 per cent) and paddy (7.4 per cent). Of the cultivated area, 4.45 per cent is under banana and other plantains. Little more than 2 per cent is under tapioca and just 0.2 per cent is under ginger and turmeric together. In 2015-16, pulses, pepper, ginger, areca nut, cardamom and rubber recorded slight increases in area under cultivation compared to the previous year while all other crops recorded a decline.

Irrigated Area

The share of net irrigated area to total cropped area was 15.75 per cent in 2015-16. Thus, only 15.75 per cent of the total cropped area was under irrigation cover whereas in states like Punjab, Uttar Pradesh and Tamil Nadu it was more than 50 per cent. The share of gross irrigated area to gross cropped area was 18.4 per cent. Coconut occupied the largest share of the irrigated area (34.25 per cent) followed by paddy (31.12 per cent). The share of other crops were banana (9 per cent), areca nut (7 per cent) and vegetables (8 per cent).

Rice

Rice is the most important food crop grown in Kerala. It occupies 7.46 per cent of the total cropped area of the state. However, the area under rice has been falling at an alarming rate ever since the 1980s. From 8.82 lakh hectare in 1974-75, the paddy area has come down to 1.96 lakh hectare in 2015-16. The production has also concomitantly declined from 13.76 lakh MT in 1972-73 (peak of production) to 5.49 lakh MT in 2015-16. Moreover, the productivity of the crop is very low in the State (2790 kg/ha), though it is higher than the national average (2424 kg/ha). There has only been a marginal increase in the productivity of rice in the past four decades. China, which is the major producer of rice in the world, reports a productivity (6744 kg/ha) more than three times the productivity of rice in Kerala. The productivity of rice in Egypt is the highest in the world (9088 kg/ha), which is nearly four-fold of our productivity. Punjab is the state with the highest yield in the country (3952 kg/ha). In the recent months, the

State government has taken a number of steps for the promotion of paddy cultivation.

There are three main rice growing seasons in the state: *(a)* Virippu season/Autumn season/First crop season, which starts in April-May and extends up to September-October; *(b)* Mundakan season/Winter season/ Second crop season, which starts in September-October and extends up to December-January; and *(c)* Puncha season/Summer season/Third crop season, which starts in December-January and extends up to March-April. In Kerala, winter crop (mundakan) has been greater than the other two crops (summer and autumn) both in terms of area as well as production. However, in 2015-16, all the three seasons showed a declining trend resulting in an overall reduction in production.

Palakkad, Alappuzha, Thrissur and Kottayam account for about 81.2 per cent of the total production of rice in the state, their individual shares being 41 per cent, 16 per cent, 14 per cent and 9 per cent respectively. In 2015-16, Alappuzha and Palakkad recorded a decline in production, while Thrissur and Kottayam recorded a slight increase in production. District-wise area under rice cultivation shows that area under rice fell for all the districts of the State between 1996-97 and 2012-13. However, the decline was sharpest for Ernakulam (93 per cent) followed by Kollam (92 per cent), Thiruvananthapuram (86 per cent) and Malappuram (78 per cent). On the positive side, in Kottayam and Alappuzha, the major rice growing districts, the decline was much less pronounced (13 and 12 per cent respectively). In 2015-16, Palakkad, Alappuzha and Wayanad, showed a decline in area as well as production of rice in the State.

Area cultivated with paddy has increasingly been converted into cultivation with other crops as well as for non-agricultural purposes. This is mainly due to the low relative profitability in paddy cultivation, which in turn is a result of increasing costs due to rising wages and relative price changes in favour of competing crops. In spite of focused interventions through the State plan and programmes like Rashtriya Krishi Vikas Yojana (RKVY), enhancement of per hectare assistance from ₹1500 to ₹4500 in the 12th plan period and the introduction of procurement in all districts, rice production has not responded positively. More proactive steps under the leadership of the Department of Agriculture and local bodies are required to revitalise rice production in the State.

Coconut

In terms of area under cultivation, coconut is the most important crop in the state with over 7.9 lakh hectare under cultivation. It accounts for the largest share in the Gross Cropped Area (GCA) followed by rubber and paddy. Kerala has the largest area under the crop in the country, but in terms of production it comes third. This indicates the low productivity of the crop in the state with just 7535 nuts per hectare compared to Tamil Nadu and Andhra Pradesh where the productivity is 14,873 nuts per hectare and 13,808 nuts per hectare respectively in 2014-15. Also, Kerala's share in area and production of coconut in the country has declined over time. While Kerala accounted for 69.58 per cent of the area and 69.52 per cent of the production in the country in 1960-61, the corresponding shares declined to 40.2 per cent and 42.12 per cent respectively in 2011-12.

The main reason for the falling productivity of coconut is the prevalence of the root wilt disease, poor crop management and the existence of senile and unproductive palms. Hence, massive replanting of palms affected by root wilt with elite palms and elimination of senile palms, setting up of nurseries for production of quality seedlings and their subsequent distribution is essential for increasing productivity. Restructuring of the cluster development programme is also essential for more effectiveness. The attempt made by the Department of Agriculture and Cooperation to restructure two coconut development programmes through convergence approach at the panchayat level, coupled with a price advantage, is expected to revive coconut production in the state. The isolated attempts at the production of dwarf coconut seedlings and hybrids need to be scaled up substantially with the support of research institutions. Entrepreneurial ventures for the production of value-added products like desiccated coconut, beverages, shell-based products, coconut cream, and neera have to be promoted with appropriate tie-ups with credit and marketing agencies. The coconut procurement system through Krishi Bhavans in association with Kerafed was introduced in 2012-13, which needs further streamlining. The initiative taken by the government in promoting neera and value addition are expected to revive coconut economy of the state.

Pepper

India comes third in the production of pepper in the world after Vietnam and Indonesia. However, the production of pepper in the country has been stagnant at around 50,000 tonnes in the last few years and hence is fast losing its status as a leading producer and exporter of pepper. Grown mostly in the slopes of Western Ghats in Kerala, Karnataka, and Tamil Nadu, the area under cultivation of pepper has come down drastically in the last decade, which has adversely affected production and export. In 2015-16, pepper production recorded a decline to 55,000 tonnes from 70,000 tonnes in 2014-15. However, Kerala, which accounts for 75 per cent of the total production in the country, recorded a slight increase in pepper production from 40.6 thousand tonnes in 2014-15 to 42.1 thousand tonnes in 2015-16.

Pepper production in the State in recent years has been affected mainly by low productivity and various diseases. In order to revive spices development in the state, the Department of Agriculture had initiated comprehensive pepper development programmes in all districts in 2014-15. An integrated action plan was prepared for the revival of the crop, covering reorientation of planting material production, expansion of grafting wherever possible, area-wide disease management, liming and nutrients management and revival of pepper samities. The increase in production achieved during 2015-16 could be because of this concerted effort by the State Government.

Cashew

In 2015-16, India continued to be the largest producer of raw cashew nuts in the world. The other main producing countries were Vietnam, Brazil, Tanzania and Ivory Coast. The production of raw cashew nuts in India declined from 725 thousand MT in 2014-15 to 670 thousand MT in 2015-16. The area under cashew cultivation, however, recorded an increase from 1027 thousand hectares to 1034 thousand hectares.

In Kerala, in the last one decade, there has been a continuous and considerable decline in both area under cultivation as well as production of cashew. It is alarming to note that the production, which stood at 60 thousand MT in 2004-05, declined to 33.3 thousand MT in 2013-14 and to 24.73 thousand MT in 2015-16. The area under cultivation dwindled from 81,000 to 49,000 hectares and to 43,000 hectares during the same period. The productivity of cashew, which was around 900 kg per hectare during the late eighties, also fell to 654 kg per hectare in 2014-15.

Plantation Crops

Plantation crops in general are either export oriented or import substituting and therefore assume special significance from the national point of view. It is estimated that nearly 14 lakh families are dependent on the plantation sector for livelihood. Each of the four plantation crops of South India has its distinct characteristics and economic problems. Consequent to the removal of quantitative restrictions on import, plantation crops in general are facing the threat of low quality imports.

Rubber

Production of Natural Rubber (NR) in India declined by 12.9 per cent from 6.45 lakh tones in 2014-15 to 5.62 lakh tonnes in 2015-16. Even though tappable area under natural rubber was 5.59 lakh ha during 2015-16, only 3.91 lakh ha of area contributed to the NR production during the year. Consequently, the average yield, measured in terms of production per hectare of tapped area, declined to 1437 kg/ha in 2015-16 as compared to 1443 kg/ha the previous year. During 2016-17, the production is estimated to be 6.54 lakh tonnes of NR. Adverse weather, high wages, lack of skilled labourers and the grower's reluctance in harvesting or maintaining trees in response to the low NR prices have affected the production of natural rubber (NR) in India in 2016.

The production scene was no different in Kerala also, as the total production dwindled from 5.07 lakh MT in 2014-15 to 4.38 lakh MT in 2015-16.

The declining rubber production in the year has affected India's ranking internationally as it has been pushed to the fifth position with countries like Vietnam and China occupying the third and fourth position respectively. Thailand continues to be the top producer followed by Indonesia in the second spot in the global rubber scene.

The declining price of rubber is a cause of concern. A revival of rubber prices is expected based on the revision of import duty and other measures taken by Government of India. However, more proactive measures by the central government are essential to support the rubber growers of Kerala. The strengthening and reorientation of Price Stabilisation Fund is essential. The Government of Kerala has introduced a rubber production incentive scheme with a financial support of ₹ 300 crores. However, to a large extent the price depends on global supply and demand of natural rubber and the price of synthetic rubber.

Coffee

Domestic coffee production for the year 2015-16 was estimated at 348,000 tonnes, which represents an increase of 21,000 tonnes compared to previous year. Initially, the Coffee Board had projected 2015-16 crop production (Post Blossom estimate) at 355,000 tonnes, which was subsequently revised downwards by 7,000 tonnes. As per the revised figure, the Arabica production was estimated at 103.5 thousand tonnes (29.7 per cent) and Robusta at 244.5 thousand tonnes (70.3 per cent). However, as per FAO estimates, yield in India at 845.6 kg per hectare is much below that of Vietnam (2499.1 kg per hectare) and Brazil (1421.5 kg per hectare). A comparison of the productivity levels in 1971 vis-a-vis 2011 suggests that India (−1.8 per cent) and Indonesia (−0.1 per cent) are the only two countries that reported a decline in yield levels in the last 40 years. Lower productivity in India is due to limited mechanization, pest infestation, existence of old/senile plants and labour shortage. Thus, on the productivity side, much more is needed to be done and towards this concerted efforts are required both at the policy and farm level. The only way to address this issue is by providing positive research and development which can directly contribute in achieving higher yield.

With regard to Kerala, the production of coffee registered a slight increase from 67,700 MT in 2014-15 to 69,230 MT in 2015-16. The share of Kerala in total coffee production in the country is around 20 per cent during the year. Major variety grown in Kerala is Robusta with a share of 97.1 per cent in planted area. Productivity of the crop in terms of bearing area in Kerala is 808 kg/ha, which is lower than the national level of 852 kg/ha during 2011-12. Among the States, Kerala stands next to Karnataka which produces 70.4 per cent of total Indian coffee production.

Tea

As one of the largest tea producing countries, India accounts for 24.8 per cent of the total world production. The Tea Board had revised the production figures during 2011 by bringing within the net all segments of tea producers, both organized and unorganized, especially North India many of whom were not reporting their crop statistics earlier, which helped India in breaching the 1 billion mark. The domestic tea production during 2015 was 1191.1 mkg lower by 16.2 mkg from previous year. The decline in production in North India and South India was 1.6 mkg and 14.6 mkg respectively. The steep fall in production in south India after a one year reprieve from the low crop trap is a matter of concern.

Kerala accounts for 5.03 per cent of the area and 6.3 per cent of the total domestic production of tea in the country. The production of tea in the State has been consistently falling since 2009-10. There was a slight improvement in 2012-13 as tea production recorded an increase of 5059 MT despite a decline in area of 18 per cent. This increase in production was mainly on account of increase in productivity. Tea production recorded an increase of 3.5 per cent in 2014-15 also but in 2015-16 there was a decline in production by 11.16 per cent.

The major issues affecting the tea industry are stagnant productivity, acute labour shortage, high cost of machines, and lack of indigenous machinery.

Cardamom

India is the second largest producer of small cardamom and plays an important role in the international trade of cardamom. The output of cardamom is dependent on prevailing climatic conditions as the cardamom plant requires intermittent spells of rains and good sunshine during the growth stage. Cardamom production in the country during 2015-16 was estimated at 22 thousand tonnes compared to 18 thousand tonnes in 2014-15, an increase of 4 thousand tonnes. The turnaround in cardamom prices since 2006-07 continued up to 2010-11 reaching the highest level, but thereafter the prices have fluctuated. During 2015-16 (August-June), the prices increased by ₹ 107.33 per kg to reach ₹ 754.00 per kg.

Meanwhile in Kerala, cardamom production has increased by 21.8 per cent in 2015-16 despite the area under cultivation remaining stagnant.

Pulses

The year 2016 was the International Year of Pulses. Pulses are important source of protein, high in fibre content and provide ample quantity of vitamins and minerals. Keeping in view large benefits of pulses for human health, the United Nations proclaimed 2016 as the International Year of Pulses. Thus, due attention is required to enhance the production of pulses not only to meet the dietary requirement of protein but also to raise the awareness about pulses for achieving nutritional, food security and environmental sustainability. Pulses are important component to sustain the agriculture production as the crops posses wide adaptability to fit into various cropping systems and improves the soil fertility.

India's share is 25 per cent in production, about 33 per cent in acreage and about 27 per cent in consumption of the total pulses in the world.

In Kerala, pulses are cultivated in autumn, winter and summer seasons. The area under the cultivation of pulses shows a declining trend in the state. During 1975-76, the total area under pulses including tur was 37,485 ha but by 2015-16 it has come down to 3764 ha. Apart from tur, the other main pulses grown in Kerala are cow pea, black gram horse gram and green gram. Major cultivation of pulses and tur is in Palakkad district and contributes to 30 per cent of the total production in the State. The production of pulses in the State was highest during the year 2005-06. More proactive steps are needed to augment pulse production in the State.

Collective Farming through Kudumbashree

Collective farming is an important area of Kudumbasree, which aims at food security both at household and community level. The major crops cultivated are paddy, vegetables, banana, pineapple and tubers. In 2013-14, area brought under cultivation of paddy was 15078.60 ha, of vegetables was 12555.60 ha and of other crops (banana, pineapple and tubers) was 22476.20 ha.

Key Initiatives of the Department of Agriculture

The annual plan schemes for 2016-17 were formulated focusing on the thrust areas and strategies for increasing the productivity in agriculture from the current levels. The key initiatives taken by the Department of Agriculture in 2016-17 for the improvement of agricultural sector included integrated food crop production programme focusing on self-sufficiency in vegetable production including comprehensive rice development, modernization of existing farms and labs and establishment of new labs, institutional mechanism for marketing, focusing initially on vegetables development of farmers markets and setting up of agriculture markets, production and distribution of quality planting materials, comprehensive fallow land cultivation with people's participation, strengthening extension activities, Agricultural Technology Management Agency (ATMA) plus model of extension, rejuvenation of spices economy, crop health management covering pests and disease surveillance, promotion of organic farming and safe food production, crop insurance, establishment of 20 Agro Service Centres (ASCs) and strengthening the existing ASCs for improved service delivery, revival package for pepper in Wayanad. In 2016-17, the Harithakeralam Mission has been launched focusing on food crop production, waste management and water resource conservation and development.

State Horticulture Mission (SHM)

The State Horticulture Mission was formed in 2005 to implement the programme of the National Horticulture Mission, a centrally sponsored scheme, with 85 per cent central share and 15 per cent state share which has been restructured as the Mission for Integrated Development of Horticulture from 2014-15 onwards. During 2015-16, Government of India (GoI) has changed the sharing pattern of the scheme as 60 per cent central share and 40 per cent state share. The main objective of the mission is a holistic development of the horticulture sector covering fruits, plantation crops, spices, flowers, aromatic and medicinal plants and mushroom. The important programmes under the mission include production and productivity improvement, post-harvest management and marketing.

The components undertaken in this mission include establishment of nurseries for production and distribution of quality seeds and planting material, establishment of new gardens, establishment of integrated pack houses, sorting and grading units, cold storage units, establishment of rural markets, strengthening wholesale markets, market intelligence, extension quality awareness and market led extension activities for fresh and processed foods.

Vegetable and Fruit Promotion Council's Programme (VFPCP)

Vegetable and Fruit Promotion Council, Kerala (VFPCK) formed in 2001, has been implementing various schemes in fruits and vegetable sector with the financial assistance from state and central Governments. The major activities of the council are formation of Self Help Groups (SHGs), awareness creation on Participatory Guarantee System (PGS), dissemination of Participatory Technology Development, campaigns/training/capacity building programmes, production of quality seeds and planting materials, participatory credit and insurance support, group marketing and Haritha nagari programmes for the promotion of vegetable cultivation in urban areas.

Rashtriya Krishi Vikas Yojana (RKVY)

In order to incentivize States to draw up comprehensive plans for their agricultural sector, taking into account the agro climatic conditions, natural resource issues and technology and by integrating livestock, poultry and fisheries, a special additional central assistance scheme was launched during 2007-08. During XIth plan, GOI had released a total amount of ₹ 22,408.76 crore to states of which ₹ 21586.6 crore was utilized in implementing 5768 projects under crop development, horticulture, agriculture mechanization, natural resource management, marketing and post-harvest management, animal husbandry, dairy development, fisheries, extension, etc. The scheme was implemented as 100 per cent centrally assisted scheme till 2014-15. From 2015-16 onwards the sharing pattern has been changed as 60:40 between GoI and GoK.

Organic Farming

Organic farming policy, strategy and detailed action plan for Kerala was declared during 2010. The Department of Agriculture has been implementing a comprehensive project on organic farming in Kasargode district and it is envisaged to cover potential areas in other districts. Under this programme, 100 vermi compost units, 625 rural compost units, 30 demonstration plots and 42 ecoshops in 13 districts were established. Also the existing 200 clusters were strengthened and 50 new clusters formed. During 2015-16, 339 vermi compost units have been established under organic farming by the State Horticulture Mission and an area of 3000 ha has been brought under organic certification.

A comprehensive assessment of the impact of interventions in organic farming on the farmer's well-being, economy and environment in the state as envisaged in the organic farming policy (2010) is required to reorient the strategies and to evolve suitable action plan for promoting organic farming in the state. Strengthening of participatory guarantee system, good agriculture practices, quality control laboratories and other certification and incentive system are also to be worked out to promote organic and nature friendly farming in the state.

LIVESTOCK DEVELOPMENT

Livestock is a major source of livelihood for the World's poor. It is an integral part of India's agricultural economy and plays a multifaceted role in providing livelihood support to the rural population. Livestock sector apart from contributing to national economy in general and to agricultural economy in particular, also provides employment opportunities, asset creation, coping mechanism against crop failure and social and financial security. Livestock is the main source of animal protein for the population. Small and marginal farmers and landless labourers own majority of the livestock resources. Also sustainable development of the livestock sector would lead to more inclusive development and empowerment of women. Livestock sector contributed 3.03 percentage of the Gross State Value Added (GSVA) and 29.18 percentage of the GSVA in Agriculture and Allied activities during 2015-16 (at constant price with base year 2011-12).

Production of Major Livestock Products

MILK : Milk production in the State increased from the level of 21.19 lakh MT at the end of the tenth plan (2006-07) to 27.16 lakh MT at the end of the eleventh plan (2011-12). Milk production during 2014-15 and 2015-16 was 27.11 lakh MT and 26.50 lakh MT respectively with an annual growth rate of 2.11 per cent and (-)2.25 per cent respectively. Annual Growth rate of milk production during 2015-16 in the State is far below that at the national level. During 2015-16, Kerala contributed only 1.70 per cent of the annual milk production of the country.

EGG/MEAT : Egg production in the State increased from 119.39 crores at the end of the Tenth Plan (2006-07) to 170.48 crores during the year 2011-12. The egg production during 2014-15 and 2015-16 was 250.36 crores and 244.25 crores respectively with an annual growth rate of 1.08 per cent and (-)2.44 per cent respectively. Meat production in the state increased from the level of 1.98 lakh MT at the end of the tenth plan (2006-07) to 4.26 lakh MT during the year 2011-12. The meat production during 2014-15 and 2015-16 was 4.46 lakh MT and 4.66 lakh MT respectively with an annual growth rate of 7.16 per cent and 4.48 per cent respectively. Growth of egg production in the state during 2015-16 is far below the national level while for meat the growth percentage during 2015-16 is almost the same as that at the national level. During 2015-16 Kerala contributed 2.9 per cent of the annual egg production and 6.64 per cent of the annual meat production of the country.

Govardhini

Govardhini is a new scheme started in the state from 2014-15 onwards with the objectives of providing total health care to the calves like reducing the age at puberty, age at first calving and inter caving period of the female calves borne in Kerala for increasing milk production in the state. Scientific Management, feeding with adequate quantity of good quality feed and health cover including prevention against common contagious diseases and insurance cover against loss due to unforeseen reasons are the basic requirement in achieving the goal. All these aspects are comprehensively covered in this scheme. Beneficiaries are selected from the calf birth register maintained at Government veterinary dispensaries on first come first serve basis.

FISHERIES DEVELOPMENT

India is the second largest fish producing nation in the world, with a share of 5.4 per cent of global fish production. India is also a major producer of Fish through aquaculture and ranks second in the world after China. Total fish production in India has increased since 1991. From 3.84 Million Tonnes (MT) in 1991, it increased to 10.06 MT in 2014-15 (provisional figures), of which 6.57 MT was from Inland sector and 3.49 MT was from Marine sector. Inland fish production constitutes about 65 per cent in total fish production of the country. Annual growth rate of production has also been high in the Inland sector. Though marine fish production has increased, the growth rate is very low during recent years.

Fisheries sector contributes significantly to the national economy while providing livelihood to approximately 8.74 lakh fishermen families in the country.

Fisheries and aquaculture contribute around 8.9 per cent of the Gross State Value Added (GSVA) from the primary sector which is of significance to the state economy. The GSVA of the State has been increasing over years, but the share of primary sector and that of fisheries sector has been declining. The share of fisheries sector in the State Value Added has declined from 1.12 per cent in 2011-12 to 1.04 per cent in 2015-16. The share of Primary Sector in GSVA has declined from 15.20 per cent in 2011-12 to 11.58 per cent in 2015-16.

Marine fish production of India during the year 2014-15 has provisionally been estimated as 3.49 million tones with an increase of about 0.05 million tonnes compared to the estimate for the last year. As per estimates of 2013-14, among the states, Gujarat was the highest contributor of Marine fish production followed by Kerala. In total fish production in 2014-15, Andhra Pradesh was the highest contributor and Kerala stands at 5th position. Marine Fish landings in Kerala during 2015-16 were 5.17 lakh tonnes. Marine fish landing in Kerala has been declining continuously since 2011-12, with the exception of a marginal increase in 2014-15. High value species among the fish catch is less. However, significant among them are Seer fish, Prawn, Ribbon fish and Mackerel. The quality of these high value species in the total catch ultimately decides the income of the fishermen.

Trend in Production

As per estimates of 2013-14, among the maritime states in India, Kerala occupies the second position in marine fish production. The total fish production in Kerala during 2015-16 was 7.27 lakh metric tonnes. The marine fishery resources of the state is said to have almost attained the optimum level of production. At National level about 65 per cent of the total fish production is contributed by the inland sector, however at the state level, the share of inland sector is relatively less than the marine sector. The current level of Inland fish production is 2.1 lakh tones, and it shows an increase of about 4 per cent over the previous year.

The marine fish production in Kerala has tended to fluctuate while the inland fish production has showed signs of improvement from 1999-2000. Marine fish production has decreased from 5.24 lakh tonnes in 2014-15 to 5.17 lakh tonnes in 2015-16. Inland production has been increasing during the recent years. During 2015-16, the share of inland fish production in the total fish production of the state was 29 per cent. Kerala has not utilized its potential in Inland fishing. Kerala has over 7 per cent of the water bodies in the country, but its share in Inland fishing is lower than that of many other states.

Agriculture Related Institutions and their Head Quarters in Kerala

Institutions	Head Quarters
Kerala Agro Industries Corporation (KAMCo)	Athani (Ernakulam)
Kerala Livestock Development Corporation	Pattom (Thiruvananthapuram)
National Seed Corporation	Karamana (Thiruvananthapuram)
Oilpalm India Limited	Kottayam
Command Area Development Authority (CADA)	Perukavu (Thrissur)
Coconut Development Board	Cochin
Bureau of Indian Standards-Ag mark	Thathamangalam (Palakkad)
Central Soil Test Centre	Parottukonam (Thiruvananthapuram)
Central State Farm	Aralam (Kannur)
Central Integrated Pests Management Centre	Kochi
Farm Information Bureau	Kowdiar (Thiruvananthapuram)
Kerala State Horticulture Development Corporation	Vellayambalam (Thiruvananthapuram)
Milma	Thiruvananthapuram
Sugandhabhavan	Kochi (Palarivattam)
Marketfed	Kochi (Gandhi Bhavan)
NABARD	Palayam (Thiruvananthapuram)
Kerafed	Thiruvananthapuram
Beefed	Pappanamcode (Thiruvananthapuram)
Serifed	Pattom (Thiruvananthapuram)
Bamboo Corporation	Angamali

Agriculture Research Centres

Rubber Institute of India	Kottayam
Cardamom Research Institute	Pampadumpara
Harvest Research Institute	Karamana
Pepper Research Institute	Panniyur
Central Plantation Crops Research Institute	Kasargode
Spices Research Institute	Kozhikode
Pineapple Research Institute	Vellanikkara
Central Tuber Crops Research Institute	Sreekaryam
Sugarcane Research Centres	Thiruvalla and Menonpara
Coconut Research Institute	Kadachalkuzhi (Balaramapuram)
Cashew Research Centre	Anakkayam
Agronomic Research Station	Chalakkudi
Rice Research Centres	Vyttila, Kayamkulam, (Pattambi and Mankomp)
Ginger Research Institute	Ambalavayal
Indo-Swiz Project	Mattupetti
Indo-Norwegian Project	Neendakara
C.P.C.R.I	Palode
Forest Research Institute	Peechi

KNOW THE FACTS

☞ *Food security project was launched in 2008–09 to increase production of rice, milk and egg.*
☞ *With a coverage of 7.7 lakh ha, coconut occupies 37 per cent of the net cropped area.*
☞ *Nearly 14 lakh families are dependent on the plantation sector for livelihood.*
☞ *Kerala accounts for 78.2 per cent of the area under rubber in the country.*
☞ *The export front cardamom has been facing competition from Guatemala although the quality of Guatemala cardamom is inferior.*
☞ *Palakkad is the district with fresh fruits largely cultivated in the State.*
☞ *The area of the cultivation of pineapple is maximum in Ernakulam district.*
☞ *Kerala's share in the national marine fish production is about 20–25%.*
☞ *Fisheries sector contribute 3% of the GSDP of the State.*
☞ *In view of increasing the inland fish production on a sustainable basis by scientifically using the Vast Inland spread available in the State, Government have initiated the new programme Matsyakeralam during 2008–09.*

TEST YOUR SELF

1. Among the following crops, which covers maximum area in Kerala?
   A. Rice   B. Pepper   C. Rubber   D. Coffee

2. Which state is the largest producer of coconut in India?
   A. Karnataka   B. Goa
   C. Kerala   D. Andhra Pradesh

3. Which district of Kerala is known as 'Rice Bowl' of the state?
   A. Alappuzha   B. Kottayam   C. Kannur   D. Thrissur

4. What is the percentage of net sown area in Kerala?
   A. 60%   B. 64%   C. 50%   D. 53%

5. Which district of Kerala record highest growth in productivity in rice?
   A. Malappuram   B. Alappuzha
   C. Kannur   D. Thiruvananthapuram

6. Which is the major crop cultivated under 'Kudumbasree' programme?
   A. Pulses   B. Rubber   C. Rice   D. None of these

7. Which type of coffee is mainly produced in Kerala?
   A. Arabica   B. Robusta   C. Liberica   D. All of these

8. Food Security Project in Kerala was launched in ....
   A. 2002-03   B. 2008-09   C. 2004-05   D. 2009-10

9. Which crop has the second largest area under cultivation in Kerala?
   A. Rubber   B. Coconut   C. Rice   D. Pepper

10. Keral Kesari Award is given to ....
    A. best cattle farmer   B. best group farming
    C. best coconut farmer   D. best women farmer

ANSWERS

1	2	3	4	5	6	7	8	9	10
C	C	A	D	B	C	B	B	A	C

❑❑❑

11

<u>IRRIGATION</u>

The uneven distribution of rainfall causes damages to crops by flooding during monsoon and by drought during the summer season. Thus it is seen that irrigation is must for the successful cultivation of crops in Kerala.

Though there are various methods for providing irrigation water, the best and the most reliable method which can be used for Kerala is the construction of storage reservoirs for impounding water during the monsoon and utilizing the water in the reservoir for critical periods of the crops when there is insufficiency.

During 1960's and 70's State faced acute storage of food grains. Hence, major and medium projects were taken up during that time to provide irrigation facility for paddy. A major portion of the cultivable land could be made as ayacut under these projects. But, in the present context, priority has changed. Almost all projects are being converted into multipurpose projects in order to maximize the utilization of existing resources.

Karapuzha Irrigation Project

Karapuzha Project is the first project for irrigation taken up in the Wayanad district of Kerala. The project is to construct an earthen dam with concrete spillway in right bank at Vazhavatta across Karapuzha stream and the saddle dam at Pakkam, Cherupetta and Cheengeri to create a reservior of 76.50 Mm^3 storage capacities. The project was originally envisaged for irrigation only and now it has turned to be a multipurpose project.

Idamalayar Irrigation Project

The Idamalayar Irrigation Project is a diversion scheme intended to irrigate an extent of 14394 hectares of wet and dry lands and the Cultivable

Command Area (C.C.A.) is 13209 hectares. The source of water for irrigation is the tail race discharge of Idamalayar Hydroelectric Project for which a Dam at Ennakkal has already been completed. This barrage was constructed in 1960–67. The canal system of the Project consists of a main canal, (32.272 km) long on the right bank of the river Periyar. The main canal bifurcates itself into 2 canal systems. The low level canal, 27.25 km long and the link canal (6.73 km) long. The total length of link canal is 7.575 km.

Banasura Sagar Irrigation Project

The project commenced in 1979 with an estimated cost of ₹ 8.00 crore to irrigate an area of 2800 ha (net) agriculture land for the second and third crops in two taluks of Wayanad district. The revised estimate of the project as per 2010 SOR is ₹ 185.5 crores.

86 per cent of the works of 2730 m long main canal have been completed. The work of both branch canals - Padinjarathara branch canal and Venniyode branch canal are in progress. Out of the total length of 5390 m of Venniyode branch canal, works of 770 m completed. Total expenditure incurred for the project is ₹ 52.78 crore (including 85 lakh paid to KSEB as share cost).

Chamravattom Regulator-cum-Bridge

A regulator-cum-bridge at Chamravattom across Bharathapuzha about 6.5 km upstream of river mouth is a multipurpose project. The targeted irrigated area is 4344 ha (Gross) and 3170 ha (Net).

As per the assessment of the Directorate of Economics and Statistics the net irrigated area in the state as on March 2010, is 3.86 lakh ha. and the gross area irrigated is 4.54 lakh ha. The net area irrigated has declined from 3.99 lakh ha during 2008–09 to 3.86 lakh ha in 2009–10. Only 16.34 per cent of the net cropped area is irrigated. The percentage of net area irrigated to net area has declined and percentage of gross irrigated area to gross cropped area records a slight increase during the year compared to the last year. During 2009–10, the net irrigated area registered a decline of 10.75 per cent and gross irrigated area by 0.64 per cent compared to the previous year. During 2009–10, among the crops, paddy tops among the major crop supported by irrigation. It accounted for about 37 per cent followed by coconut (33%), banana (8%), arecanut (8%) and vegetables (4%).

Muvattupuzha Valley Irrigation Project

The Muvattupuzha Valley Irrigation Project, one of the major projects in

Kerala envisages the utilization of the tailrace discharge from the Moolamattom Power House of the Idukki Hydro-Electric Project and the dependable runoff from the catchments of Thodupuzha River. MVIP was started in 1974 with an estimated cost of ₹ 20.86 crore. The estimated cost of the project based on current CPWD rate is ₹ 945.00 crore. Project was partially commissioned in 1994.

The expenditure of the project as on October 2016 is ₹ 918 crore AIBP Central Loan Assistance of ₹ 154.96 crore was released during 2000-2009. Balance work is to be done for completion of the project.

Minor Irrigation

Schemes having a cultivable command area up to 2000 ha are treated as Minor Irrigation schemes. Out of these, schemes having an ayacut below 50 ha are classified as Minor Irrigation Class II and those having ayacut area of 50 ha or more are Minor Irrigation Class I schemes. The role of Minor Irrigation is quite significant to Kerala. Works generally taken up under Minor Irrigation are construction of check dams, construction and renovation of irrigation tanks, regulators and bunds, and lift irrigation works.

Focus on minor irrigation and development of minor irrigation structures in critical agro ecological zones for the development of agriculture was one of the thrust areas during 12th plan period. During the 12th plan period, 19.63 per cent of the total budgeted outlay was earmarked for Minor Irrigation.

Haritha Keralam Mission

Conservation and protection of the environment and thereby natural resources such as land and water have been an inseparable part of Indian heritage and culture. Over the years, the water use scenario has changed drastically impacting the water systems adversely. This necessitates a major campaign focusing on the restoration of all types of water resource system and management of all resources in a sustainable and equitable manner.

Some of the major objectives of Haritha Keralam Mission are - restore and improve the existing water resource systems including water resource structures, maximize rain water harvesting and ground water recharge within each micro water-shed of the State, conservation of land and water to prevent soil erosion and enhancing the carrying capacity of river systems.

Development and preservation of water resources of the State following a water shed based approach with integration to river basins is the basic strategy for action in the water sector. By using water shed maps as scientific tools, watershed development plans can be prepared. The focus at the watershed level will be on the effective management of run off water and improved soil and moisture conservation activities.

Ground Water Development

Ground Water is a vital resource for meeting the water requirements of irrigation, domestic and industrial sectors of the country. Ground Water is an annually replenishable resource but its availability is non-uniform in space and time. The annual replenishable ground water resources of the area is the sum of recharge during monsoon and non-monsoon seasons.

Ground Water level is one of the basic elements which reflects the condition of the ground water regime in an area. Ground Water levels are being monitored by Central Ground Water Board and State Ground Water Departments. The assessment of Ground Water draft is carried out based on Minor Irrigation census data and sample surveys carried out by the State Ground Water Departments. The annual Ground Water draft of the entire country for 2010-11 has been estimated as 245 bcm. There has been marginal (2 bcm) increase in the overall estimate of Ground Water draft of the country in 2011 compared to 2009. Agricultural sector remained the predominant consumer of ground water resources. About 91 per cent of total annual ground water draft *i.e.,* 222 bcm is for irrigation use. Only 23 bcm is for domestic and industrial use which is about 9 per cent of the total draft. In several states including Kerala, Ground Water draft for domestic and industrial purposes are more than 15 per cent.

As on March 2011, total annual Ground Water recharge of the State is 668601.72 ha.m. and the net annual ground water availability is 607407.22 ha.m. The net annual ground water availability for future irrigation development of our State is 306634 ha.m. The stage of ground water development of our State is 47 per cent. Among the districts, Kasargod and Wayanad ranks maximum and minimum with 71 per cent and 18 per cent respectively.

KNOW THE FACTS

☞ *Karapuzha Project is the first project for irrigation taken up in the Wayanad district of Kerala.*

☞ *Banasura Sagar Irrigation Project was commenced in 1971 with an estimated cost of ₹ 1137.07 lakhs to irrigate an area of 2800 ha agriculture land.*

☞ *Dug wells are the major ground water extraction structure in Kerala.*

☞ *A Regulator-cum-bridge at Chamravattom across Bharathapuzha is a multipurpose project.*

☞ *The availability of the ground water level between the post and pre-monsoon levels varies widely.*

☞ *The ground water storage is the best method for water harvesting.*

TEST YOUR SELF

1. Which among the following is the major source of irrigation in Kerala?
   A. Wells
   B. Tanks
   C. Canal
   D. Lift Canals

2. Which crop covers the maximum area under irrigation in Kerala?
   A. Coconut
   B. Rice
   C. Pulses
   D. Banana

3. Muvattupuzha Valley Irrigation Project was started in ....
   A. 1981
   B. 1979
   C. 1974
   D. 1983

4. Which of the following is largest earthen dam in India located in Kerala?
   A. Banasura Sagar Dam
   B. Idamalayar Dam
   C. Mangalam Dam
   D. Chimmony Dam

5. Which of the following project provides irrigation facilities to Ernakulam, Kottayam and Idukki districts?
   A. Idamalayar Irrigation Project
   B. Muvattupuzha Valley Irrigation Project
   C. Karapuzha Irrigation Project
   D. Banasura Sagar Irrigation Project

6. Karapuzha Irrigation Project is located in ....
   A. Thiruvananthapuram
   B. Thrissur
   C. Wayanad
   D. Kannur

7. Kerala Irrigation and Water Management Act was passed in ....
   A. 2003
   B. 2005
   C. 2008
   D. 1998

8. Minor Irrigation in Kerala received considerable attention from ....
   A. Fifth Plan
   B. Sixth Plan
   C. Third Plan
   D. Seventh Plan

9. Minor Irrigation Project in Kerala received external assistance from ....
- A. Dutch Government
- B. World Bank
- C. EEC
- D. Both A and C

10. A regulator-cum-bridge Project was constructed on river ....
- A. Bharathapuzha
- B. Karapuzha
- C. Periyar
- D. Idukki

ANSWERS

1	2	3	4	5	6	7	8	9	10
A	B	C	A	B	C	A	D	D	A

❑❑❑

12

DAMS IN KERALA

Neyyar Dam

Neyyar is a dam on Neyyar river in Thiruvananthapuram district of Kerala, located on the foot of the Western Ghats about 32 km east of Thiruvananthapuram. Neyyar dam is included in the province of Kallikkad Panchayath of Neyyattinkara Taluk. It was established in 1958. The Neyyar dam has

adjacent sanctuary which is a home for wildlife including gaur, sloth bear, Nilgiri tahr, jungle cat and Nilgiri langur, wild elephants and sambar deer. The prime attractions at the Neyyar dam are the adjacent Lion safari park, Crocodile Farm, Deer park, Miniature wildlife sanctuary and Lake garden. There is a swimming pool within the limits. Boating facilities are available at the reservoir. The watch tower offers a panoramic view of the river and the reservoir. The dam was built for irrigation purposes.

Thenmala (Parappar) Dam

It is located on Kallada river in Quilon district of Kerala. Dam is a centre of attraction at Thenmala—an ecotourism destination. Built under the Kallada Irrigation and Tree Crop Development Project, it is the second largest irrigation project in Kerala (India). The dam impounds the longest reservoir in the State. Waters from the reservoir is now used for power generation also. The trees of Shendurney Wildlife Sanctuary line up on both sides of the reservoir. Irrigation is the main way of utilization of dam water. It also supports the power generation.

Idukki Dam

Located in Idukki district on Periyar river in Kerala. The dam stands between the two mountains—Kuravanmala (839 feet) and Kurathimala (925 feet).

The construction of the dam was commenced on April 30, 1969 and the inauguration of the run of first machine was on 4th October, 1975.

This is the world's second and Asia's first arch dam constructed across the Kuravan and Kurathi hills. The dam rises to an elevation of 167.68 metres and is one of the highest arch dams in Asia, at 555 feet in height. It was constructed and owned by the Kerala State Electricity Board. Construction of this arch dam and two other dams at Cheruthony and Kulamavu has created an artificial lake of 60 sq.km width. Idukki Wildlife Sanctuary is near to the dam.

Kundala Dam

It lies in Kundala town 20 km away from Munnar. Kundala dam is relatively a small dam having curved shape. A narrow road on the top of the dam offers a panoramic view of the catchment area of the Kundala dam. The reservoir adjoined to the dam has boating facilities. Kundala lake and Aruvikkad waterfall are the nearby attractions of this tourist spot. The dam benifits the Kundala town by providing water for irrigation.

Mattupetty Dam

It is situated near Munnar in Idukki district. Munnar is located near the confluence of the mountain streams of Muthirappuzha River, Chanduvarai river and Kundali river. The reservoir is also known to be one of the visiting grounds of elephants of the region. It is a storage masonry dam built in the mountains of Kerala, to conserve water for hydroelectricity. It has been a vital sources of power, yielding along with other such dams, huge revenue to the states. The large amount of perennially available water allows wild animals and birds to flourish. However salinity caused by irrigation and water-logging are of concern to environmentalists.

Mullaperiyar Dam

It is situated in Idukki district of Kerala. The name of Mullaperiyar dam is derived from a portmanteau of Mullayar and Periyar. As the dam is located in the convergence of the Mullayar and Periyar rivers, the river was called Mullaperiyar. The Periyar National Park, Thekkady is located close to the park Periyar reservoir. The backwaters of this dam form this park. The water utilization is mainly for irrigation purpose.

Challakudy Dam

It is located on Challakudy river, 65 km east of Challakudy town, Thrissur district in Kerala. This dam is also known as Sholayar dam. The name Challakudy is taken from the word "Shallakudy" depicting a place where sacrifices were made. The people coming to Sholayar city often visit this dam and Athirappilly waterfall which are famous picnic spots. This route is a well known tourist spot where two water theme parks are the main attraction. The water in the dam is mainly utilized for hydroelectric power generation.

Peechi Dam

It is situated on Manali river in a village 23 km outside Thrissur city in Kerala.

Peechi is a good picnic spot. The dam is a vast catchment area of nearly 3,200 acres (1,300 ha) with extensive botanical gardens and cascading fountains offer numerous inviting avenues for tourists. This dam project started as an irrigation project, offers boating facilities at the reservoir. Boating is permitted in the reservoir and on lucky days one can see wild tuskers on the forested banks, part of which forms a reserved forest (Peechi Wildlife Sanctuary).

Vazhani Dam

It is situated 23 km from Thrissur city on Vadakkancherry Puzha river in Kerala.

It has a length of 792.48 metres. The project was completed during the year 1962. It is one of the biggest clay dams. Vazhani dam and its garden is a splendid spectacular view. It is one of the tourist attraction of Thrissur district. The water is used mainly for irrigation and drinking purposes. The Vazhani dam is an integral source of water for the people of Thrissur district.

Chaliyar (Chulliyar) Dam

It is located on Chaliyar river in Muthalamada panchayath in Palakkad district in Kerala. It is a charming spot for tourists. The dam offers a superb view of Nelliyampathy hills. The water from the dam is mainly utilized for irrigation.

Kanjirapuzha Dam

It is located on Kanjirapuzha river, a major tributary of the Chaliyar river, in Kanjirapuzha village 40 km away from Palakkad district in Kerala.

Just beyond the reservoir and surrounded by the hills, is the evergreen forest, 'Vettilachola'. During winter season, mist-wrap mountains creates a picturesque landscape which provides a visual treat. The main purpose is to support irrigation in the area.

Malampuzha Dam

It is located on Malampuzha river, a tributary of Bharathapuzha, near Palakkad district in Kerala. The canal systems serve to irrigate farm land while the reservoir provides drinking water to Palakkad and surrounding villages. Malampuzha dam has brought prosperity to the district, making Palakkad the 'rice bowl of Kerala'. Paddy is cultivated in 50,000 acres (200 km^2) in two seasons each using waters from the Malampuzha dam. The water from the dam is also utilized for mini hydroelectric project. The dam was conceived as a multipurpose project to provide water for irrigation, drinking, industries, power generation, fish farming and water transport.

Mangalam Dam

It is constructed across the river Cherukunnapuzha which is a tributary of Mangalam river. The dam project consists of the spillway and a network of canal system, completed and opened in 1966. The main use of the dam is to meet the needs of irrigation of various plantations like rubber, pepper, coffee, and tapioca which spread across 3639 hectares length and breadth of the catchment area.

Meenkara Dam

It is on Parambikulam river about 32 km south-east of Palakkad. The water from this dam is mainly used for irrigation purpose through a large network of canal system spreading out through the whole Palakkad district.

Parambikulam Dam

Parambikulam is located in Udumalaipettai in the Palakkad district in the Western Ghats of Kerala. Parambikulam dam is located at the extreme end of Parambikulam Wildlife Sanctuary. It is on the Parambikulam river. It ranks number one in India as well as in the top ten embankment dams in the world in volume capacity in the year 2000. As per the agreement with Tamil Nadu, Kerala was supposed to receive 7.25 TMC feet of water per year from the Parambikulam Aliyar Project of which the Parambikulam dam is a part. The Parambikulam Aliyar Project starts from Parambikulam dam. It is connected to the Aliyar dam through a series of canals and underground tunnels which connect each one of the dams in the sanctuary. The surrounding areas are excellent for bird-watching. The main utilization of water is for irrigation purpose.

Pothundi Dam

The dam is located in Chittur taluk, about 42 km from Palakkad; around 17 km away from Nelliyanpathy, and 8 km from Nemmara. Pothundi is the oldest dams of State of Kerala which was constructed in the 19th century. It is the second dam in Asia constructed without using cement mixture. The dam is unusual in being constructed without a conventional concrete core, which is employed in most earth dams to counteract the force exerted by high water pressure. The core is, instead, an unusual mixture of jaggery and quick lime. The strength of the Pothundi dam is one of the wonders for the present technology. The Pothundi dam is a nice site for tourists, covered with mountains. The well known Nemmara Vallengi Vela festival is organised on the banks of this dam where people visit in large number.

The Pothundi dam was constructed with the main aim of providing water for irrigation to Palakkad district in Kerala. The dam is one of the major water sources for agricultural and drinking in the Chittur taluk.

Siruvani Dam

It is located 65 km east of Challakudy town, Thrissur district in Kerala. It is on Siruvani river.

The water of Siruvani river is known for its tasty water, and it is typically known to be the second sweetest lake water in the world. It is one of the main water source of Coimbatore city. The panoramic view of the dam and the falls is enchanting with beauty. Sadivayal Checkpost is the gateway to the waterfalls. It is enclosed with lush green trees and beautiful rivulets of waters flowing all around. It is the main source of water for domestic purpose for the inhabitants of Coimbatore.

Walayar Dam

It is located about 15 km away from Palakkad district of Kerala, south India. It is on Walayar river which is a tributary of Kalpathipuzha river. It was completed and opened in 1964. The dam site is perfect for site seeing as Loknayak J.P. Smrithivanam and Deer park is closeby. It is one of the major sources of irrigation in the region. Most of the water in this river is passed to the inner places of Walayar. The dam holds a larger reservoir area, and the persons living near the reservoir area utilizes the water from the Walayar dam as their main water source. But currently the water holding inside the reservoir is less due to lesser rain at Walayar. Several industries like Malabar Cements depend on this dam for daily water requirement.

Banasura Sagar Dam

The Banasura Sagar Dam is located 21 km from Kalpetta, in Wayanad district of Kerala in the Western Ghats. It is on Karamanathodu tributary of the Kabini river, which is a part of the Indian Banasura Sagar Project consisting of a dam and a canal project started in 1979. It is the largest earthen dam in India and the second largest in Asia and an ideal starting point for hikes into the surrounding scenic mountains. It is an important tourist attraction. In the dam's reservoir there is a set of islands that were formed when the reservoir submerged the surrounding areas. The islands with the Banasura hills in the background provide a spectacular view. The goal of the project is to support the Kakkayam Hydroelectric Power Project and satisfy the demand for irrigation and drinking water in a region known to have water shortages in seasonal dry periods.

KNOW THE FACTS

☞ *Thenmala (Parappar) Dam is the second largest irrigation project in Kerala (India).*

☞ *Idukki Dam stands between the two mountains—Kuravanmala (839 feet) and Kurathimala (925 feet). This is the world's second and Asia's first arch dam constructed across the Kuravan and Kurathi hills.*

☞ *Kundala dam is relatively a small dam having curved shape.*

☞ *Mattupetty Dam is situated near Munnar in Idukki district.*

☞ *Mullaperiyar Dam is situated in Idukki district of Kerala.*

☞ *Challakudy Dam is located on Challakudy river, 65 km east of Challakudy town, Thrissur district in Kerala.*

☞ *Vazhani Dam is situated 23 km from Thrissur city on Vadakkancherry Puzha river. It is one of the biggest clay dams.*

☞ *Kanjirapuzha Dam is located on Kanjirapuzha river, a major tributary of the Chaliyar river.*

☞ *Meenkara Dam is on Parambikulam river about 32 km south-east of Palakkad.*

☞ *Parambikulam Dam ranks number one in India as well as in the top ten embankment dams in the world in volume capacity.*

☞ *The Pothundi dam was constructed with the main aim of providing water for irrigation to Palakkad district in Kerala.*

☞ *The Banasura Sagar Dam located 21 km from Kalpetta, in Wayanad district of Kerala in the Western Ghats is the largest earthen dam in India and the second largest in Asia.*

TEST YOUR SELF

1. Banasura Sagar Dam Project was started in the year ....
   A. 1975   B. 1977
   C. 1979   D. 1981

2. Chimmony Dam is situated in which of the following districts?
   A. Thrissur   B. Idukki
   C. Kottayam   D. Alappuzha

3. Which among the following is a gravity masonry dam?
   A. Malampuzha Dam   B. Idamalayar Dam
   C. Mangalam Dam   D. Mattupetty Dam

4. Which among the following is built across the Manali river?
   A. Peechi Dam   B. Parambikulam Dam
   C. Neyyar Dam   D. Mullaperiyar Dam

5. Kakki Reservoir is an artificial lake located in district ....
   A. Kollam   B. Ernakulam
   C. Pathanamthitta   D. Palakkad

6. Which among the following is the largest reservoir in Kerala?
   A. Idamalayar Dam   B. Neyyar Dam
   C. Parambikulam Dam   D. Mulampuzha Dam

7. Which Dam is located near the confluence of the Muthirappuzha, Chanduvarai and Kundali river?
   A. Mullaperiyar   B. Mattupetty
   C. Mangalam   D. Idamalayar

8. Which among the following is the embankment dam located in Kerala?
   A. Neyyar Dam   B. Mattupetty Dam
   C. Parambikulam Dam   D. Peechi Dam

9. Which of the following is correct?

Dam		**Districts**
A. Walayar	—	Palakkad
B. Pothundi	—	Thiruvananthapuram
C. Neyyar	—	Thrissur
D. Parambikulam	—	Kannur

10. Which among the following is one of the biggest clay dams in Kerala?
   A. Pothundi Dam   B. Thenmala Dam
   C. Vazhani Dam   D. Walayar Dam

ANSWERS

1	2	3	4	5	6	7	8	9	10
C	A	B	A	C	D	B	C	A	C

13

<u>MINERAL RESOURCES</u>

Kerala State is endowed with a number of occurrences/deposits of minerals such as Heavy Mineral Sands Ilmenite, Rutile, Zircon, Monazite, Sillimanite, Gold, Iron ore, Bauxite, Graphite, China Clay, Fire Clay, Tile and Brick Clay, Silica Sand, Lignite, Limestone, Limeshell, Dimension Stone (Granite), Gemstones, Magnesite, Steatite etc. However, mining activities on large scale are confined mainly to a few minerals—Heavy Mineral Sands, China Clay and to a lesser extent Limestone/ Limeshell, Silica Sand and Granite. In fact, Heavy mineral sand and China Clay contribute more than 90% of the total value of mineral production in the State.

Gold

Gold occurs in Kerala both as primary and placer deposits. The known occurrences are mainly in Wayanad-Nilambur regions. Discovery of gold in Attapady valley of Palakkad district is new and promising. Mining activity in the Wayanad Gold Field was abandoned in the early part of the 20th century. The main reason for this appears to be the discovery of the very rich gold deposits in Kolar Gold Field in Karnataka around that time.

United Nations assisted Kerala Mineral Exploration & Development Project of the State (now merged with Department of Mining and Geology) studied the gold placers in Chaliyar and Punnapuzha rivers draining Nilambur valley. Exploration for primary gold was also taken up which resulted in delineating the Maruda prospect. Two other prospects of interest have also been identified close to Maruda viz. Mannucheeni and Thannikkadavu.

Iron Ore

Five iron ore deposits of banded magnetite quartzite type have been identified in Kozhikode District and one in Malappuram District. These deposits are estimated to contain 84 million tonnes of reserve (geological reserves) with iron content varying from 32 to 41%.

Bauxite

Bauxite occurs in close association with laterite all along the west coast of the State. Traces of bauxite are seen in almost all laterite cappings. But bauxite deposits of economic significance in south Kerala are a few and are located at Sooranad, Vadakkumuri, Chittavattom, and Adichanallur in Kollam district and Mangalapuram, Chilambil, Sasthavattom and Attipra areas of Thiruvananthapuram district. The total bauxite reserves in the State are estimated at 12.5 million tonnes. The largest bauxite deposits are in Nileswaram with a reserve of 5.32 million tonnes of grade around 45% Al_2O_3 and SiO_2 less than 5%.

China Clay

China clay (kaolin) consisting dominantly of kaolinite is one of the most sophisticated industrial minerals with a host of applications, viz., in ceramics, refractories, paper coating, filler for rubber, insecticides, cement, paint, textiles, fertilizers and others including abrasives, asbestos products, fibreglass, chemicals, cosmetics, pharmaceuticals, electrical ware, foundry and glass. There are two major china clay zones viz., the southern china clay zone between Thiruvananthapuram and Kundara (Thiruvananthapuram and Kollam districts) and the northern china clay zone between Kannapuram Madayi-Cheruthazham in Kannur district to Nileswaram-Manjeshwaram in Kasargode district. An estimated reserve of 172 million tonnes (probable reserve of 80 million tonnes and possible reserve of 92 million tonnes) of china clay of sedimentary and residual origin has been arrived at. Kerala china clay is one of the finest quality clay and is world class. In fact, Kaolin marketed by English Indian Clays Ltd. (EICL), Thiruvananthapuram claims to have similar or even better properties compared to imported clays.

Ball Clay

Ball clay (inferred reserve of 5.67 million tonnes) is found in certain areas in Kollam, Alappuzha, Ernakulam, Thrissur and Kannur districts. Though it does not confirm to specification of ball clays, yet it is considered to be a good substitute. At present, there is no commercial production.

Fire Clay

The fire clay occurrences are in association with Tertiary sediments in the coastal land and the inferred reserve stands at 11.50 million tonnes. However, this resource is waiting to be exploited.

Tile And Brick Clays

The tile and brick clays are usually of low grade and red burning. The main requisites are that they should mould easily and burn hard at low temperature. There are about 400 tile factories and about 5000 brick kilns spread over the entire state to manufacture tile and bricks. The vast resources of alluvial clays in the paddy land and valley fill areas are used by this industry in the State. Clays available for the manufacture of tiles are mostly found in the districts of Thrissur, Kozhikode, Ernakulam, Kollam, Thiruvananthapuram, Kannur and Palakkad Districts.

There are two main types of tile and brick clays in the State, lacustrine and floodplain. The former are confined to Kannur district. Clays are generally fine plastic to dull white to variegated colours and occur in the depressions in the laterite near Pattuvam, Alakode, Thaliparamambu etc. The flood plain deposits, which occur in the neighbourhood of rivers are found in a number of districts.

Graphite

Graphite occurs in nature in the form of vein, dissemination (flaky) and amorphous variety. The first two types of occurrences are found in Kerala. The vein - type graphite mined earlier around Veli, Vellanad and Changa is confined only to the Thiruvananthapuram district. The flake type of graphite is extensive in occurrence in Thiruvananthapuram, Kollam, Kottayam, Idukki and Ernakulam districts. The studies of the bulk samples collected from the flaky graphite deposits of Vadakode, Nagapuzha (Muvattupuzha taluk, Ernakulam district) and Chirakkadavu (Kanjirappally taluk, Kottayam district) point to good beneficiation characteristics, a high recovery of fixed carbon (about 85%) and preservation of suitable flake size facilitating their use in key value added industrial application like crucible manufacture etc.

Silica Sand

The coastal tract between Alappuzha and Aroor in Alappuzha District contain extensive deposits of silica sand. The best deposits are confined to the narrow strip of land sandwiched on either side by Vembanad lake and stretching from Cherthala to Arookutti over a distance of about 35 kms. Besides there are also smaller deposits in other districts of Kerala.

Varanad sand could be used for making high grade colourless glass such as crystal glass, table ware etc. The scope for beneficiation of the sand established its usefulness in optical and ophthalmic glass industry. The products suit to the specification of sheet rolled and polished glass manufacture.

Mineral Sand

The Heavy Mineral Sand deposits in Kerala contain an assemblage of Ilmenite, Rutile, Leucoxene, Monazite, Zircon and Sillimanite. The State possesses one of the world class deposits of mineral sands in the coastal tracts between Neendakara and Kayamkulam. This, commonly known as the *Chavara deposit,* after the main locality, covers a total length of 22 kms and a whidth of about 8 km in the northern side and 6 kms in the southern side. The Chavara barrier beach portion contains concentration of heavy minerals above 60%. The Chavara deposit is estimated to contain 127 million tonnes of heavy minerals with ilmenite content of 80 million tonnes from the total reserve of raw sand of the order of 1400 million tonnes. In the northern portion beyond Kayamkulam Pozhi extending up to Thottappally in Alappuzha district, the total reserve of heavy minerals estimated to the order of 17 million tonnes with ilmenite content of 9 million tonnes from the raw sand of 242 million tonnes.

Lignite

Lignite, the only fuel mineral discovered recently in the State assumes special significance. Since no coal deposits have been identified and the landed cost of coal remains high, the possibility of substitution of coal and fire wood by lignite in the user industries would be worth pursuing.

Lignite occurs in multiple seams having an average cumulative thickness of 4.65 m. Calorific values ranges from 1583 to 4556 K cal/kg and the average is 2830 K cal/kg. A reserve of 5.40 MT have been estimated from Madai area, Kannur of 1.19 sq.km. Small as well as pilot scale tests on the lignite samples established fluidised bed combustion and a high combustion efficiency (more than 96%) of lignite.

Drilling at Kadankottumala, near Cheruvathur has indicated that lignite seams of average cumulative thickness of 2.85 m occur in the sedimentaries in the depth range from 16.70 m and 33.40 m. A reserve of 1 million tonnes of lignite has been estimated tentatively. In Kayyur— layicode area east of Nileswaram a reserve of 0.55 million tonnes of lignite with clay has also been estimated.

Limestone

Crystalline Limestone

Kerala State is deficient in crystalline limestone and only a few bands of crystalline limestone in Palakkad and Idukki districts have been located in addition to the limestone deposit proved at Pandarathu, Walayar, Palakkad district. The Pandarathu limestone deposit (24 million tonnes) is now the captive mine producing limestone for M/s. Malabar Cements Ltd., the Portland cement plant in Kerala.

A number of small bands have also been identified in other localities in Nattuvanki, Athurasram, Vannamadai, Thavalam in Palakkad district and in a few localities in Idukki district.

Kankar Limestone

Limestone of Kankar variety has been reported from Chittoor-Kozhinjampara area in Palakkad district. The economic significance of low-grade limestone has not been indicated by the studies conducted so far. The 16 km^2 area between Thavalam and near Anaiketty shows that kankar caps the amphibolite over 0.3 km^2.

Fossiliferous Limestone

Fossiliferous Limestone is known to occur in various parts of Kollam district such as Kallurkadavu, Mughathala, Kannanallur, Kottiyam, Mayyanad, Nedumgandam and Edava in Thiruvananthapuram district. The occurrence of shell limestone is in the form of discontinuous lenses intercalated with black carbonaceous clay in the Tertiary formations.

Lime Shell

The State is deficient in high-grade limestone. Consequently the requirement of lime for chemical industry is depended on the limeshell resources occurring in the backwaters/estuaries, river mouths and lagoons along the coastal tract.

By far the largest reserves of lime shell are known to occur in Vembanad lake and adjoining portions comprising parts of Alappuzha, Ernakulam and Kottayam Districts.

The lime shell resources next in importance to Vembanad lake are those in Kannur and Kasargode districts in North Kerala.

Magnesite

A total possible reserve of 0.037 million tonnes has been estimated in Mulli-Salayur areas, Attappadi in Palakkad District. In Salayur area, magnesite veins varying in thickness from 10 to 30 m were observed in pits. The average recovery of magnesite was assessed as 100 kg/m^3 of magnesite-bearing rocks.

Steatite / Talc

It is consumed in many manufacturing industries of paper, insecticide, textile, fertilizers, ceramics, rubber products, cement, asbestos etc.

Several steatite occurrences have been identified in Thalassery Taluk of Kannur district. The total reserves estimated are of the order of 7.94 million tonnes. The major granite belt of Kerala can be classified by its geologic setting into three categories:

- Charnockite-Khondalite belt of Thiruvananthapuram, Kollam, Pathanamthitta and Kottayam districts (colour ranges from pale green with mottled red, bluish green with cordierite, deep dark green, greyish white).

- True intrusive or anatectic granites and associated magmatites of Proterozoic age from Idukki, Palakkad, Kannur, Kasargode and Wayanad districts (colour : Pink, light pink, Gray, yellowish white and bluish pink with wavy patterns).

- Dolerite-Gabbro dykes, Proterozoic intrusive hypabasal dyke swarms from Kottayam, Palakkad, Malappuram and Kozhikode districts (colour: dark greenish blue, black and dark gray with black spots).

Gemstones

There are three different geological setting in which gemstones occurs in Kerala viz.

- The pegmatites traversing the crystalline rocks.

- In association with gravels in the river channels of the present day.

- In the older gravels which are often consolidated and lateritised.

- These settings have fairly extensive geographical distribution in Thiruvananthapuram district, the localities of importance are Andoorkonam, Aruvikkara, Balaramapuram, Bonaccord Estate, Braemore Estate, Changa, Chullimanur, Madathara, Manickkal, Pirappancode, Venjaramoodu, Venganoor, Vembayam, Thonnakkal, Uzhamalakkal, Manvila, Mudakkal, Nedumangad, Vellanad, Nettani, Ooroottambalam, Pothencode and in Kollam, the main gem bearing localities are Adukkalamula, Podiattuvila, Kulathupuzha, and Talachira. Besides these localities several stretches of rivers like Kallar- Vamanapuram Ar, Karamana Ar, Neyyar in Thiruvananthapuram District and Kulathupuzha, Kallada rivers in Kollam district are also subjected to sporadic mining activities, though there is no legalized gem mining in the State.

KNOW THE FACTS

☞ *Gold occurs in Kerala both as primary and placer deposits. The known occurrences are mainly in Wayanad-Nilambur regions.*

☞ *Iron ore deposits of banded magnetite quartzite type have been identified in Kozhikode and Malappuram District.*

☞ *Bauxite occurs in close association with laterite all along the west coast of the State. The largest bauxite deposits are in Nileswaram with a reserve of 5.32 million tonnes.*

☞ *China clay (kaolin) consisting dominantly of kaolinite is one of the most sophisticated industrial minerals. There are two major china clay zones viz., the southern china clay zone between Thiruvananthapuram and Kundara (Thiruvananthapuram and Kollam districts) and the northern china clay zone between Kannapuram Madayi-Cheruthazham in Kannur district to Nileswaram-Manjeshwaram in Kasargode district. Kerala China clay is one of the finest quality clay and is world class with an estimated reserve of 172 million tonnes.*

☞ *Ball clay is found in certain areas in Kollam, Alappuzha, Ernakulam, Thrissur and Kannur districts.*

☞ *The fire clay occurrences are in association with Tertiary sediments in the coastal land and the inferred reserve stands at 11.50 million tonnes.*

☞ *There are two main types of tile and brick clays in the State, lacustrine and floodplain.*

☞ *Graphite occurs in nature in the form of vein, dissemination (flaky) and amorphous variety.*

☞ *The coastal tract between Alappuzha and Aroor in Alappuzha District contain extensive deposits of silica sand.*

TEST YOUR SELF

1. Attapady Valley of Palakkad district is famous for ....
   A. gold mining
   B. coal mining
   C. bauxite
   D. fire clay

2. Iron ore deposits in Kerala are located in ....
   A. Kozhikode
   B. Kannur
   C. Malappuram
   D. Both A and C

3. Sooranad and Vadakkumuri regions are famous for ....
   A. China clay
   B. Fire clay
   C. Bauxite
   D. Tile Clay

4. China clay is used in which of the following industries?
   A. ceramies
   B. paper coating
   C. cement
   D. All of these

5. Fire clay occurrences are found in association with tertiary sediments in ....
   A. coastal area
   B. hilly area
   C. plain area
   D. None of these

6. Which among the following occurs in nature in the form of vein, dissemination and amorphous?

A. sillica sand

B. lignite

C. graphite

D. limestone

7. Nileswaram—Manjeshwaram region is famous for ....

A. bauxite

B. iron ore

C. gold

D. china clay

8. Vadakode and Nagapuzha are famous for graphite mining located in ....

A. Ernakulam

B. Alappuzha

C. Kannur

D. Idukki

9. Where does the Magnesite reserve occur?

A. Kannur

B. Palakkad

C. Thiruvanthapuram

D. Alappuzha

10. Vembanad lake is famous for which of the following occurrence?

A. Magnesite

B. Steatite

C. Lime shell

D. Gemstones

ANSWERS

1	2	3	4	5	6	7	8	9	10
A	D	C	D	A	C	D	A	B	C

❏❏❏

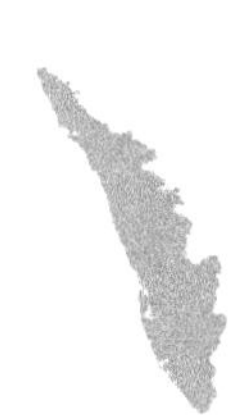

14

INDUSTRIES

The growth of manufacturing sector in the state has been curbed due to the high cost for skilled labor, the rapidly propelling land prices and the preference of the local population for white collar jobs. Also being a traditionally service oriented economy with a high density of population, the state hasn't been able to find a balanced growth strategy for manufacturing sector. The state has been successful to some extent in ensuring private capital in these sectors. Village and traditional industries have been revived and rejuvenated for healthy growth thereby bringing substantial relief to lakhs of workers depending on them for their livelihood. Medium and large industry sector have also witnessed substantial hike in public investment and with its help the KSIDC and KINFRA have initiated the setting up of mega projects. The loss making State PSUs have initiated steps for generating decent profits. For the manufacturing sector to sustain in Kerala it should aim at bringing about environmentally sustainable practices, better waste management technology, sensible use of water and forest resources, and follow a stringent quality and environment norms.

Industrial & Commercial Policy 2007

To achieve high and sustainable economic growth, with specific thrust to social objectives, through rapid industrialization and big leap in commercial activities, without affecting ecology and environment and to create large-scale employment opportunities for the people of Kerala and ensuring them fair wages and to convert Kerala into an investment friendly destination is the vision of the Industrial & Commercial Policy announced by the Government during 2007. The main features of the Industrial Policy 2007 are as follows:

- Convert Kerala into a favoured destination for Manufacturing, Agro-Processing, Health Services, Knowledge-based Industries and Services.

- Strengthen the State Level Public Enterprises (SLPEs) by technological upgradation, diversification, efficient management system and synergizing with Central Public Sector Undertakings.
- Make Traditional Industries competitive by modernization, value addition and skill development.
- Promote and support SMEs as ancillaries to large scale industries as well as a self-sustaining entity considering its role as a largest employment provider in the State.
- Make use of the abundant and highly rich mineral resources of the State to the fullest extent protecting environment and ecology and restricting the mining activity in the Public Sector.
- Generate massive employment in industrial, commercial and service sectors.
- Attract huge capital investment on mutually beneficial terms.
- Tap the rich industrial potential of biotechnology.

State Scenario

As per Quick Estimate of Gross State Domestic Product for 2015-16 by Economics & Statistics Department, the manufacturing sector of Kerala grew by 9.28 per cent at current prices compared to 5.02 per cent in the previous year. At constant prices (2011-12), the sector registered a growth of 12.65 per cent in 2015-16 as against 2.46 per cent in 2014-15. The shares of manufacturing sector in GSDP at constant and current prices in 2015-16 were 9.97 per cent and 8.72 per cent respectively.

Large Industries

Food Processing

Food processing industry has been recognized as a priority sector in Kerala due to its potential for future growth, diversification and possibility of generating substantial employment. Kerala Industrial Infrastructure Development Corporation (KINFRA) has been playing a proactive role for the promotion of food processing industry in the State. KINFRA has adopted 'Theme based parks' in the State. KINFRA has set up industrial parks to suit the specific needs of the food processing sector.

KINFRA Food Processing Park at Kakkancherry, Special Economic Zone (Food Processing) at Kakkancherry, Food Processing Zone in KINFRA Small Industries Park, Mazhuvannur, KINFRA Food Processing Park at Adoor and Seafood Park India Private Ltd at Aroor are the five Food Processing Industries parks already set up by KINFRA.

New Initiatives of KINFRA in Food Processing

- Marine Park in Beypore for Seafood pre-processing activity.
- Kera Park in Thrissur for Coconut based Industries.
- Spices Park in Idukki for Spice Processing Industries.
- Integrated Food Zone (Mega Food Park) in Wayanad
- Mega Food Park in Kinaloor under the new Mega Food Park Scheme of Ministry of Food Processing Industries, Government of India.

Handloom Industry

Kerala's textile industry comprises traditional handloom sector, weaving and spinning sector. The Handloom Sector in Kerala stands second to the coir sector in providing employment among the traditional industries of the state. The Handloom Industry in the state is mainly concentrated in Thiruvananthapuram and Kannur District and in some parts of Kozhikode, Palakkad, Thrissur, Ernakulam, Kollam and Kasargode Districts. The Industry is dominated by the Co-operative sector covering with 96% of total looms. The remaining four per cent of Handlooms units is owned by Industrial entrepreneurs. The Co-operative sector consists of factory type and cottage type societies. The number of registered Primary Handloom Weavers Co-operative Societies in the State as on October, 2016 is 600 as against 575 during March 2015. Of this, 167 are factory type and 433 are Cottage type societies. Of these 600 societies, 402 are in working condition as on October 2016.

The major varieties produced in the handloom sector of the State are dhothis, furnishing material, bed sheets, grey saree and lungi. About 77.62% of the major items are produced in the southern region followed by the North (12.81%) and Central (5.33%) regions. Of the total production, 95.76% are contributed by the cooperative sector and the balance of 4.24% is by the units in the entrepreneurial sector.

Promotional measures of handloom sectors such as procurement, sales and marketing of handloom fabrics are done by two state level organisations namely Hantex and Hanveev.

Hantex is the apex society of handloom co-operative societies in the state. Number of PHWCS registered under Hantex is 489. Despite grants and loans are being given to the society, the organisation is running in loss and the accumulated loss of Hantex is ₹ 1998.48 lakhs during the 2015-16.

Hanveev assist handloom weavers outside the co-operative fold by providing necessary raw materials at reasonable price and making arrangements for marketing their products. This organisation is also running in losses and the net loss at the end of 2015-16 is ₹ 7808.58 lakhs.

The Integrated Handloom Development Scheme is a Centrally sponsored Scheme introduced to the growing competitiveness in the textile industry both at the national and international markets and the free trade opportunities emerging in the post MFA environment. A growing need has been felt for adopting a focused yet flexible and holistic approach to the sector to facilitate handloom weavers to meet the challenges of a globalised environment. A need has also been felt to empower weavers to chart out a sustainable path for growth and diversification in line with the emerging market trends. The Integrated Handlooms Development Scheme (IHDS) is an attempt to facilitate the sustainable development of handloom weavers located in and out side identified handloom clusters in to a cohesive self managing and competitive socio - economic unit.

Textile Sector

The Textile Industry in Kerala is spread over in public sector as well as in Co-operative Sector and there exist thirteen Spinning Mills jointly in the public/ co-operative sector. Kerala State Co-operative Textile Federation (TEXFED) have seven Co-operative Spinning Mills in its member fold. Five of them are administered by the Government and two have elected boards. Due to various reasons consequent to globalization, Spinning Industry was facing deep crisis and the Mills in Co-operative Sector slipped into the huge accumulated losses amounting to ₹132.52 crore. From 2006 onwards the Government interfered in the day-to-day activities of these mills and turnaround the units in a big way enforcing financial as well as technical discipline.

The main handicaps faced by the Mills were the lack of working capital and availability of raw materials. The Government through a centralized purchase system interfered in this area and pumped ₹7 crore and is now procuring cotton for the entire textile sector through professionally constituted committee comprising of RIAB, TEXFED and KSTC. Also the sale of Yarn carried out through depot system is being monitored by the same committee. Due to this raw material cost was brought down heavily and sufficient savings in this area accelerated revenue and turnover.

The Co-operative Spinning Mills in the State were formed with a social objective to provide raw material support to the traditional handloom sector in Kerala. But from 1999 onwards due to various reasons this has been stopped. The Government took up the issue seriously and to have an integrated approach for the industry decided to establish three hank yarn production centres in the State. Now Cannanore Co-operative Spinning mills, Alleppey Co-operative Spinning Mills and the Trichur Co-operative

Spinning Mills have hank yarn production centres established with an outlay of ₹2.00 crore each.

Powerloom

Kerala consumes cloth to the tune of Rs. 2000 crores every year. The four integrated power loom co-operative societies in the state at Calicut, Wayanad, Neyyattinkara and Kottayam have been accelerated by providing budgetary support.

The Calicut Integrated Power loom Co-operative Society Ltd., has been converted as a textile park comprising all the segments of a composite mill i.e., weaving, processing and garment making. Here semi automatic power looms, automatic looms and highly sophisticated machines are working. The value added products manufactured from these units is being exported through merchant vendors to Europe and other parts of the world. They manufacture terry towels, high quality home furnishings, shirts, dothies, blazers etc. for domestic as well as export market.

Handicrafts

Kerala State Handicrafts Apex Co-operative Society (SURABHI), Handicrafts Development Corporation and Artisans Development Corporation (KADCO) are the major promotional agencies in the handicraft industry. SURABHI is the apex organization of primary handicrafts co-operatives established with a view to uplift the artisans by marketing the product produced by the primary co-operatives and implementing welfare schemes with the assistance from State and Central Governments.

Handicrafts Development Corporation of Kerala was established in 1968. It is engaged in procuring and marketing handicraft products by giving fair returns to artisans through its Kairali emporia spread all over India. At present it is having a net work of 19 such sales emporia. The Corporation provides loans to OBC groups of artisans / member of artisans family below double the poverty line for starting small business, carpentry, blacksmith, weaving, grocery shops, pottery, tailoring, jewellery making etc. The Kerala Artisans Development Corporation (KADCO) was established in 1981. It is one of the State agencies to provide assistance to artisans for establishing production units, promoting marketing of products and providing employment opportunities through schemes of trade fairs and marketing centres.

Bamboo Industry

Kerala State Bamboo Corporation was set up in 1971. The main objective of the Corporation is to develop and promote industries based on bamboo, reed, cane and rattan and to undertake manufacture and trading of the above products, provide financial, technical and other such assistance, guidance to the bamboo workers. Collection of good quality reeds from Government forest, distributes the reeds to the registered bamboo mat weavers of the Corporation on credit basis and to procure woven mats are the major activities of the Corporation.

As part of diversification, Corporation has initiated an innovative project viz. Bamboo Flooring Tiles Project with the financial support of Central and State Governments.

The Kerala State Bamboo Mission was constituted in 2003 with the broad aim of marshalling the scattered resources of the State adopting a focused approach to revitalize the Bamboo Sector thereby promoting value addition, enhancing income generation and alleviating poverty.

Coir Industry

The Coir Industry is the largest agro based Traditional & Cottage industry in Kerala and concentrated mainly in the rural areas. It provides livelihood to nearly 2 lakh families, out of which women constitutes 76 per cent. The industry consists of three sub sector, namely, fibre extraction, spinning and weaving sections. Co-operative Sector dominates the Coir Industry in Kerala. Coir yarn producers, product manufactures, public sector undertakings, exporters, and workers are the other major stake holders of the Coir industry.

Government of Kerala has laid emphasis for developing this industry by increased utilization of coconut husk for production of coir fibre, market intervention through branding techniques, strengthening of R & D facilities to find innovative uses of coir and acquiring new technologies, encouragement to co-operativisation and providing social welfare, civic amenities and medical facilities to workers. Modernization is encouraged through incentives to make the coir industry more competitive.

The Kerala State Coir Cooperative Marketing Federation (COIRFED) is an apex federation of primary coir co-operative societies with an objective to procure the entire products of the member societies and marketing the same throughout the country and thereby providing fair wages and subsistence to the coir workers.

Khadi and Village Industries

Khadi and Village Industries Board (KVIB) is the statutory body vested with the responsibility of organizing, developing and promoting Khadi and

Village Industries in the State. It carries out its activities through co-operative societies, registered institutions and departmental units by availing financial assistance from State Government, Khadi Commission and Nationalized Banks.

Cashew Industry

Cashew is an important commercial horticulture crop of India. India's production of cashew nut in 2014 was 7,37,000 metric tons, which accounted for 18 per cent of the total cashew production in the world. In fact, India is the largest producer of raw cashew nut in the world. The important cashew growing states in India are Kerala, Karnataka, Goa, Maharashtra, Tamil Nadu, Andhra Pradesh, Odisha and West Bengal. Maharashtra is the top among the states with high production and productivity (31.85%). Kerala has a long tradition both in cashew cultivation and cashew nut processing.

The Cashew Industry in Kerala is mainly concentrated in Kollam District. The Central Government recognises Kollam as a "Centre of Cashew Industry". The industry is highly labour intensive and employs more than 2 lakh workers, a majority of them women (above 90 per cent). Thus the industry provides a source of income for a large number of low-income families. In 2014-15, the export of cashew and cashew Kernels through Cochin port was 68150 MT. Kerala accounts for 11 per cent of cashew production and 35 per cent of all cashew nut processing units in India. The state needs around 6 lakh MT of raw cashew in a year for catering to the needs of its 800 factories.

The Cashew Export Promotion Council of India (CEPCI, Govt. of India), a not-for-profit company, was established at Kollam, with the objective of promoting exports of cashew kernels and cashew nut shell liquid from India. The council operates plan schemes of Government of India, and offers various services to its member exporters.

Beedi Industry

Beedi Industry in Kerala is concentrated in Kozhikkode, Kannur and Kasargode. The Kerala Dinesh Beedi Workers Central Co-operative Society Ltd. was the only agency in the State to promote beedi industry in the organized sector. The society concentrated on the upliftment of units for the diversified products for the rehabilitation of about 7000 beedi workers under the society.

Micro Small and Medium Enterprises (MSMEs)

In Kerala, MSME sector which has been provided special support by the Government, contributes greatly towards domestic needs, export marketing and foreign exchange earnings by producing varieties of products ranging from traditional to modern. Being the volume of production of MSME sector is very large, the quality of production, diversification of products, energy consumption, and environmental effects were considered all through.

The MSME sector almost overcame the Neo-liberal policies of GOI which cause huge inflow of consumer goods from neighboring nations and the post recession era thrust; and improved in terms of quality infrastructure development and social welfare of the state during the year 2010-11. It was reflected in the growth performance of the MSME sector that the sector was highly contributed in terms of investment, value of production and high employment potential for the year 2007-08 among the last 5 years.

With a view to promote Kerala as a prime destination for industrial investments with environmental protection, various programmes were implemented during the year 2010-11. As part of developing quality industrial infrastructure in Kerala, new industrial parks with all facilities are promoted and existing Parks updated. Also adequate support is given to promote employment intensive industries like agro based and food processing, textiles and garments and handicrafts to ensure job creation. Besides, Skill development programmes are promoted. Cluster development programme is one of the key areas for MSME promotion. Separate fund from State head is provided for the development of clusters.

As on September 17, 2015, the total number of working SSIs/MSMEs registered in Kerala are 2,57,466. Out of the total SSIs/MSMEs, 3.84 per cent were promoted by SC entrepreneurs, 0.72 per cent by STs and 24.97 per cent by women entrepreneurs. The total investment was ₹ 17,98,646.38 lakh while the total value of goods and services produced was ₹ 67,65,143.93 lakh and the total number of employment generated was 13,18,666 Nos.

Small Industries Development Bank of India (SIDBI)

Small Industries Development Bank of India (SIDBI) is the principal financial institution for the promotion, financing and development of MSME industries. It also acts as the nodal agency for the scheme sponsored by Government of India in this regard. It also extends indirect financial assistance by way of refinance facilities to primary lending institutions viz., KFC, KSIDC and Commercial Banks against their loans granted to small scale units.

Kerala Small Industries Development Corporation (SIDCO)

Kerala Small Industries Development Corporation was established for strengthening the Small Scale Sectors in the State. It provides infrastructure facilities such as land, work shed, water, distribution of scarce raw materials, marketing the products etc. by setting up of industrial estates, mini industrial estates and industrial parks. Execution of construction works for Industries department and public sector undertakings are the other activities of SIDCO.

MSME Development Institute

MSMED Institute provides technical, managerial consultancy services besides attending to revival of small scale sick units in all the districts of Kerala and the Union Territory of Lakshadweep. The prime motto of MSMED Institute is to provide timely and adequate techno-economic and managerial assistance to prospective and existing entrepreneurs. It also acts as a technology resource centre, training centre, service provider of industry, implementing agency of MSME schemes and assistance of Government of India.

Industrial Financing

Kerala Financial Corporation (KFC)

It is one of the oldest Industrial Financing Agencies in the State and it has been providing finance to a large number of projects and enterprises.

Kerala State Industrial Development Corporation (KSIDC)

Kerala State Industrial Development Corporation (KSIDC) is a Government agency for industrial and investment promotion in Kerala. Established in 1961 with the objective of promoting, stimulating, financing and facilitating the development of large and medium scale industries in Kerala, KSIDC acts as a promotional agency involved in catalyzing the development of infrastructure required for constant growth of industry in the State. It offers professional guidance and support for potential investors through a comprehensive set of services that include developing business ideas, identifying viable projects, providing financial assistance, guidance and assistance for implementation. KSIDC has a proven track record of attracting a commendable volume of investment to the State.

Kerala Industrial Infrastructure Development Corporation (KINFRA)

Kerala Industrial Infrastructure Development Corporation (KINFRA) was set up by an Act of the State Legislature in February 1993, aiming at accelerating the industrial development of the State by providing infrastructure facilities to industries. KINFRA's thrust has been to facilitate the development of industrial infrastructure in the State.

KINFRA has been focusing on industrial infrastructure development, specifically aimed at the economic development of the industrially backward regions of the State, by setting up Industrial Parks/Townships/Zones etc., which provide all the facilities required for the entrepreneurs to start an industry.

Cochin Special Economic Zone (CSEZ)

The Cochin Special Economic Zone (CSEZ) is one among the seven Government of India owned Special Economic Zones set up as a multi-product Export Processing Zone to boost exports from the State. The Cochin Export Processing Zone was converted into a Special Economic Zone in November 2000.

CSEZ is a multi-product zone with 108 working units and 18 under implementation units as on September 2011, in sectors as varied as electronic hardware, software, engineering, readymade garments, food processing, plastics and rubber products gem and jewellery manufacturing with more than 12000 employees. It is the single largest employment destination in the State. Both multinational corporations and domestic corporate have set up their units in the Zone.

Information and Communication Technology

The repute of the country as a favored IT/ITES destination has been growing phenomenally even in times of recession. The size of Indian IT-BPO industry has crossed 70 billion USD, contributing 5.8% of country's GDP. In the last 5 years Kerala too has witnessed the emergences of the IT & ITES business as a key contributor to the economy. The growth of the knowledge economy has been beneficial for the state as it enjoys many natural vantages that can be utilized effectively. The high density of technology graduates, lower salaries and lower employee attrition rates have also helped the states progress.

Kerala State Information Technology Mission (KSITM)

Kerala State IT Mission (KSITM), the nodal IT implementation arm of the Government was established in the year 1999. KSITM was registered as a Society under the Travancore, Cochin, Literary, Scientific and Charitable Societies Act (Act 12 of 1955). The Key Objectives of KSITM include e-governance, disseminating Information across citizens and Government, interfacing between Government and Industry, bridging digital divide, investor interactions and device strategies in achieving speed and transparency in governance. The thrust activity is e-governance, KSITM has conceptualized and implemented many citizen centric E-governance Projects directly or helped the departments indirectly.

Kerala State IT Infrastructure Limited

Kerala State Information Technology Infrastructure Ltd (KSITIL) is a public limited company formed for the creation of infrastructure for IT/ITES in the State. The company has been incorporated under the Companies Act on January 2008 and has commenced business on March 2008.

The business model for the company is to acquire land, create value addition by providing basic infrastructure like electricity, water, and road, obtain SEZ status and such other Government approvals that may be required and then allot land to private developers for development of either IT SEZs or IT parks, realizing value of land based on market prices. Revenue so generated is reinvested in projects it promotes as company's share capital. The company holds upto 26% in the projects.

Technopark

Technopark was set up under the auspices of Electronics Technology Park, Kerala an autonomous body under the Department of Information Technology, Government of Kerala. The Park is home to over 240 Companies employing more than 32,000 professionals. Technopark's aim was to create infrastructure and provide support required for the development of high technology companies.

Infopark

Infoparks Kerala is a society registered under Travancore Cochin Literary Scientific and Charitable Society Act XII of 1955 and fully owned by Government of Kerala. The main objectives include creation of state-of-art infrastructure facilities such as space for IT/ITES companies, supply of power, water, connectivity etc. Since its inception in 2004 Infopark has created over 34 lakhs sq.ft. of IT space and has provided employment to over 15,000 IT professionals through around 104 IT companies who have taken space in its Parks. Currently, Infoparks Kerala has the following IT Parks.

	Park	Area	District/Village
1.	Infopark Kochi – Phase I In operation	100 acres	Kakkanad village, Ernakulam District–
2.	Infopark Kochi – Phase II (125 acres taken possession) - under development	160 acres	Kunnathunad/Puthencruz villages, Ernakulam District
3.	Infopark Thrissur–in operation	30 acres	Koratty

4.	Infopark Cherthala– operation started	66 acres	Pallippuram village, Alappuzha district –
5.	Infopark Ambalapuzha		Ambalapuzha

Cyber Park

Cyber Park is strategically positioned to provide the benefits of large pool of skilled resources, the lower infrastructure cost and the high quality of living combined with its location and benefits to investors around the world. Further the number of reputed universities and educational institutions in the region has made it even more compelling to start the next phase of IT Parks developments in this region. The purpose of Cyberpark is to provide a friendly, cost effective and top of the line infrastructure to the IT/ITES investors, there by acting as a catalyst for the social and infrastructure development of the region with a vision to provide unlimited employment opportunities and a substantial contribution to economic development of the state especially the Malabar Region.

KNOW THE FACTS

☞ *Kerala's textile industry comprises traditional handloom sector, weaving and spinning sector.*

☞ *The Handloom Sector in Kerala stands second to the coir sector in providing employment among the traditional industries of the State.*

☞ *The Handloom Industry in the State is mainly concentrated in Thiruvananthapuram and Kannur District and in some parts of Kozhikode, Palakkad, Thrissur, Ernakulam, Kollam and Kasargode Districts.*

☞ *Hantex is the apex society of handloom co-operative societies in the state.*

☞ *Hanveev assist handloom weavers outside the co-operative fold by providing necessary raw materials at reasonable price.*

☞ *The Integrated Handloom Development Scheme is a Centrally sponsored Scheme introduced to the growing competitiveness in the textile industry.*

☞ *The Textile Industry in Kerala is spread over in public sector as well as in Co-operative Sector.*

☞ *The Calicut Integrated Power loom Co-operative Society Ltd., has been converted as a textile park comprising all the segments of a composite mill.*

☞ *SURABHI is the apex organization of primary handicrafts co-operatives established with a view to uplift the artisans by marketing the product produced by the primary co-operatives.*

☞ *Handicrafts Development Corporation of Kerala was established in 1968.*

☞ *Kerala State Bamboo Corporation was set up in 1971. The main objective of the Corporation is to develop and promote industries based on bamboo, reed, cane and rattan.*

☞ *The Kerala State Bamboo Mission was constituted in 2003 with the broad aim of marshalling the scattered resources of the State.*

☞ *The Coir Industry is the largest agro based Traditional & Cottage industry in Kerala and concentrated mainly in the rural areas.*

☞ *Khadi and Village Industries Board (KVIB) is the statutory body vested with the responsibility of organizing, developing and promoting Khadi and Village Industries in the State.*

☞ *Beedi Industry in Kerala is concentrated in Kozhikkode, Kannur and Kasargode.*

☞ *Kerala State IT Mission (KSITM), the nodal IT implementation arm of the Government was established in the year 1999.*

TEST YOUR SELF

1. In which year Cochin Export Processing Zone was converted into SEZ?
   A. Nov. 2000   B. Nov. 2001   C. Dec. 2000   D. Dec. 2001

2. Hanveev is related to which industry in Kerala?
   A. Coir Industry   B. Handloom Industry
   C. Handicraft Industry   D. Cashew Industry

3. Which Industrial sector in Kerala provides maximum employment?
   A. Handloom Industry   B. Coir Industry
   C. Beedi Industry   D. Bamboo Industry

4. In which year KINFRA was established?
   A. 1991   B. 1992   C. 1993   D. 1994

5. Women in Kerala are mainly employed in which industry?
   A. Beedi Industry   B. Handicrafts
   C. Coir Industry   D. Handloom Industry

6. Small Industries Development Corporation in Kerala was established in ....
   A. 1968   B. 1970   C. 1972   D. 1975

7. Which among the following is the role played by KINFRA?
   A. Industrial infrastructure development
   B. Financial support to industries
   C. Managerial support to industries
   D. Both B and C

8. Coir industry in Kerala faces which of the following problems?
   A. Non-professional management system
   B. Reluctance to adopt mechanisation
   C. Shortage of raw materials
   D. All of these

9. Handloom industry in Kerala is mainly concentrated in ....
   A. Thiruvananthapuram   B. Kannur
   C. Thrissur   D. Both A and B

10. Surabhi Handicrafts Development Corporation was started in ....
    A. 1964   B. 1968   C. 1972   D. 1970

ANSWERS

1	2	3	4	5	6	7	8	9	10
A	B	B	B	C	B	A	D	D	A

15

ENERGY

Power Sector in Kerala plays a vital role in all developmental activities in Kerala. Obviously power crisis is the prime obstacle to start new initiatives in the industrial field. The need for power is increasing and the production of power should also be increased accordingly.

After the commissioning of the Pallivasal hydroelectric station in 1940 and until the commissioning of Brahmapuram (106 MW) LSHS based power station in 1996–97, Kerala had 100 per cent generation from hydel projects and it was able to generate and supply power at the lowest rates possible in the country. Even during the late seventies, the state depended on its surplus supply of inexpensive hydropower to attract energy-intensive industries and to promote industrialization. The State earned revenue from exporting surplus power until the early 1980's.

During the first three decades of the post-independence period, there were sharp increases in installed capacity. One of the major landmark in the development of the power sector in Kerala was the commissioning of the Idukki hydroelectric project with an installed capacity of 780 MW.

Total installed capacity of power in the State as on March 2016 is 2880.20 MW. Of which, hydel contributed the major share of 2104.3 MW (73.06 per cent); while 718.46 MW was contributed by thermal projects, 43.27 MW from wind and 14.1 MW from Solar. The total additional capacity added from all sources during 2015-16 was 44.5 MW and scheme wise addition details are presented in the table :

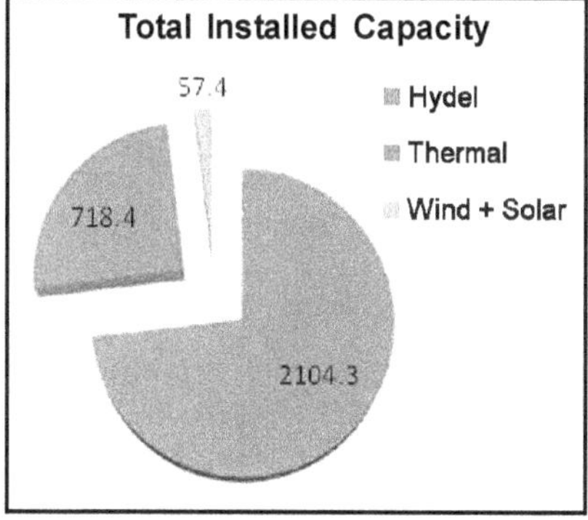

Capacity Addition, 2015-16

Sl.No.	Name of Power Stations	Installed Capacity (MW)			Date of Commissioning
		Hydel	Solar	Wind	
1.	Chimmony HEP	2.5			22.05.2015
2.	Adyanpara HEP	3.5			03.09.2015
3.	Barapole HEP	15			29.02.2016
4.	Peringalkuthu HEP (capacity enhancement)	1			29.05.2015
5.	Solar Kanjikkode		1		20.08.2015
6.	Solar Power Project at Chalayoor Colony, Agali		0.096		31.08.2015
7.	Solar Power Project at Peringalkuthu Power House		0.05		10.09.2015
8.	Solar Power Project at Banasura Sagar, Wayanad		0.01		21.01.2016
9.	Wind Power Project by M/s. Ahali Alternate Energy Pvt. Ltd. (IPP)			8.4	22.02.2016
10.	Solar Power Project by M/s. CIAL (IPP)		13		18.08.2015
	Total	**22**	**14.156**	**8.4**	

Source: KSEBL

Kerala State Electricity Board Limited (KSEBL)

KSEBL is one of the driving forces behind the economic development of the State of Kerala. It has been responsible for the generation, transmission and supply of electricity in the State, with particular mandate to provide electricity at affordable cost to the domestic as well as for agriculture purposes.

Pattern of Power Consumption

Kerala's consumption is predominantly domestic, which account for 51 per cent of the total consumption. Revenue from Domestic consumers is only 36 per cent of the total revenue. The domestic category consumers showed a growth rate of 1.52 per cent from 89,87,947 in 2014-15 to 91,24,747 in 2015-16. Per capita consumption has increased by 3.86 per cent, that is, to 565 KWh in 2015-16 against 544kWh in 2014-15. During

2015-16, 19,325 MU of energy valued at ₹ 10,44,601 lakh was sold (internally) showing an increase of 899 MU as compared to the previous year's 18,426 MU. Total consumption and per capita consumption of electricity in Kerala show a fluctuating pattern of growth.

Power Projects in Kerala

Kerala State Electricity Board (KSEB) is a public sector agency established in 1957 under the authority of the Department of Power of Kerala government. KSEB is responsible for generation, distribution and regulation of the electricity supply in Kerala State. Main source of Energy generation in Kerala is Hydroelectric Power. First Power Project in Kerala was Pallivasal during the year 1940, biggest Hydroelectric Project in Kerala is Idukki. Idukki Power Project includes Idukki, Cheruthonni and Kilivallithode dams. Important hydel projects on river Periyar include: Pallivasal, Chenkulam, Idukki, Panniyar, Neryamangalam, Idamalayar and lower Periyar. Wind farm power projects of Kerala are at Kanjikode and Ramakkalmedu. Thermal Power Plant is at Kayamkulam under the control of NTPC. Two Diesel Power Plants are at Brahmapuram and Nallalam.

Cheemeni Power Plant

The Kerala State Electricity Board (KSEB) is seriously contemplating the setting up of a 2400 MW thermal power project at Cheemeni in Kasargode district. The coal for this project will come from the coal field of the Union Government in Odisha allotted for Kerala. A company for undertaking the mining operations has already been set up there by the KSEB in association with outside public sector power utilities. The centre would provide all assistance for the project. The centre was attaching top priority to power capacity addition all over the country.

With the commissioning of the LNG Terminal in Kochi, expected by 2012, natural gas would be available as fuel for power generation here. The plant now is to upgrade the KSEB's Brahmapuram Power Project to 1000 MW capacity, in addition to setting up one more project with a capacity to generate 1000 MW of electricity with LNG as fuel. KSIDC has been appointed as the nodal agency for setting up the project. A special purpose vehicle will be formed between KSIDC and KSEB with 50:50 participation for implementing the project. Board has decided to transfer its share of 5 MT per annum of coal produced from Baitarni West Coal Block to the Cheemeni Project.

Projects in the Pipeline

Under the purview of KSEB, 28 hydel projects are in the pipeline.

Projects in the Pipeline

Sl. No.	Name of the Project	Installed Capacity (MW)	Energy Potential (MU)
1	Pallivasal Extension	60.00	153.90
2	Adyanpara	3.50	9.01
3	Athirappally	163.00	233.00
4	Sengulam Augmentation		85.00
5	Sengulam Tailrace	3.60	12.57
6	Chathankottunada II	6.00	14.76
7	Vilangad	7.50	22.63
8	Thottiar	40.00	99.00
9	Mankulam	40.00	82.00
10	Ranni-Perunadu	4.00	16.73
11	Perumthenaruvi	6.00	25.77
12	Chimoni	2.50	6.03
13	Peechi	1.50	3.30
14	Barapole	15.00	36.00
15	Achankovil	30.00	75.81
16	Chinnar	24.00	78.00
17	Anakkayam	7.50	22.83
18	Poringalkuthu	24.00	45.02
19	Pazhassi Sagar	15.00	42.14
20	Kakkayam	3.00	10.39
21	Upper Kallar	2.00	5.15
22	Peechad	3.00	7.74
23	Western Kallar	5.00	11.23
24	Chembukadavu III	6.00	14.92
25	Olikkal	4.50	10.18
26	Poovaramthodu	2.70	5.88
27	Vakkallar	24.00	45.00
28	Pambar	40.00	84.79
	Total	**543.30**	**1258.78**

Source: KSEB

MAJOR PROJECTS IN THE PIPELINE

Solar Park

As per the renewable purchase obligation notified by Regulatory Commission, the solar power purchase obligation for distribution licensees is 0.25 per cent of the total energy consumption for the year 2010-11 which will increase every year to reach 3 per cent by 2022. KSEBL proposes to implement solar power plants at vacant lands available at the sites of existing substations, powerhouses and rooftops of Vydyuthi Bhavanams and also in various government buildings.

The KSEBL has executed memorandum of understanding with Solar Energy Corporation of India (SECI) to develop different types of Solar Power Projects within/outside the State of Kerala. The proposal for setting up of 200 MW Solar Park at Kasargode District had been approved in-principle by Ministry of New & Renewable Energy (MNRE) on March 19, 2015. Government of Kerala has accorded sanction for the incorporation of the Joint Venture Company namely Solar Power Park Developer (SPPD) between Solar Energy Corporation of India and KSEBL for the implementation of the project in Kerala. Out of the 200 MW, implementation of 50 MW had been awarded on October 29, 2015. The work has commenced.

Integrated Power Development Scheme (IPDS)

Integrated Power Development Scheme (IPDS) was launched by Ministry of Power, Government of India for improving the distribution infrastructure of urban areas. The scheme include construction of 33kV substations, construction of 11kV overhead lines and underground cables, construction of LT lines, installation of transformers, and replacement of electro-mechanical meters with electronic meters. An amount of ₹ 592.07 crore has been sanctioned for the scheme. Out of this ₹ 32.82 crore has been received by KSEBL as central share.

Deen Dayal Upadhyay Gram Jyoti Yojana (DDUGJY)

This is another programme launched by Ministry of Power for reducing AT & C loss, providing electricity to all households and for ensuring 24 × 7 power supply. Government of India has sanctioned an amount of ₹ 485.37 crore on January 5, 2016 for implementing DDUGJY in the 14 districts of Kerala. As per the scheme, 1,61,199 rural households are proposed to be electrified. Among these, 41,884 numbers belong to BPL category. Work include construction of 33kV substations & 33kV lines, 11kV lines & LT lines, installation of distribution transformers, replacement of energy meters and effecting BPL service connections.

The erstwhile Rajiv Gandhi Grameen Vidyutikaran Yojana (RGGVY) scheme for village electrification and providing electricity distribution infrastructure in the rural areas has been subsumed in the DDUGJY scheme.

Non-Conventional Energy

The major programmes targeted by ANERT during 2011 comprises of Baseline studies on energy demand, renewable energy potential and energy conservation potential, implementation of renewable energy and energy conservation programmes and infrastructure development for sustaining interactive energy planning and development programmes with local governments.

The programmes of ANERT can be brought under five categories of activities as follows:

- Baseline Energy Studies
- Energy Resource Assessment
- Energy Conservation Programmes
- Decentralised Energy Generation Programmes
- Other Supporting and Institution Building Programme

As part of the baseline energy demand studies ANERT had carried out a detailed study of the households that are yet to be electrified. The total houses registered as un-electrified counts to 2,03,694 from the 454 local bodies. The direct survey conducted in these households covers the reason for non-electrification as well as the distance of existing grid from the surveyed houses as well, along with an estimation of power requirement. The data being consolidated forms a firm basis for charting out programmes for the coming years with a focus to achieve the long cherished dream of the State to achieve 100% household electrification, through collaborative functioning with Local Self Governments and KSEB.

Energy Management Centre (EMC)

Kerala is an autonomous body under Department of Power, Government of Kerala, registered under the Travancore-Cochin Literary, Scientific and Charitable Societies Act of 1955. The Centre is devoted to the improvement of energy efficiency in the State, promotion of energy conservation and encouraging development of technologies related to energy conservation and management through research, training, demonstration programmes and awareness creation. The centre is networking with institutions within and outside the State for research and training activities.

Government of Kerala, with the concurrence of Bureau of Energy Efficiency, Ministry of Power, government of India designated EMC as the State Designated Agency to enforce, regulate, coordinate and to implement the provision of the Energy Management Centre. The United Nations Industrial Development Organisation (UNIDO) has opened its first Regional Centre for Small Hydro Power Development in EMC in the year 2003.

Challenges in the Energy Sector

- Inadequate capacity addition over the years leading to massive in-house demand supply gap,
- Hydel power dominated supply scenario,
- Negligible share of renewable energy in the energy mix,
- High Aggregate Technical and Commercial (ATC) Losses,
- Losses/inefficiencies of the main power utility,
- Gap between energy conservation potential and its realisation,
- Limited presence of Independent Power Producers (IPPs) and Co-Generating Stations (CGS),
- Limited penetration of star labelled products,
- Insufficient interventions/incentives to promote energy conservation and thereby manage demand,
- No coal based plant, no gas based plant,
- Energy price volatility.

KNOW THE FACTS

☞ *Hydel energy is the most reliable and dependable source in Kerala.*

☞ *Kerala State Electricity Board (KSEB) is a public sector agency established in 1957 under the authority of the Department of Power of Kerala government.*

☞ *First Power Project in Kerala was Pallivasal during the year 1940.*

☞ *Biggest Hydroelectric Project in Kerala is Idukki Power Project which includes Idukki, Cheruthonni and Kilivallithode dams.*

☞ *Wind farm power projects of Kerala are at Kanjikode and Ramakkalmedu.*

☞ *Thermal Power Plant is at Kayamkulam under the control of NTPC.*

☞ *Two Diesel Power Plants are at Brahmapuram and Nallalam.*

☞ *The United Nations Industrial Development Organisation (UNIDO) has opened its first Regional Centre for Small Hydro Power Development in EMC in the year 2003.*

TEST YOUR SELF

1. Which among the following is the most reliable and dependable source of energy in Kerala?
   A. Hydel Power
   B. Thermal Power
   C. Wind Power
   D. Solar Power

2. Which among the following sector has the maximum installed capacity?
A. Central sector
B. State sector
C. Private sector
D. Both A and C

3. Pallivasal hydroelectric station was commissioned in ....
A. 1945
B. 1938
C. 1940
D. 1950

4. Kerala State Electricity Board is a public sector agency established in ....
A. 1950
B. 1961
C. 1957
D. 1953

5. Which among the following is the biggest hydroelectric power project in Kerala?
A. Panniyar
B. Idukki
C. Pallivasal
D. Idamalayar

6. Where is the wind farm power project in Kerala located?
A. Kanjikode
B. Ramakkalmedu
C. Kayamkulam
D. Both A and B

7. Which among the following is not a diesel power plant in Kerala?
A. Brahmapuram
B. Nallalam
C. Kayamkulam
D. None of these

8. The Cheemeni Thermal Power Project in Kasargode district will get coal from ....
A. Karnataka
B. Odisha
C. Chattisgarh
D. Jharkhand

9. The LNG terminal is expected to commission in ....
A. Kochi
B. Brahmapuram
C. Nallalam
D. Kanjikode

10. Rajeev Gandhi Grameen Vidyuthikaran Yojana in Kerala has been implemented in ....
A. 5 districts
B. 8 districts
C. 7 districts
D. 12 districts

ANSWERS

1	2	3	4	5	6	7	8	9	10
A	B	C	C	B	D	C	B	A	C

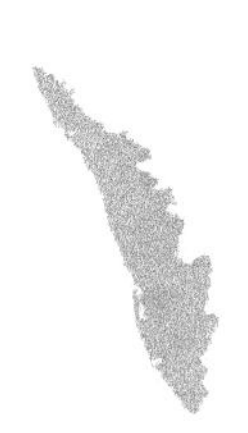

16

POPULATION

Census 2011 had put Kerala's population at 3,34,06,061, consisting of 1,60,27,412 males and 1,73,78,649 females. The population density is 860 people per square kilometres, two times the national average. Kerala is one of the densest state in the country and it recorded a decadal population growth of +4.86%. Kerala, with a sex-ratio (females per 1000 males) of 1084, is the only State with a positive figure.

Districtwise Population of Kerala 2011

Code	District	Population (2011)		
		(Persons)	(Males)	(Females)
32	**Kerala**	**3,34,06,061**	**1,60,27,412**	**1,73,78,649**
1	Kasaragod	13,07,375	6,28,613	6,78,762
2	Kannur	25,23,003	11,81,446	13,41,557
3	Wayanad	8,17,420	4,01,684	4,15,736
4	Kozhikode	30,86,293	14,70,942	16,15,351
5	Malappuram	41,12,920	19,60,328	21,52,592
6	Palakkad	28,09,934	13,59,478	14,50,456
7	Thrissur	31,21,200	14,80,763	16,40,437
8	Ernakulam	32,82,388	16,19,557	16,62,831
9	Idukki	11,08,974	5,52,808	5,56,166
10	Kottayam	19,74,551	9,68,289	10,06,262
11	Alappuzha	21,27,789	10,13,142	11,14,647
12	Pathanamthitta	11,97,412	5,61,716	6,35,696
13	Kollam	26,35,375	12,46,968	13,88,407
14	Thiruvananthapuram	33,01,427	15,81,678	17,19,749

Net addition to population has been continuously falling in Kerala since 1980. The trend has been visible in all the districts of the State. Among the districts, Malappuram had the highest growth rate in 2001-2011 with 13.39%. It was 17.09% in 1991–2001. Kasargode, Kozhikode, Malappuram, Palakkad and Ernakulam are the five districts having a growth rate higher than the average growth rate of the State in 2001-2011.

Child population in the age-group of 0-6, which stood at 37.93 lakh in 2001, declined to 34.72 lakh in 2011. A net decline of about 3.21 lakh at the rate of about 30,000 per year, on an average, is thus, noticed. Interestingly, it had been negative growth in all districts except Malappuram. Even in Malappuram district, the rate of growth in child population had been negligible. The district that had the lowest growth rate, according to Census 2011, was Pathanamthitta (–3.0%). Incidentally, the district had the lowest decadal growth rate in population.

Decadal Growth

An analysis of the decadal growth rate of all-India population shows that it increased from 1921 to 1981 and since then declined gradually. As for Kerala, the decadal growth rate had been higher from 1941 to 1971 and since then it had been sliding down.

Population and its Growth from 1901 to 2011

Census year	Population (lakhs)		Total	Decadal Growth Rate (%)
	Rural	Urban		
1901	59.4	4.5	63.9	—
1911	66.2	5.3	71.5	11.89
1921	71.2	6.8	78.0	9.09
1931	85.9	9.2	95.1	21.92
1941	98.3	12.0	110.3	15.98
1951	117.2	18.3	135.5	22.85
1961	143.5	25.5	169.0	24.72
1971	178.8	34.7	213.5	26.33
1981	206.8	47.7	254.5	19.20
1991	214.1	76.8	290.9	14.30
2001	235.7	82.7	318.4	9.45
2011	174.7	159.3	340.6	4.9

Sex Ratio

Kerala State has a very unique position with regard to sex ratio by dint of the fact that in all the censuses, the number of females outnumbered the number of males in the State, contrary to the pattern shown at the all-India level. The trend had a legacy of at least 100 years. In the Census 2011 also, sex ratio in the State registered an increase of 26 points and thus achieved a ratio of 1084 females per 1000 males.

Sex Ratio—India and Kerala (1951 to 2011)

Year	Sex Ratio	
	India	Kerala
1951	946	1028
1961	941	1022
1971	930	1016
1981	934	1032
1991	927	1036
2001	933	1058
2011	943	1084

In 2001 Census, Pathanamthitta district topped with a sex ratio of 1094, followed by Thrissur with 1092 and Kannur with 1090. This order underwent a change in 2011 when Kannur (1136) replaced Pathanamthitta (1132). Idukki continued to enjoy the lowest rank in 2011 Census also.

Sex Ratio

State/ District	Sex Ratio (No. of Females) per 1000 Males) 2001			Sex Ratio (No. of Females) per 1000 Males) 2011		
	Total	Rural	Urban	Total	Rural	Urban
Kerala	**1058**	**1059**	**1058**	**1084**	**1078**	**1091**
Kasargode	1047	1042	1070	1080	1059	1113
Kannur	1090	1067	1112	1136	1072	1171
Wayanad	995	995	994	1035	1034	1051
Kozhikode	1057	1059	1055	1098	1091	1102
Malappuram	1066	1067	1061	1098	1096	1101
Palakkad	1066	1068	1056	1067	1068	1063
Thrissur	1092	1096	1079	1108	1099	1112
Ernakulam	1019	1014	1024	1027	1021	1029
Idukki	993	992	1012	1006	1005	1036
Kottayam	1025	1022	1038	1039	1034	1051
Alappuzha	1079	1087	1060	1100	1108	1094
Pathanamthitta	1094	1095	1078	1132	1132	1126
Kollam	1069	1075	1042	1113	1128	1096
Thiruvananthapuram	1060	1070	1042	1087	1111	1068

Child Sex Ratio

Data on child sex ratio is very prominent since it is an indicator of future trends. A comparison of child sex ratio of the State with 2001 Census indicates that there was very little increase in child sex ratio in 2001–2011, *i.e.*, from 960 in 2001 to 964 in 2011. In many districts, child sex ratio had been negative and in the four districts of Thrissur (950), Ernakulam (961), Kasaragod (961) and Alappuzha (951), it was below State average (964). Pathanamthitta reported the highest sex ratio of 976 female children for 1000 male children in the age-group 0–6. In 2001 Census, the corresponding position was occupied by Idukki district (969). Thrissur district is reported to have the lowest child sex ratio (950) in 2011 Census whereas in 2001 Census, the lowest position was claimed by Ernakulam district (954).

Density of Population

Kerala has a high density of population which, according to Census 2011, is 860 persons per sqkm, against 819 in Census 2001. The State had only 134 persons per sq. km. in 1881. The present density figure shows a six-fold increase in the last 130 years.

Density

State/District	Population Density per sq km.	
	2001	2011
Kerala	819	860
Kasaragod	604	657
Kannur	812	852
Wayanad	366	384
Kozhikode	1228	1316
Malappuram	1021	1157
Palakkad	584	627
Thrissur	981	1031
Ernakulam	1012	1072
Idukki	259	255
Kottayam	885	895
Alappuzha	1492	1504
Pathanamthitta	468	452
Kollam	1038	1061
Thiruvananthapuram	1476	1508

Literacy

Kerala has been the most literate state in the country. An analysis of the literacy data brings to light the fact that after a gap of 60 years, the literacy rate of the State has nearly doubled from 47.18% in 1951 to 94.0% in 2011 Census. Kottayam district ranked first (97.2%) and Wayanad (89.0%) the lowest.

Literacy Rate 1951–2011

Year	Persons	Males	Females
1951	47.18	58.35	36.43
1961	55.08	64.89	45.56
1971	69.75	77.13	62.53
1981	78.85	84.56	73.36
1991	89.81	93.62	86.17
2001	90.86	94.24	87.72
2011	94.0	96.1	92.1

The profile of literacy in the State throws up interesting trends. Of course, male literacy has been quite high, it being as high as 96.1% in Census 2011. But, unlike in many other states, literacy among women has also been quite high, as much as 92.1%, as per Census 2011. Quite importantly, it reflects a healthy social status being enjoyed by women in the State. That apart, it is seen as a precursor to other demographic indicators.

The continuous geographical belt of Pathanamthitta (95.8%), Kottayam (96.5%) and Ernakulam (94.5%) districts top in female literacy. The district which are having lower female literacy rate are Wayanad (85.7%), Palakkad (85.8%) and Kasaragod (86.5%). In 10 districts, the female literacy rate is above 90%. The district of Thiruvananthapuram is having literacy rate lower than the State average in the case of total literacy, male literacy and female literacy.

Urbanization in Kerala

The Union Government has recognized urban areas as generators of economic momentum. But the economic potential of urban areas may depend on a number of factors like geographical location, availability of economic infrastructure, regional linkages and propensities for accepting further investments and creating spread effects.

As per the 2011 Census, 47.72% of the populations live in urban areas. This is higher than the national average of 31.2%. However, unlike the other parts of the country, urbanization in Kerala is not limited to the designated cities and towns. Barring a few panchayats in the hilly tracts and a few isolated areas here and there, the entire State depicts the picture of an urban rural continuum. The Kerala society by and large can be termed as urbanized.

KNOW THE FACTS

☞ *Kerala, with a sex-ratio (females per 1000 males) of 1084, is the only State with a positive figure.*

☞ *Malappuram had the highest growth rate in 2001-2011.*

☞ *Kasargode, Kozhikode, Malappuram, Palakkad and Ernakulam are the five districts having a growth rate higher than the average growth rate of the State in 2001-2011.*

☞ *Thrissur district is reported to have the lowest child sex ratio (950) in 2011.*

☞ *Kerala has been the most literate state in the country.*

☞ *Kottayam district ranked first (97.2%) and Wayanad (89.0%) the lowest.*

☞ *Kottayam (96.5%), Pathanamthitta (95.8%) and Ernakulam (94.5%) districts top in female literacy.*

☞ *The district which are having lower female literacy rate are Wayanad (85.7%), Palakkad (85.8%) and Kasaragod (86.5%).*

☞ *As per the 2011 Census, 47.72% of the populations live in urban areas.*

TEST YOUR SELF

1. Which district of Kerala has the highest decadal growth rate?
   A. Thiruvananthapuram
   B. Ernakulam
   C. Malappuram
   D. Kollam

2. Which is the largest district of Kerala in terms of population?
   A. Malappuram
   B. Kollam
   C. Thiruvananthapuram
   D. Alappuzha

3. What is the sex-ratio in Kerala?
   A. 1,084
   B. 1,059
   C. 1,058
   D. 1,050

4. What is the population density of Kerala?
   A. 860
   B. 820
   C. 829
   D. 830

5. What is the rank of Kerala in India in terms of Population?
   A. 13th
   B. 15th
   C. 11th
   D. 14th

6. Which district of Kerala has the lowest decadal growth rate?
   A. Pathanamthitta
   B. Wayanad
   C. Idukki
   D. Kasargode

7. Which district of Kerala has the highest female population?
   A. Malappuram
   B. Kannur
   C. Ernakulam
   D. Thiruvananthapuram

8. Which district of Kerala has the lowest sex-ratio?
A. Idukki
B. Kasargode
C. Wayanad
D. Ernakulam

9. First census of the state of Kerala was taken in which year?
A. 1961
B. 1951
C. 1971
D. 1981

10. Which district of Kerala has the highest sex-ratio?
A. Malappuram
B. Kasargode
C. Kannur
D. Kollam

ANSWERS

1	2	3	4	5	6	7	8	9	10
C	A	A	A	A	A	A	A	A	C

❑❑❑

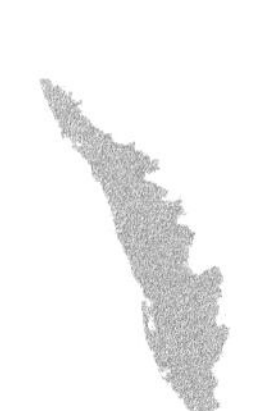

17

PEOPLE & RELIGION

The Origins

Kerala is one of the most populated states in India. There are no evidences of the very early human settlement in the region. It see ms that Stone-Age people deliberately avoided the forests of Kerala infested by Malaria-bearing mosquitoes and man-eating tigers. No relic of the Stone Age, not a single authentic Neolithic implement, has been discovered in any parts of Kerala. Mankind appeared on Kerala soil as an Iron-Age builder of megaliths.

Megaliths or huge burial stones carved by iron implements are scattered all along the Ghats of Wayanad in the north to Trivandrum in the south. There is a pattern in the distribution of these stones extending all the way from Kashmir and Himachal Pradesh along the Nepal Valley down through the Vindhya Mountains to Tamil Nadu and the High Ranges of Kerala. This pattern indicates that Kerala's early people were originally from the Northwest of India.

The remarkable thing about the Kerala megaliths is that they are not as old as the Harappan culture (2500-1500 B.C.). According to Sir Mortimer Wheeler and many historians, the megalith culture was introduced into Kerala between 300 B.C. and 50 A.D. Megalithic evidence shows that the builders came originally from Northwestern India and entered Kerala's High Ranges around 200 B.C.

Though it is to identify these early inhabitants of Kerala with any certainty, we can be certain that their descendants are alive and well in Kerala today. These people of Kerala and elsewhere, are, in the view of anthropologists, "an ethnological museum." Several racial strains are easily recognized in the racial composition of the Keralites of different communities. There are still a number of "white" or fair-skinned Brahmins of the Aryan stock; according to the Kannada tradition. King Mayura Varma sent Brahmin families to Kerala from Ahichatra in North India.

A school of anthropologists are of the opinion that the Negrito element as representing the earliest inhabitants of Kerala; some members of the hill tribes of Kadar, Kanikkar, Uralis, and Paniyar have curly to frizzy hair, black skin, broad noses, thick lips, and round heads that are characteristic of the Negroes of the Andaman Islands, Malay Peninsula, and Africa. However, the Australoids also have similar features; the Australoid group is the major racial element in the Munda or Kolarian population of North and Central India and in the Dravidian population of South India. Some anthropologists even notice distinctive Mongoloid features in Kerala Dravidians.

Inter-racial Mixing

The history of race-mixing in Malabar is of significant interest for our understanding of the pre-historic race-blending of Keralites. Race-blending was brought about by the opendoor policy of the Malabar chieftains who brought the Chinese, the Egyptians, the Arabs, and the Europeans to mingle freely with the indigenous population. The Zamorins of Calicut encouraged the Arabs and the Mukkuvan fisherfolk to mix together socially and sexually, and, as a result, a half-breed Muslim population grew up along the Calicut Coast. With the Nairs it has been a case of hypergamy to give their women to the immigrant Aryan Nambutiri Brahmins who forced it on them. As a result, physically, the Nairs became taller and light-skinned; culturally, they became very Brahminical in their Hindu beliefs and cults; economically, they became prosperous.

The small town of Thankasserri near Quilon has a large number of Anglo-Indians and Portuguese Indians; the local women whom the Portuguese and British converted and married were mostly Ezhavas and Mukkuvans. It has been pointed out that the Directors of the East India Company encouraged the marriage of local women to the soldiers because they found that the half-breeds were more reliable than the local people to serve the Company as soldiers, commercial agents, and political agents. The half-breeds became Christians and received preferential treatment at the hands of the British administrators. Such is the story of the Ezhava, the "white Tiyas" found chiefly in Tellicherry and Cannanore. This historical race-mixing experienced in Malabar during the past three hundred years is only a re-enactment of the pre-historic racial blending of Keralites between the Munda and Dravidian and between the resultant Munda-Dravidian and the Aryan. The vast majority of Keralites carry three racial strains in their genetic make-up; Munda, Dravidian, and Aryan.

Kerala and the Munda Race

The Munda people belong to the Australoid race and speak a family of languages called the Munda family: Korku, Santali, Mundari, Kharia,

Saora, Parengi, Gutob, Bonda, and Didey. Today they live in the Chhotanagpur geographical region of Eastern India though once they occupied the whole of India, that is, before the arrival of Dravidians and Aryans. A comparative study of Malayalam, the language of Keralites, and the Munda languages shows the presence of a large number of Munda words in Malayalam. Physical and cultural anthropology shows significant similarities between Keralites and Mundas. A comparative study of Munda and Kerala folklore also suggests numerous similarities.

Certain tribal folk traditions maintain that the people of Kerala originally came from the east of the Western Ghats through gaps like Palghat, Thamarasserri, and Aramboli. They were known then as Cheras. Already by the time of Emperor Ashoka, they were settled down south of the Mauryan Empire. But the Cheras, according to their traditions, came from the Chhotanagpur region where they lived among other Mundas and spoke Munda languages. There is still a formerly Munda ethnic group southeast of Gorakhpur who are called "Cheras"; today these Cheras speak Indo-European languages as a result of large-scale assimilation with the Aryan immigrants. Members of this Munda-Chera tribe gradually moved south to Tamil Nadu carrying with them their Munda language and megalith tradition. After settling down in Tamil Nadu for hundreds of years, they accepted Dravidian as their spoken language while retaining many Munda words in their speech which later came to be known as Malayalam. During the political upheavals in the eastern plains among the Pandyas, Cholas, Pallavas, and Rashtrakutas, during the long period between the fourth and eighth century A.D., many Cheras and related tribes fled west across the Western Ghats and settled down in different parts of Kerala. It is these Munda-Chera immigrants who left most of the megaliths all along their travel route.

The Dravidians Lineage

Consensus exists among ethnologists that the Dravidian population is a branch of the Mediterranean race, or at least a closely allied one. While the Mediterranean race is White, the Dravidians are much darker. There is also a wide range of difference in the shape of the skull, the colour and texture of the hair, the colour of the eyes, and the shape of the nose. These deviations can be explained with a probable interbreeding between the Dravidians and Mundas, as it is still taking place in the Chhotanagpur region between the Dravidian Oraons and the neighbouring Mundas.

The Dravidians are said to have entered India before the Aryans, before 2000 B.C., after passing through Mesopotamia, Iran, and Baluchistan where the Brahuis, a Dravidian race, still live. On grounds of cultural affinities such as inheritance through women, snake cults, organization of society, and structure of temples, some historians connect the Dravidians with the Elamites and Mesopotamians. The evidence of Indian skulls from the Indus Valley indicates that the Mediterranean stock became established in north India before the Harappa Civilization came into existence around 2000 B.C.

The Advent of the Aryans

The arrival of the Aryans in Kerala in the eighth century changed significantly the racial, social, political, and cultural landscape of Kerala. Though the Aryans conquered the Mundas and the Dravidians of Kerala, it was ultimately the Aryans who were conquered and absorbed by Kerala, creating a new brand of Hindu religion, a hybrid race, and a new culture--a blend of Munda, Dravidian, and Aryan cultures.

The mixing of different races resulted in the four major ethnic groups in Kerala namely Brahmins, Nairs, Ezhavas, and Scheduled Castes and Tribes. There are also several other (around five hundred) castes and sub-castes like the Kshatriyas, Ambalavasis, Samantans, Kammalans, Mukkuvans, and outcastes like the Nayadis.

Brahmins

Brahmins, who constitute only 4% of the Kerala population, are the most recent immigrants to Kerala; they are not all pure-bred Aryans or a homogeneous community. They are divided into several groups. The highest are the Namboothiris who regard themselves as pure Aryan Brahmins, faithful to the Vedic traditions. They claim to have descended from the sixty-four families of the original inhabitants (swadeshi) brought over by Parasurama. Most likely they came from North India, but today many of them have the dark complexion and look like other Keralites. All other Brahmins are considered aliens (paradeshi) and inferior in status to the Namboothiris. They came after the eighth century from Tulu Nadu in the north and Tamil Nadu in the east in search of better employment opportunities at the invitation of royal patrons and local temples who preferred Brahmin teachers, administrators, and priests. They are the Embrantini and the Pattar or Potti Brahmins. By profession, all these Brahmins were mostly priests and teachers; they controlled the temples and lived mainly on temple revenues.

The Nair Heritage

The Nairs were in Kerala before the Brahmins arrived in the seventh century A.D. The Chera kings were Nairs, and the Nairs were also Dravidians and not Kshatriya Aryans; the Brahmins, in fact, considered them as Sudras. However, the younger sons of Brahmin families could form morganatic relationships (Sambandham) with Nair women, the children remaining Nairs and thus introducing a new element in the race. This helped the junior members of the Brahmin family to be relieved of their life-long bachelorhood without the responsibility for supporting their wives and children from their family property. It was, on the other hand, to the advantage of the children to carry the genes of the Brahmins, apparently. It does not mean that the Nairs had loose marriage morals; it only means that this type of relationship was tolerated as an exception for its advantages for the Brahmins and Nairs; the rule of real marriage was endogamous monagamy between Nairs especially between the daughter of a maternal uncle and his nephew. The Nairs used to practice polyandry, a custom that can be traced to Tibet.

The Ezhavas and Tiyas

The largest ethnic group (40%) of Kerala is the Ezhavas. For long they were treated as outcastes by the Brahmins and the Nairs; nevertheless, these earliest sons of the soil--the first Munda-Dravidian immigrants— retained their pride and ethnic identity and rose above adversity by means of Hindu religion which was first used to reduce them to the status of outcastes. They gradually accepted the Hindu religion and followed the teachings of their leaders like Sri Narayana Guru; they sought education and established their own schools; in all this they were encouraged by the British who admitted them into civil service in Malabar. Many of them sought advancement through political parties; for decades now Ezhavas have remained the hardcore supporters of the Marxist parties in Kerala. Today they are no longer an "untouchable" scheduled caste, but a proud and powerful ethnic group to be reckoned within Kerala.

Scheduled Tribes

In Kerala there are still 37 Scheduled Tribes out of 48 tribal communities; they occupy only 1.5% of the state's population. What this figure indicates is that the rate of the assimilation of the aboriginals of Kerala has been extremely rapid. In the past few years 11 tribal communities have been declassified on account of the social and cultural progress they have made.

Among the Scheduled Tribes of Kerala the numerically dominant ones are the Pulayans, Paniyans, Maratis, Malayarayar, Kurumans, Kurichiyans, and Irulas. The numerical strength of each remaining tribes is more or less 1,000. Most of these tribes are forest-dwellers and food-gatherers. Increasingly, they are found living on the fringes of the forests near the highways and the villages of the plainspeople, yet apart from them. This frontier existence of the tribals is highly symbolic. They are caught between two worlds. Their forest home cannot support them any longer, for food in forests is getting scarce because of the state policy against deforestation.

Religion

Kerala is famous for its communal harmony. From very ancient times people who practised several religions inhabited the land of Kerala. It is pluralistic society where no one ethnic community or religious group has dominance. Unlike many other states in India, Kerala has a long tradition of secularism and communal amity, though there have been a few stray and minor instances of communal riots in certain parts of northern Kerala. The religious minorities, especially Christians and Muslims, enjoy prominent positions in Kerala society. The major religions are Hinduism, Christianity and Islam. There are also the presence of Jews, Budhists and Jains, though very very negligible.

The Buddhist

Tamil Sangam-works like *Manimekhalai* indicate that there were Buddhist in Tamil Nadu and that the Buddhist missionaries were active in spreading their religion. According to the Sangam tradition, there was a famous Buddhist chattya (temple) at Vanchi (Karur) and a Palli Bana Perumal became a Buddhist.

The Cheras were originally Mundas, many of whom were Buddhists even before their arrival in Tamil Nadu. It was they as well as the Buddhist missionaries from the Maurya Empire that brought the religion of Buddha to the South. They were distinctly a powerful minority in Tamil Nadu and were subjected to persecution by the Brahmin Counsellors of the Dravidian Hindu Kings during the ascendancy of Brahminical Hinduism in the South. Aalavaipathikam records that around 640 A.D., Sambanda Murti, a Brahmin, won over the Pandya royal family and caused the massacre of 8,000 Buddhist monks in Madurai; Buddhist nuns were reportedly made into devadasis and relocated in the Hindu temple precincts.

The Buddhists came to Kerala and established their temples and monasteries in different parts of the country. The following Hindu temples were once Buddhist shrines: the Vadakkunnathan Temple of Trichur, the Kurumba Bhagavathi Temple of Cranganore, and the Durga Temple at Paruvasseri near Trichur. A large number of Buddha images have been discovered in the coastal districts of Alleppey and Quilon; the most important Buddha image is the famous Karumati Kuttan near

Ambalappuzha. Buddhism probably flourished for 200 years (650-850) in Kerala. The Paliyam Copper Plate of the Ay King, Varaguna (885-925 A.D.) shows that the Buddhists enjoyed some royal patronage even in the tenth century.

The decline of Buddhism started in the eighth century with the arrival of the Aryan missionaries and the Brahminical religion. The Brahmin scholars defeated Buddhist monks in debates and established the superiority of the Hindu religion. Adi Sankaracharya, the Hindu revivalist, was also responsible for the fall of Buddhism; he founded Hindu monasteries and trained Hindu priest-scholars to combat his Buddhist adversaries. Buddhism faded away gradually and completely disappeared during the reign of the Vaishnavite Kulasekharas in the eleventh century. What actually happened was that Buddhism was reabsorbed into Hinduism from which it broke away. Many Keralites, like the Ezhavas, who were most likely Buddhists once, gradually became Hindus.

Buddhism has left its impact on Kerala. The images and tall *rathas* (cars) used in temple processions, and utsavams (fairs) are said to be Buddhist legacies. The Ayurvedic system of medical treatment is also a gift of Buddhism.

Buddhists opened schools in *pallikudam* and *ezhuthupally. Pally* is the Buddhist term for school near their monasteries. Kerala temples shows traces of Buddhist art and architecture. Amarasimha, the author of the popular Sanskrit text-book used in Kerala schools until recently, was a Buddhist. Kumaran Asan, the great Kerala poet, was influenced by the great Buddhist religion and wrote the famous, Buddhist poems: *Karuna, Chandala Bhikshuki,* and *Sri Buddha Charitam.*

The Jews

There is no consensus of opinion on the date of the arrival of the first Jews in India. The tradition of the Cochin Jews maintains that after 72 A.D., after the destruction of the Second Temple of Jerusalem, 10,000 Jews migrated of Kerala. A second tradition says that the Jews are the descendants of the Jews taken into captivity by Nebuchadnezzar and then released by Cyrus of Persia in the sixth century B.C.

The jews, like the rest of the Keralites, came from the East Coast in the sixth century and after. They came to India as political refugees and/ or as traders. Because of the paucity of their numbers at any time in their history in India, it is very likely that they came only in small numbers to India and remained small unless most of them became Christians at one time. According to one tradition, St. Thomas converted many of them to Christianity. It seems likely that the fate and fortune of the jews were tied in with the fate and fortune of the Christians. The clearest evidence for their view is found in the Aramaic language once spoken by the Kerala Christians and used even today in the prayer books of Kerala's Syrian Christian community. It was the language of the Iraqi Jews and of some Iraqis even today. In the sixteenth century White Jews from Spain and Portugal came to Kerala.

The Portuguese did not look favourable on the Jews. They destroyed the Jewish settlement in Cranganore and sacked the Jew town in Cochin and partially destroyed the famous Cochin Synagogue in 1661. However, the tolerant Dutch allowed the Jews to pursue their normal life and trade in Cochin. According to the testimony of the Dutch Jew, Mosss Pereya De Paiva, in 1686 there were 10 synagogues and nearly 500 Jewish families in Cochin. During the British times, too, the Jews enjoyed peace and protection. After the creation of the State of Israel in 1948, most Jews (85%) decided to depart for Isarael. All the Black Jews and Brown Jews, about 3,000, went to Israel between 1948 and 1955; they are known as Cochini in Israel today. Only a few hundred Jews remained in Kerala; they were all White Jews. In 1961 there were only 359 Jews in Kerala with only two synagogues open for service: the Pardesi Synagogue in Mattancherry built in 1567 and the synagogue in Parur.

Today the number of the Jews has dwindled down to a mere 50; most of them are elderly people, and women outnumber men. According to the prominent Jewish businessman of Kerala, S. S. Koder, the main problem for the Kerala Jews is to find bridegrooms and brides for their young people in Kerala. When it is time for them to get married, they leave for the Kiriath Shemona settlement in Israel where most of the Cochin Jews resettled. Another problem is the absence of a good shoeth (butcher) to prepare kosher meat after ritual slaughter. Fortunately, they have found one recently.

The Christians

The St. Thomas Christians of Kerala firmly believe that St. Thomas the Apostle is the father of Christianity in India. According to their tradition, he landed at Maliankara, near Cranganore in 52 A.D. He preached Christianity first among the Jews and then converted twelve Brahmin families from whom the Syrian Christians trace their genealogy. St. Thomas also founded seven churches at the following places: Maliankara, Palayur, Kottakavu, Quilon, Niranom, Nilakkal, and Chayal. After several years of work in Malabar, the Apostle went to the Coromandel Coast (East Coast) where he was assassinated by irate Brahmins (or by a hunter) in 72 A.D. This tradition along with many others legends is found in ancient Christian songs (seventeenth century and later) like the Veeradian Pattu, Thomma

Parvom, and Margom Kali Pattu. The Acts of St. Thomas, an apocryphal work by the Syrian Bardesan (220 A.D.) also mentions the missionary work and martyrdom of St. Thomas in India.

There is no historical evidence for the missionary work of St. Thomas on the West Coast of India. But there is enough evidence to believe that St. Thomas probably was buried at Mylapore. It is, then more likely that he preached Christianity and made Christian converts at Muziris on the mouth of Kaveri in Tamil Nadu rather than in Kerala. The early Christians were probably from the Jewish community, and the mainstream of the St. Thomas Christians are most likely composed of Munda-Dravidian converts and of Jewish converts, but not of Brahmins. These St. Thomas Christians fled west across the Western Ghats in the sixth and seventh centuries, carrying with them their religious traditions except the tomb of St. Thomas.

It is important to mention here that a group of Christians in Kerala, the *Thekkumbhagar* (Southists), call themselves Jewish Christians. They claim that their ancestors made up of 72 Jewish Christian families from around Baghdad, Nineveh, and Jerusalem came to India under the leadership of one Thomas of Cana (the place where Jesus turned water into wine), a blood-relative of Jesus. These new colonists settled down on the southern shore of the Periyar; hence they received the name "Southists," as opposed to the local "Northist" Christians who lived north of the river in Cranganore.

These St. Thomas Christians followed the Aramaic language in their liturgy and were under the ecclesiastical jurisdiction of the Oriental Patriarch of Celusia-Ctesiphon of Persia (Babylon) up until the arrival of the Portuguese in the fifteenth century. Until that time the Christians of Kerala were very Indian in their culture, though Middle-Eastern in worship. The Portugues considered it their duty to bring these Oriental Christians under the supremacy of the Pope of Rome by Latinizing their Syrian liturgy and by purging them of their errors or "heresies."

Dom Menezes persuaded the Synod delegates to pass several decrees which admitted that their Church had been heretical in some tenets and practices. The Synod severed the connection between the Kerala Church and "heretical" Persian Church and declared their fealty to the Pope of Rome. Oom Menezes then appointed a Portuguese bishop over the Syrian Church.

A large number of the Syrian Christians resented this foreign incursion in the internal affairs of their Church. They wanted their own Syrian bishops. In 1653, Ahatulla, A Syrian bishop, arrived in Kerala, but he was detained illegally by the Portuguese, who—it was rumored—even assassinated him on his way from Mylapore to Kerala. The enraged Syrian

Christians believing the rumors were true, assembled in thousands in front of the ancient cross (*koonan kurisu*) at Mattancherry and took a solemn pledge with oath that they would never again obey the Latin Archbishop or the Jesuits. These defiant Christians came to be called Puthencoor (Protestant) Syrians and those who remained loyal to the Roman Pontiff came to be called Pazhyacoor (Orthodox) Syrians.

The Portuguese missionaries introduced the Latin Church in Kerala and made many converts from among the untouchables of the coastal area. Today the Latin Church has several dioceses and parishes in Kerala.

Protestant missionaries from England came to Kerala with the English colonists in the seventeenth century. The Church Mission Society of London (CMS) made many converts from among the untouchables and the Syrian Christians. Some Syrian Christians who were impressed by Protestant Christians wanted to introduce like them the vernacular language in the liturgy. For this purpose they formed a reform Church called "The Marthomite Church," which is a very progressive and prosperous Church today. The Christians of Kerala today are divided into several branches: (1) the Latin Catholic Church, (2) the Syro-Malabar Catholic Church, (3) the Jacobite Syrian Church, (4) the Nestorian Church, (5) the Anglican Church which is now part of the Church of South India, (6) the Marhoma Syrian Church, (7) the Syro-Malankara Catholic Church. In addition, there are also a number of minor Churches and Missions.

The early Christians have, indeed, made significant contributions to the culture of Kerala. The Portuguese missionaries introduced printing in Kerala besides opening several theological seminaries for the education of the clergy. Chavittunatakam is a Portuguese-Christian art-form. The Protestant missionaries from Germany and England laid the foundations of western education in Kerala by opening English grammar schools, high schools, and colleges. Some of the early Christian missionaries had performed valuable services for the development of the Malayalam language: the grammatical works and dictionaries by Arnos Patiri (Johann Ernestus Hanxleden), Angelo Francis, Rev. Bailey, Rev. Richard Collins, and Dr. Gundert are substantial contributions to the study of Malayalam.

Islam

There had been much trade and commerce between India and Arabia even before the time of Prophet Muhammad. Unlike the Jews and Christians, the Arabs settled down primarily on the West Coast, which indicates that they arrived in large numbers only in the eighth and ninth centuries.

The first Muslim merchant who visited Kerala was Sulaiman in 851 A.D. As trade between Kerala and the Muslim countries increased, many

Arab Muslims came to Kerala and settled down on the Malabar Coast where the Zamorin of Calicut welcomed them. He encouraged them to marry with the local women and serve on his armed forces. Mention must be made here of the legend that the last of the Chera emperors, the Cheraman Perumal, became a convert to Islam and went on a pilgrimage to Mecca. There is among the Malabar Muslims a tradition about a devout Arab Muslim, Ibn Dinar. He was like Apostle Thomas before him. He came to Kerala to spread Islam; he established the first mosque in Cranganore; afterwards he built mosques in Quilon, Madayi, Kasargode, Srikantapuram, Dharmapattanam, and Chaliyam.

The travelogue of Ibn Batuta who visited Kerala between 1342 and 1347 gives detailed information on Muslims in different parts of Kerala. His journey from Calicut to Quilon lasted 10 days. During the fifteenth, sixteenth, and seventeenth centuries Muslims flourished economically and numerically. Many untouchables were attracted to Islam. At one point (twelfth century) the Muslims even had their own rulers; the Arakkal royal family of the Ali Raja; he was the son of a wealthy Arab and a prince of the Kolathiri royal house. One of his descendants, Azi Raja (master of the sea) conquered in 1183-84 some of the Maldive Islands for the Kolathiri Raja.

During the Mysorean invasions of Tipu Sultan (1782-1792), many Keralites became Muslims. Many Nairs and high-caste Hindus were seized and forcibly converted to Islam. The Mysore Sultan Tipu is the reason why there are so many Muslim Mappilas in the districts of Cannanore, Tellicherry, Calicut, and Malappuram. The Mysorean invasions and Muslim converstions deeply affected the old caste-controlled social order of Malabar. It shattered the myth of the social superiority of the Brahmins and the Nairs and improved the self-image of the lower classes.

In this century, Muslim leader like Vakkam Abdul Kadir, Ummer Kazi, Seethi Sahib, and E.K. Maulavi Sahib tried to bring the relatively backward Muslim community to the twentieth century through educational and social reforms. They opened service-oriented institutions like orphanages, Madrasas (school for teaching Arabic and Islam), primary schools, high schools, and Arabic colleges. Of all the institutions the most important under Muslim management is Farook College established in 1948. The Thangal Kunju Missaliar College of Engineering has also done great service to the Muslim community by training engineers and technicians. The recently established (1964) Muslim Educational Society is running colleges, schools, and hospitals today. The Mappila Muslims are increasingly becoming more Indian and less Islamic. Most Kerala Muslims are Sunnis and patriotic Indians have come a long way since the ninth century and the nineteenth century.

KNOW THE FACTS

☞ According to Sir Mortimer Wheeler and many historians, the megalith culture was introduced into Kerala between 300 B.C. and 50 A.D.

☞ Race-blending was brought about by the opendoor policy of the Malabar chieftains who brought the Chinese, the Egyptians, the Arabs, and the Europeans to mingle freely with the indigenous population.

☞ The Zamorins of Calicut encouraged the Arabs and the Mukkuvan fisherfolk to mix together socially and sexually.

☞ The small town of Thankasserri near Quilon has a large number of Anglo-Indians and Portuguese Indians.

☞ Tribal folk traditions maintain that the people of Kerala originally came from the east of the Western Ghats through gaps like Palghat, Thamarasserri, and Aramboli.

☞ The Dravidians are said to have entered India before the Aryans, before 2000 B.C.

☞ Brahmins are the most recent immigrants to Kerala; they are not all pure-bred Aryans or a homogeneous community. The highest are the Namboothiris who regard themselves as pure Aryan Brahmins, faithful to the Vedic traditions.

☞ The largest ethnic group (40%) of Kerala is the Ezhavas.

☞ A large number of Buddha images have been discovered in the coastal districts of Alleppey and Quilon.

☞ Buddhism probably flourished for 200 years (650-850) in Kerala.

☞ The Paliyam Copper Plate of the Ay King, Varaguna (885-925 A.D.) shows that the Buddhists enjoyed some royal patronage even in the tenth century.

☞ The jews, like the rest of the Keralites, came from the East Coast in the sixth century and after. They came to India as political refugees and/or as traders.

☞ The Portuguese did not look favourable on the Jews. They destroyed the Jewish settlement in Cranganore and sacked the Jew town in Cochin.

☞ Dutch allowed the Jews to pursue their normal life and trade in Cochin.

☞ St. Thomas the Apostle is the father of Christianity in India. He preached Christianity first among the Jews and then converted twelve Brahmin families.

☞ St. Thomas also founded seven churches at the following places: Maliankara, Palayur, Kottakavu, Quilon, Niranom, Nilakkal, and Chayal.

☞ St. Thomas probably was buried at Mylapore.

☞ In 1653, Ahatulla, A Syrian bishop, arrived in Kerala, but he was detained illegally by the Portuguese.

☞ The Portuguese missionaries introduced the Latin Church in Kerala and made many converts from among the untouchables of the coastal area.

☞ Protestant missionaries from England came to Kerala with the English colonists in the seventeenth century.

☞ Unlike the Jews and Christians, the Arabs settled down primarily on the West Coast, which indicates that they arrived in large numbers only in the eighth and ninth centuries.

☞ The first Muslim merchant who visited Kerala was Sulaiman in 851 A.D.

☞ Arab Muslims came to Kerala and settled down on the Malabar Coast where the Zamorin of Calicut welcomed them.

TEST YOUR SELF

1. Which district of Kerala has the highest Hindu population?
   A. Thiruvananthapuram
   B. Kollam
   C. Palakkad
   D. Malappuram

2. Which district of Kerala has lowest Hindu population?
   A. Wayanad
   B. Pathanamthitta
   C. Alappuzha
   D. Kochi

3. In which district of Kerala Sabarimala pilgrim centre is located?
   A. Thiruvananthapuram
   B. Kochi
   C. Trichur/Thrissur
   D. Pathanamthitta

4. The famous Guruvayoor temple of Kerala is dedicated to
   A. Lord Ayyappa
   B. Lord Shiva
   C. Lord Krishna
   D. Lord Vishnu

5. The pilgrim centre of Kalady Adi Sankaracharya is situated on the banks of which river?
   A. Periyar
   B. Pamba
   C. Bharathappuzha
   D. Chalakudy

6. Which pilgrim centre of Kerala is known as 'Dwarka of South'?
   A. Sabarimala
   B. Varkala
   C. Thiruvananthapuram
   D. Guruvayoor

7. Which district of Kerala has the highest Muslim population?
   A. Kasargode
   B. Malappuram
   C. Kannur
   D. Wayanad

8. What is endogamous marriage?
   A. to marry outside ones own caste
   B. to marry outside ones own religion
   C. to marry with ones own caste and religion
   D. None of the above

9. In which district of Kerala Jewish synagogue is situated?
   A. Kochi
   B. Thiruvananthapuram
   C. Kasargode
   D. Palakkad

10. The month of Chingam in Kerala's calendar is from
    A. February-March
    B. June-July
    C. August-September
    D. November-December

ANSWERS

1	2	3	4	5	6	7	8	9	10
A	A	D	C	A	D	B	C	A	C

❏❏❏

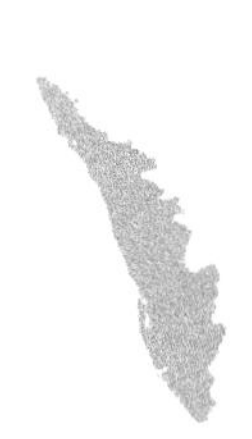

18

EDUCATION

Literacy is a basic step towards education, which is a process of life learning and an entry point to the world of communication and information. Traditionally literacy has been commonly defined as the ability to read and write at an adequate level of proficiency that is necessary for communication.

As literacy development is concerned; Kerala has the distinction of being a historic State in India so far. Kerala's literacy rate is comparable to the most advanced regions of the world. Kerala's literacy rate which was only 47.18% in 1951 has almost doubled to 94.0% in 2011. The male, female literacy gap which was 21.92% in 1951 has narrowed down to 4.0% in 2011.

Public spending on education has been more or less equitably distributed between the sexes and among different social groups and regions in the State. The State is making concerted efforts in sustaining the achievements in the elementary education sector and improving the quality of secondary, higher, technical education and research.

School Education

There were 12,882 schools in Kerala in 2015-16: 4619 (36 per cent) government schools, 7140 (55 per cent) aided schools and 1123 (9 per cent) unaided schools. More government schools are functioning in lower primary section than the upper primary or high school sections. Aided schools outnumber government schools in all sections. Malappuram District has the largest number of schools (1548) in the State followed by Kannur (1305) and Kozhikode (1269). Malappuram also has the largest number of government (546) and unaided schools (221) in the State. But the largest number of aided schools is functioning in Kannur district (959).

Sarva Shiksha Abhiyaan (SSA)

Sarva Shiksha Abhiyaan was introduced in 2000-2001 as a flagship programme of Government of India to provide useful and relevant elementary education for all children in the age group of 6 to 14 by 2010. The programme seeks active participation of the community in the management of schools without social, regional, economic and gender barriers. It comprises all activities of school education: providing physical infrastructure, free textbook for children, encouraging enrolment of girls and teacher training. The sharing of funds between the central and the state governments was 75:25. The funding pattern has now been modified to 60:40.

Higher Secondary Education

Education after the first 10 years was a part of the higher education system for many decades. Higher Secondary courses were introduced in the state during 1990-91 to reorganize the secondary level of education in accordance with National Education Policy. Higher Secondary Course is the turning point in the entire school education in the state. The department serves as a professional institution in formulating and maintaining the standards of Higher Secondary Education and in providing need based timely, scientific, effective and sustainable services to the students and teachers at the Higher Secondary level.

There were 2073 Higher Secondary Schools in 2016 in the State. Out of these 833 (40.18 per cent) are Government schools, 854 (41.2 per cent) are Aided schools and the remaining 386 (18.62 per cent) are Unaided and technical schools. Among the districts, Malappuram has the largest number of Higher Secondary Schools (248) in the State followed by Ernakulam (209) and Thrissur (204) respectively.

There are 7248 batches of higher secondary classes in 2016. The enrolment in Higher Secondary Schools was 383,582. Kozhikode has the largest number of batches (1051) with an enrolment capacity of 55914 students. The pass percentage of students in higher secondary courses decreased to 73.18 per cent in 2015-16 from 74.19 per cent in 2014-15. During 2016, 10,391 students secured A+ for all subjects and 317,887 students were eligible for higher studies.

Vocational Higher Secondary Education

Vocational Higher Secondary Education was introduced in the State in 1983-84. Vocational Higher Secondary Education in the State impart education at plus two level with the objective to achieve self/wages/direct employment as well as vertical mobility. The course is designed to prepare skilled workforce at middle level in one group or more of occupations, trade or job after matriculation at 10+2 stage of education. 389 Vocational Higher Secondary Schools are there in the State with a total of 1100 batches.

Out of the 389 Vocational Higher Secondary Schools 261 are in the Government sector and 128 in the Aided sector. Kollam District (52 nos) has the largest number of Vocational Higher Secondary Schools in the State.

University and Higher Education

There are a total of 14 universities functioning in the state. Out of these four universities viz. Kerala, Mahatma Gandhi, Calicut and Kannur are general in nature and are offering various courses. Sree Sankaracharya University of Sanskrit, Cochin University of Science and Technology and Kerala Agricultural University offer specialized courses in specified subject areas. Besides these, the National University of Advanced Legal Studies (NUALS) established in 2005 and the Central University established in Kasargode district are also functioning.

Universities in Kerala

University	Year of Founding
Kerala University	1937
Calicut University	1968
Cochin University	1971
Agrilcultural University	1971
Mahatma Gandhi University	1983
Sri Sankara University	1993
Kannur University	1996
National University of Advanced Legal Studies	2006

Inter University Centres within the universities in Kerala were established in 2009. These centres provide academic support to the faculties and students of various universities and coordinate major projects undertaken in their respective fields. The Inter University Centre has the objective of developing post graduate programmes in the relevant discipline and serving as an Inter University Centre for research in the relevant discipline and strengthening the ongoing Ph.D programmes and research activity in the concerned areas of advanced study. The establishment of the Inter University Centres has a significant impact. The Inter University Centres are interdisciplinary centres for conducting cutting edge research programmes synergizing available academic expertise in the universities.

Several scholars have expressed their willingness to work in these centres and the researchers of the various research institutions within Kerala are invited as adjunct professors in these centres. A cluster of such centres has been established in the field of Bio Sciences. The centres are Centre for Bio-Informatics (Kerala University), Centre for Bio Science (Kannur University), Centre for Plant Biotechnology (Calicut University), Centre for Marine Biotechnology (CUSAT), Centre for Genomics and Gene Technology (Kerala University) and Centre for Bio Medical Science (MG University).

Arts and Science Colleges

Including 153 Private Aided Colleges and 60 Government Colleges there are 213 Arts and Science Colleges in the State. Ernakulam district (25 nos) has the largest number of Arts and Science colleges in the State followed by Kottayam (22 nos), Thiruvananthapuram (22 nos) and Thrissur (22 nos) districts. A new Government Arts and Science college has started functioning in Ambalapuzha, Alappuzha district with BSc. Maths, BA Economics, and B.Com. Thiruvananthapuram district has the largest number of Government colleges (10 nos) in the State.

Engineering Colleges

There are 183 engineering colleges in the State with a sanctioned intake of 60,376 in 2016. Out of these engineering colleges, 171 (93.44 per cent) are self-financing colleges (unaided), 9 (4.92 per cent) are government colleges and 3 (1.64 per cent) are private aided colleges. Largest number of the unaided engineering colleges are functioning in Ernakulam (31) followed by Thiruvananthapuram (26). There is no government engineering college in Kollam, Pathanamthitta, Alappuzha, Ernakulam, Malappuram and Kasargode. The sanctioned intake of government colleges during 2016 was 3283 (5.44 per cent), in aided colleges was 1850 (3.06 per cent) and in unaided colleges was 55,243 (91.5 per cent).

Technical Education Quality Improvement Programme (TEQUIP)

In 2002-03, the Government of India with the financial assistance from the World Bank launched Technical Education Quality Improvement Programme (TEQUIP) as a long term Programme for 10-12 years to be implemented in three phases for systematic transformation of the Technical Education System. The first phase of TEQUIP commenced in March 2003 and ended in March 2009, covering 127 institutions in 13 States. Five Engineering Colleges of Kerala were included in Phase I. TEQUIP II, the second phase of the project commenced in 2010-11 and is likely to be over by March 31, 2017 covering 190 institutions in the State.

₹ 10 crore for 19 institutions plus ₹ 5.7 crore for State Project Facilitation Unit (SPFU) was sanctioned for the State and out of this, ₹ 156.16 crore has already been released. Under TEQUIP III, 250 institutions will be competitively selected from the States based on the pre-notified criteria and quality of the proposals submitted by the institutions.

Polytechnics and Technical High Schools

Forty five Government polytechnics and 6 private aided polytechnics are functioning in Kerala. The annual intake of students in government polytechnics and private aided polytechnics during 2016-17 were 9,708 and 1,475 respectively. The total number of students in government polytechnics during the year 2016-17 is 27,861 and that of private aided polytechnics is 4,448.

Punarjjani

Punarjjani, as the term denotes, is a unique programme designed by National Service Scheme, Technical Cell, Kerala to restore and reinstate the assets of institutions such as government hospitals, educational institutions and other government institutions, as a consolidated effort to achieve greater results. As a pilot programme, the cell has undertaken the rejuvenation works of discarded and unusable instruments, tools and other materials including operation tables and polluted water tanks on the premises of selected government hospitals across the State. The volunteers have repaired, painted and put them back into service. The volunteers have also attended electrical wiring, plumbing works and repaired the dilapidated buildings and toilets, and removed waste and cleaned the premises. The hospitals chosen for the Punarjjani operation include medical colleges, general hospitals, district hospitals, taluk hospitals, community health centre, primary health centres, mental hospitals and ayurveda hospitals. The efforts of the volunteers were widely appreciated. This has boosted the morale of team of NSS Technical Cell to undertake more result oriented community development projects. The team conducted 100 programmes with 6460 volunteers and created assets with value of around 10 crores during 2015-16.

Information Technology Education

Indian Institute of Information Technology and Management—Kerala (IIITM–K) was set up by Government of Kerala in the year 2000, as a premier institute of excellence in post graduate education and research in the area of Information Technology and allied areas. The Institution is a non-profit making autonomous institution and is registered under Section 25 of the Companies Act. All the shares of the Company is held by

Government of Kerala and the management of the Institute is vested in a Board of Directors.

The Institute currently offers a Master of Science programme in Information Technology, M.Phil programme in Eco-Informatics and a Post Graduate Diploma programme in e-Governance.

Centre for Continuing Education

Kerala State Civil Service Academy under Centre for Continuing education is offering free coaching for Civil Service mains and interview for all Keralites who cleared the preliminary examination and mains examination respectively. The Centre has given free coaching to all SC/ST students and BPL category students for the State Level Engineering/ Medical entrance examinations. During 2011, 86 candidates were undergoing the free coaching programme for the Civil Service main examination.

Kerala Council for Historical Research (KCHR)

Kerala Council for Historical Research is an autonomous academic institution committed to scientific research in History and Social Sciences. It is a recognized research centre of the University of Kerala and has academic affiliations with leading research institutions and universities inside and outside the country. Major activities which are undertaken by KCHR in the past include creating and maintaining people's archives of Kerala, writing local/micro histories, life histories and institutional histories, archives on family histories, biographies etc. KCHR has planned to publish a comprehensive volume on the scientific history of Kerala from pre-historic to the present times.

Institute of Human Resource Development (IHRD)

IHRD is an autonomous institution fully owned and controlled by Government of Kerala. IHRD was established in 1987 for imparting quality education especially in the technical education sector for development of manpower of the required level of competence to match the growing demand of the industry in the field of Electronics, Computer, IT and other emerging technologies. IHRD has a network of 94 institutions which include 9 Engineering Colleges, 7 Model Polytechnics, 35 College of Applied Science, 4 model colleges, 26 Technical Higher Secondary Schools, 6 extension/study centres, 2 model finishing schools, 1 skill development centre, 1 academic staff college, 1 information technology division and 2 regional centres. The college of applied science at Mananthavady in Wayanad has been set up to bring up the educational standards of the SCs and STs. 50% of the total seats have been reserved for ST students and 30% for SC students.

LBS Centre for Science and Technology

LBS Centre for Science and Technology was constituted in 1976 with the main objective of acting as a link between technical institutions, universities and other professional bodies in the State and industry including public utility undertakings. For the last three decades, the centre is actively involved in consultancy services and its core capacity is civil engineering with emphasis on site surveying, preparation of architectural design, geo-technical investigation, foundation design, structural design, quantity survey and preparation of tender documents. Two Engineering Colleges one at Thiruvananthapuram and the other at Kasargode are functioning under the LBS.

Kerala Forest Research Institute (KFRI)

Kerala Forest Research Institute is one of the leading forestry research institutes dedicated to tropical forestry research. KFRI had 50 R & D projects and 8 consultancy programmes. It conducted 14 training programmes. An important achievement was the establishment of 32 km long coastal bio-shield at Vadanappalli under the coastal bio-shield programme. KFRI also studied the distribution, species and population dynamics of mikenia micrantha and succeeded in developing a biologic control using a natural fungal pathogen. The important research projects consisted of improving productivity of plantation, preparation of management plan for high value biodiversity area, biodiversity conservation and nature education programmes.

National Transportation Planning and Research Institute (NATPAC)

NATPAC is a centre of excellence concerned with all areas of transportation planning, research and development, training and consultancy to meet the safe transportation needs of the public. NATPAC has undertaken 14 plan project and 10 sponsored projects. The important achievements consist of preparation of Integrated Development of Transport Infrastructure for an emerging town (Kottarakkara), preparation of inventory of roads for Grama Panchayat, road connectivity to the proposed Kannur airport, traffic and transportation studies for 23 towns in Kerala State, use of waste plastics in road construction, resource mapping for road construction materials, inland water transport of west-coast canal in Kerala, road safety measures, etc.

Jawaharlal Nehru Tropical Botanical Garden and Research Institute (TBGRI)

Jawaharlal Nehru Tropical Botanical Garden and Research Institute was founded with the main objectives of conservation of the tropical plant genetic resources and development of improved scientific methods for their sustainable use to the maximum extent for human welfare. TBGRI has 50 plan projects, 36 externally funded projects along with 2 consultancy projects. A comprehensive account on the current status of the flowering plants of the Western Ghats was successfully completed.

Kerala School of Mathematics (KSOM)

The Kerala School of Mathematics has been set up at Kozhikode as a joint venture of KSCSTE and National Board of Higher Mathematics (NBHM), under the Department of Atomic Energy, Government of India. The main objective of the institute is to promote Mathematical research in the country and particularly in Kerala.

Regional Cancer Centre, Thiruvananthapuram

Regional Cancer Centre, Thiruvananthapuram (RCC), is an autonomous scientific institution sponsored jointly by the Government of Kerala and the Government of India. The centre was established in the year 1980 as a tertiary referral centre for the diagnosis and treatment of cancer. RCC rated amongst the top three of the 28 Regional Cancer Centres in the country. It is the only comprehensive, dedicated centre for diagnosis, treatment and control of cancer in Kerala. In average 32,000 new patients occur every year in the State and out of this more than one-third comes to RCC for treatment.

KNOW THE FACTS

- ☞ *A Prussian protestant Missionary by name W.T. Ringle Taube established the first English School in Kerala in 1806 (Thiruvananthapuram).*
- ☞ *First government owned English School in Travancore was opened in 1834 during the period of Swathithirunal.*
- ☞ *The school started by Rev. Dasan in 1818 in Mattancherry was the first school in Cochin state.*
- ☞ *In 1903 primary education was made free of cost.*
- ☞ *DPEP was started in Kerala in 1994.*
- ☞ *Education was made without caste discrimination and free in Travancore in 1904.*
- ☞ *Study of Hindi was made compulsory from 1953 onwards.*
- ☞ *Foundation of Modern Muslim Education in Kerala was laid by Vakkom Abdul Khadar Maulavi.*
- ☞ *Rani Gauri Parvati Bai made primary education compulsory in Travancore.*
- ☞ *First Minister of Education in Kerala was Joseph Mundassery.*

TEST YOUR SELF

1. Which is the first district to achieve full literacy-rate in India?
   A. Palakkad   B. Pune   C. Kottayam   D. Chennai

2. What is the percentage of female literacy rate in Kerala according to 2011 census?
   A. 93%   B. 92.98%   C. 92.1%   D. 94%

3. In which district of Kerala Mahatma Gandhi University is situated?
   A. Kottayam   B. Kannur   C. Kasargode   D. Ernakulam

4. Which district of Kerala has the highest female literacy-rate?
   A. Pathanamthitta   B. Kottayam
   C. Alappuzha   D. Thrissur

5. Which district has the highest male literacy rate?
   A. Pathanamthitta   B. Kottayam
   C. Kollam   D. Wayanad

6. Which district of Kerala has the largest number of higher secondary schools?
   A. Ernakulam   B. Malappuram
   C. Thrissur   D. Thiruvananthapuram

7. Vocational Higher Secondary Education was introduced in the state in ....
   A. 1960-61   B. 1965-66   C. 1983-84   D. 1972-73

8. Central University in Kerala is established at ....
   A. Kasargode   B. Malappuram   C. Wayanad   D. Palakkad

9. Which university has the largest number of engineering college?
   A. Sankaracharya University
   B. Mahatma Gandhi University
   C. Cochin University of Science and Technology
   D. None of these

10. Indian Institute of Information Technology and Management—Kerala was set up in ....
    A. 1998   B. 1983   C. 2000   D. 2005

ANSWERS

1	2	3	4	5	6	7	8	9	10
C	C	A	B	B	B	C	A	B	C

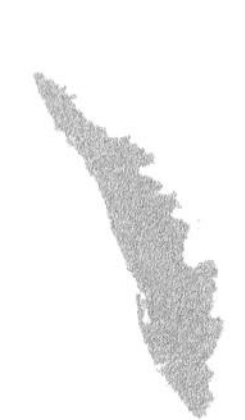

19

FAIRS AND FESTIVALS

Many colourful festivals are celebrated in Kerala. Most of these festivals are imbued with religious fervour and commemorate some event or are held in honour of some deity. Nearly all the major temples have a special festival and fair associated with it e.g., the Pooram Festival at Vadakkunatha Temple at Thrissur (Trichur). Festivals like Thiruvonam, Vishnukani, Tiruvathiru and Arattu are celebrated with great fervour and enthusiasm in Kerala.

Every season turns up new festivals, each a true celebration of the bounties of nature. The festivals exhibits an eternal harmony of spirit. Packed with fun and excitement, festivals are occasions to clean and decorate houses, to get together with friends and relatives and to exchange gifts.

New attire, dance, music and ritual, all add to their joyful rhythm. It is a time for prayer, for pageantry and processions and time to rejoice.

Aranmula Uthrittathi

The famous snake boat carnival on the Pamba, held annually at Aranmula on the day of Uthrittathi asterism, in connection with the Onam festival is to commemorate the crossing of the river by Lord Krishna on that day. The deity is supposed to be in all the boats that take part in the carnival and all of them are expected to arrive at their destination simultaneously.

Thiruvathira Festival

The festival falls on the asterism Thiruvathira in the Malayalam month of Dhanu (December-January). On Thiruvathira morning, devotees specially unmarried woman, throng Shiva temples for an early worship which is reckoned as highly auspicious. The girls adorn themselves and relax on swings hung from trees.

Tradition says Thiruvathira is celebrating the death of Kamadeva, the mythological God of Love. According to another version, Thiruvathira is the birthday of Lord Shiva. The festival has similarities to adra darshan celebrated in Tamil Nadu.

Major Fairs and Festivals of Kerala

Fair/Festival	Venue	Special Feature
Makara Vilakku	Sabarimala	Colourful Elephant processions
Great Elephant March	Thrissur and Thiruvananthapuram	A recreation of rural Kerala
Village Fair	Near Kovalam	
Uthram Festival	Tripunithura	Special Poojas & Cultural Events
Sivaratri	Aluva, Tripunithura	Delicious Indian food fest
Flavour and Nishagandhi Dance Festival	Thiruvananthapuram	
Kodiyettu	Guruvayoor	Elephant processions and elephant races
Ashtami festival and Elephant races	Guruvayoor	
Pooram	Thrissur, Arattupuzha	Elephant umbrella competition and Fire works
Vishu Vilakku	Sabarimala & Kannur	Prayers and lighting of lamps
SankaracharyaJayanthi	Kaladi	Birth anniversary of Adi Sankara
Boat races & processions	Ambalapuzha	Spectacular boat races
Nehru Trophy Boat Race	Punnamada Lake (Alappuzha)	World famous Snake Boat Race
Onam & Tourism week Celebrations	Throughout Kerala	Most important Festival of Kerala
Boat races	Alappuzha, Aranmula, Kumarakom etc.	Boat races
Sree Krishna Jayanthi	Guruvayoor	Lord Krishna's birth anniversary
Mahanavami	Thiruvananthapuram	
Mandalam Festival	Sabarimala	Elephant processions, dance and music fest
Ashtami	Vaikom	
Mandala Pooja	Sabarimala	Fasting and devotional exercises
Ekadasi Festival	Guruvayoor	Ritual dance form of Kerala
Sivagiri Festival	Varkala	
Theyyam	North Kerala	
Christmas	All over the state	Major Christian Festivals

Makaravillakku at Sabarimala

For centuries, Sabarimala in Pathanamthitta has been a major pilgrim centre attracting lakhs of devotees from all over India, more so from southern States. The presiding deity is Lord Ayyappa known as Dharma Sastha, a considered symbol of unity between Vaishnavites and Saivites. Dharma Sastha is believed to have fulfilled his mission in life and rejoined his Supreme Self, enshrined at Sabarimala. This 41 days festival at Sabarimala attracts devotees not only from all parts of India but also from abroad.

Onam

This is the most celebrated festival of Kerala. Celebrated in the month of Chingom, the celebration lasts for 4 to 10 days. It is a harvest festival and has a legend associated with it. According to the legend Mahabali, an Asura king who once rules over Kerala, was pushed into hell by Lord Vishnu (in the form of Vamana). The first day of the festival marks his homecoming. Homes are decorated for welcoming him back from his exile. Onam Tourist Week (Sept) is celebrated in all the major towns of Kerala. Dance performances, fireworks, water carnivals, elephant procession and the famous snake boat race mark the celebration. Onam is now celebrated as a National Festival under Government auspices.

Vishu

This is another major festival. It marks the new year. The Malayalam new year is celebrated by bursting crackers and going to temple.

Mahashivrathri

It is celebrated with great fervour in Kerala. In fact the celebration held to mark this festival on the banks of the Periyar river, is comparable to the Kumbha Mela of Prayag.

Vallamkali

This boat race is typical of Kerala. Except the Nehru Trophy Boat Race, which is held annually in the Punnamada Lake, all the boat races have a religious origin.

Pooram Festival

This festival is celebrated at the Vadakkunnatha Temple in Thrissur in the month of April. The celebration are marked by an impressive procession of richly caparisoned elephants and a remarkable display of pyrotechnics.

Christmas and Easter

Nearly 22% of the population in Kerela are Christians. The main Christian festivals celebrated are Christmas and Easter. The Maramon Convention is held every year on the Pamba River bed. It is the biggest gathering of Christian in Asia.

Easter is the oldest Christian festival, as old as Christianity itself. The central tenet of Christianity is not the birth of Jesus, but his resurrection. Easter is derived from this paschal mystery and from the events of Good Friday.

Arattu

This festival is celebrated in number of temples across Kerala. It marks the closing ceremony of the 10 days long celebrations of the Padmanabhaswami Temple in Thiruvananthapuram. Offering of the sweet prasad "Milk Payasam" is made in the temples.

Nishigandhi Dance Festival

On weekends, during this period, dance performances by leading proponents of all the important dance forms takes place at the Nishigandhi open air auditorium at the Kanakakkunnu palace.

Soorya Dance Festival

This dance festival takes place from the 1st to the 10th of October.

Chandanakuda Festival

This ten days festival begins on the first of the Hijri month of Jamadulakhar (Mar-Apr) at the shrine of Beemapalli dedicated to Beema Bivi. Beema Bivi was a Muslim woman, believed to be endowed with divine powers. A procession is taken out by Muslims holding pots and incense sticks. Beside there is a display of sword fighting, singing and dancing.

Navrathri or the Saraswati Festival

It is celebrated here at a special mandapam in the Padmanabhaswami Temple. Several musical concerts are held here.

Classical Music Festival

This festival is held from 27th Jan. to 3rd Feb. The venue for this festival is the Puthe Mumga Palace.

Besides these festivals, which all have religious significance, Kerala Tourism Department organizes some festivals especially for the entertainment of the tourists.

The main festival organized by them is during the month of January (17-20). This four-days festival starts at Thrissur with a spectacularly colourful procession of heavy 100 brightly caparisoned elephants. Tourists are allowed to ride on these elephants and also to feed them. In Alapuzha, there are snake boat races and rides. On the final day display of martial arts and an elephant pageant is held. A seaside barbecue and a display of firework mark the end of this carnival.

KNOW THE FACTS

- ☞ *Thiruvathira Festival falls on the asterism Thiruvathira in the Malayalam month of Dhanu (December-January).*
- ☞ *Thiruvathira is the birthday of Lord Shiva.*
- ☞ *Onam is the most celebrated festival of Kerala. Celebrated in the month of Chingom, the celebration lasts for 4 to 10 days.*
- ☞ *Vishu is another major festival. It marks the new year.*
- ☞ *Mahashivrathri is celebrated with great fervour in Kerala.*
- ☞ *Pooram Festival is celebrated at the Vadakkunnatha Temple in Thrissur in the month of April.*
- ☞ *Arattu marks the closing ceremony of the 10 days long celebrations of the Padmanabhaswami Temple in Thiruvananthapuram.*

TEST YOUR SELF

1. Which among the following festivals is associated with Vadakkunatha temple at Thrissur?
   A. Thiruvonam B. Pooram   C. Arattu   D. Vishnukani

2. The famous snake boat carnival on the Pemba is held annually at Aranmula on the day of ....
   A. Onam   B. Nag Panchami
   C. Ram Navami   D. Saraswati Puja

3. Which festival falls in the Malayalam month of Dhanu?
   A. Uthram   B. Thiruvathira
   C. Theyyam   D. None of these

4. Sabarimala is the venue of which famous fairs/festivals?
A. Great Elephant March   B. Kodiyettu
C. Makara Vilakku   D. Mahanavami

5. Which is the most celebrated festival of Kerala?
A. Vishu   B. Mahashivarathri
C. Vallamkali   D. Onam

6. Which festival of Kerala marks the new year?
A. Onam   B. Vishu
C. Arattu   D. Pooram

7. Which among the following is a closing ceremony of the 10-days long celebrations of the Padmanabhaswami Temple in Thiruvanantha-puram?
A. Arattu   B. Pooram
C. Onam   D. Mahashivarathri

8. Where does the Sankaracharya Jayanthi festival held?
A. Guruvayoor   B. Sabarimala
C. Thrissur   D. Kaladi

9. Which among the following is known as harvest festival?
A. Vishu   B. Onam
C. Arattu   D. Vallamkali

10. Which among the following is a boat race festival of Kerala?
A. Arattu   B. Pooram
C. Onam   D. Vallamkali

ANSWERS

1	2	3	4	5	6	7	8	9	10
B	A	B	C	D	B	A	D	B	D

20

<u>ART AND CULTURE</u>

Culturally, Kerala presents a pageant not found anywhere else in India. The famous pantomime dance-drama, Kathakali, the Sopana style of music, the contributions of Swathi Thirunal and Raja Ravi Varma in the realms of music and painting respectively are some of Kerala's unique contributions which have enriched the cultural heritage of India.

Kerala's folk music, though not refined, is rich with a rugged beauty that is really genuine, with its rhyme and rhythm. These are mostly devotional in nature, like the Sarpapattu, Bhadrakalipattu, Ayyappanpattu etc. The Thullalpattu demands the skill and artistry of a professional.

Music

Although Carnatic music is in vogue in Kerala as the classical music, Kerala appears to have evolved a somewhat distinctive style of singing known as the Sopana style. It is believed that this style derived its name from the sopana or flight of steps leading to the sreekovil (sanctum sanctorum) the place for the ritual singing of Ashtapadi. Kathakali has adopted this style of singing which is low in tempo and emotional in content.

Kerala has produced great masters in the realm of music. The greatest composer is Swathi Thirunal, the Maharaja of Travancore (early 19th century) who left a rich legacy of songs in six languages-Sanskrit, Malayalam, Tamil, Telugu, Kannada and Hindi. They represent the finest flowering of the Carnatic tradition in Kerala. Irayimman Thampi, a contemporary of Swathi Thirunal, was another great composer Kerala has produced. The greatest musician in Kerala history, Shadkala Govinda Marar, who lived during the days of Swathi Thirunal, was a wonderful genius who elicited admiration even from the great Thyagaraja.

Music like dancing, had its origin in the primitive dances and plays, developed by the ancient people in propitiation of the deities of the hills and forests. The development of such art forms as Kuthu Kudiyattam, Ashtapadi Attan, Krishnanattam, Ramanattam, Kathakali etc., gave a fillip to music in later days. An indigenous classical music called the Sopanasangita developed itself in the temples of Kerala, in the wake of the increasing popularity of Jayadeva's Gita Govinda or Ashtapadi. The Kathakali padas composed by scholars like Irayimman Thampi and the Tullal songs of Kunjan Nambiar also enriched the musical culture of Kerala.

The tradition of Kerala in the field of music has continued unsullied in modern times. To the galaxy of modern Kerala musicians belong such stalwarts as Vina Kalyanakrishna Bhagavatar (Bhagavathar), Kathakalashepam Anantarama Bhagavatar, Palghat Mani and Chembai Vaidyanatha Bhagavatar who have substantially enriched Carnatic music by their valuable contributions.

Kerala has developed its own typical temple arts in which instrumental music plays an important part. Chenda Melam which is played with such instruments as Chenda, Kombu, Kuzhal etc., is a feature of all temple utsavams. Tayambaka (Tayambakam) which involves the elaborate display of talas on a classical piece of drum (Chenda) is also typical of Kerala. It is performed in several sessions, each session having its climaxes and anticlimaxes. Panchavadyam is another unique art in which the sounds emanating from five musical instruments, (Maddalam, Edakka, Timila, Kombu and Elathalam) and two auxiliaries, Sankku (Conch) and Kuzhal, in varying pitches are synchronized. As in Tayambakam so too in Panchavadyam, each session lasts for hours. Nagaswaramelam, otherwise called Pandimelam, is another set of Vadyams played in connection with temple pujas and on such auspicious occasions as marriages.

Sopana Sangeetham

Sopana Sangeetham is a very ancient form of temple music in Kerala. The word Sopana means a flight of steps leading up to the sanctum sanctorum of a temple. Devotional recitals rendered on these steps came to be known as Sopana sangeetham. Besides, the musical notes (ragas) too have an ascending (aarohana) and descending (avarohana) nature. Even though over fifty types of musical instruments can accompany Sopana sangeetham, Edakka is most commonly used.

Kathakali Sangeetham

Kathakali music belongs to the Sopana category of music which is typical of Kerala and is characteristically slow, strictly adhering to the tala (rhythm) giving full scope for abhinaya (acting). The Bhagavatar or the singer plays a key role in the staging of the art form. The Bhagavatar plays a key role in a Kathakali performance. He is not just the singer, but also the manager of the entire show. Among the noted Kathakali singers of yester years are Appukuttan Bhagavatar, Thiruvilwamala (1851-1930), Ettiravi Namboothiri (1809-1908), Kannappa Kurup (1845-1921), Kunjiraman Nambisan (1871-1916), Kunju Podhuval (1879-1940) and Krishnankutty Bhagavatar. Kathakali, especially its verses and music are an enormous contribution to Malayalam literature and music. Aattakkatha, the literature part of Kathakali, forms a separate division in Malayalam literature. There are around 500 Aattakkathas and a few among them are Nalacharitham aattakkatha, Keechakavadhom aattakkatha, Dhuryodhanavadhom aattakkatha etc. Compared to others, Kathakali music is more involved and complex clarifying the meanings of mudras or hand gestures, describing the context and expressing the depth of emotions enacted by the artist.

With Kelikottu, an orchestration, the performance begins percussion music—Suddha Maddalam marks the ritualistic beginning of a Kathakali performance. Two back up artists hold up a curtain and remove it to signify the start and finish of each scene. Vocal musicians or Bhagavatars standing at the corner of the stage sing, the lead singer called Ponnani Bhagavatar keeps time with a resounding gong called the Chengila. He is assisted by Shankidi who plays a pair of Ilathalam (small cymbals).

Folklore

Kerala has a folklore which is unique in its richness and variety. Innumerable are the traditions which are current in Kerala. There are traditions about the origin of the State, religious, festivals, temples, etc. The Parasurama legend relating to the origin of Kerala, the St. Thomas tradition relating to the origin of Christianity and the Mahabali legend relating to the origin of Onam have the pride of place among these traditions. Each temple in Kerala has a Sthalapurana which throws light on some aspect or other of early Kerala culture.

Kerala has its own folk tales which deal with certain interesting personalities and their lives. A famous character who figures as the hero of a typical folk tale is Naranath Bhrandan (the eccentric Naranath) whose main pastime was to roll heavy stones up to the top of the hill and then roll them down in order to emphasise the truth that it is not easy for man to reach the top but not at all difficult to lose the position. It is worth mentioning in this connection that the Aithihyamala by Kottarathil Sankunni is a treasure house of folklore and legends current in different parts of Kerala.

The people of Kerala belonging to all castes and communities have their rich collection of folk songs which deal with a variety of themes. They mirror the joys and sorrows and the hopes and aspirations of the common people. The Vanchipattukal or boat songs sung by those who row the boats either during boat festivals or ordinary trips deal with diverse themes of human interest to the common man. The labouring classes who earn by the sweat of their brow have their own characteristic songs which inspire them to put in their best by singing them in chorus. Special mention may be made in this context of the Vadakkan Pattukal (Northern Ballads), the Tekkan Pattukal (Southern Ballads) the Palli Pattukal and the Mappila Pattukal. The Vadakkan Pattukal and the Tekkan Pattukal deal with the exploits of the heroes and heroines of old. The Palli Pattukal composed by Christians for being sung on marriage occasions contain a large admixture of Syriac, Latin and Tamil words. Many of them deal with Church history and lives of Saints. The Mappila Pattukal are the folk songs of the Mappilas (Muslim) of Malabar composed in colloquial Malayalam and sung in a distinctive tune. They are composed in a mixture of Malayalam and Arabic and have a special charm of their own. They deal with diverse themes such as religion, love satire, heroism, etc. The Mailanchi Pattu, the Oppana Pattu and the Ammayi Pattu belong to the category of Mappila Pattukal dealing with love and marriage and they were sung in chorus in connection with marriage festivals till recently. The Mappila songs of various types form part of the heritage of Malayalam today.

Theatre

Kuthu and Kudiyattom are the earliest of the theatrical arts of Kerala. The Tamil epic *Silappathikaram* refers to the performance of 'Kuthu' in the theatre hall by a Kutta Sakkaiyan of Paraiyur in order to entertain the Chera king Senkuttuvan and his queen. This is clear evidence of the antiquity of 'Kuthu' as an art form. 'Kuthu' is a monoact in which a single  actor, the Chakiar, acts the role of all the characters to the accompaniment of mizhavu (a close - necked copper metal drum) played by the Nambiar and cymbals played by the Nangiar (Woman of the Nambiar community). The Chakiar expounds puranic stories punctuating his narration with illustrations from contemporary life.

He enjoys unfettered privilege to crack jokes even at the expense of the dignitaries present in the audience and the latter have no right to report. Kudiyattom is a theatrical art which presents a full-fledged drama or select portions thereof. More than two or three actors appear on the stage at the same time as in a modern drama. The Chakiar performs the role of the male characters and the Nangiar that of the female characters. The Nangiars also sound the cymbals and recite the Sanskrit verses which the Chakiar enacts. A feature of Kudiyattom is that there is a *Vidushaka* or clown who recites the Malayalam translation of every Sanskrit verse enacted by the Chakiar. The Attaprakarams and Kramadipika of poet Tolan give detailed guidance in regard to the mode of acting.

Kudiyattom is not today such a popular art as Kathakali and it is performed only in a few major temples like Irinjalakuda, Perumanam, Kottiyur etc. Its failure to reform itself in response to the needs of changing times is responsible for the decline in its popularity as a performing art. Nevertheless, the contribution of Kudiyattom to the evolution of the Kerala stage is substantial. It is performed in temples within multi-pillared theatres called Kuthambalams built by expert architects according to the norms laid down in Bharatamuni's Natyasastra.

Chavittunatakam which is now almost defunct is theatrical art evolved by the leaders of the church, under the guidance of the Portuguese missionaries, as a Christian alternative to the Hindu Kathakali. It presents stories from the lives of Christian saints and the history of Christianity. Unlike in Kathakali, the actors in Chavittunatakam not only speak and sing but also stamp on the wooden platform with their feet to the tune of songs and beating of drums. It is because acting and stamping from important elements in Chavittunatakam that it has come to be called so. The movements of the actors on the stage are more lively and vigorous than graceful or artistic. Women are not allowed to participate in Chavittunatakam. Music, vocal and instrumental, has an important place in this art. Though it developed as the Christian counter part of Kathakali, the Chavittunatakam is modeled more after the European Opera and Ballet than after Kathakali. The stage in Chavittunatakam was an unusually large one and it could accommodate as many as fifty actors at a time along with the members of the orchestra.

In modern times, Malayalam drama as a form of popular entertainment has acquired enormous popularity. In the latter half of the 19th century the translation of Abhijnana Sakuntalam by Kerala Varma Valia Koyi Tampuran and its successful presentation on the stage gave a fillip to Malayalam drama. The successful enactment of Tamil musical plays by drama troupes from Tamil Nadu in different parts of Kerala helped to hasten this trend. The composition of a series of short plays with historical themes by C.V. Raman Pillai and their enactment by amateur clubs in Trivandrum marked a turning point in the evolution of modern Malayalam theatre. Dramas with social themes soon replaced historical plays. Special mention may be made of V.T. Bhattatiripad's Adukkalayil Ninnu

Arangathekku and K. Damodaran's Pattabakki. With the increasing popularity Malayalam drama as a medium of popular entertainment professional troupes like the KPAC, the Kalidasa Kala Kendram and Kalanilayam have made their mark in the field in recent times. Thus the professional theatre has come to acquire its place in the social and cultural life of modern Kerala.

Dance

Folk Dances

Kerala has a rich variety of folk dances. They are highly developed and reflect the temperaments and moods of the localities in music and costume. Nature silently and unobstrusively has moulded these dances just as the lives of the people who dance them.

Religious colouring is seen in almost all of these folk dances, even in those performed in connection with harvests, sowing of seeds, festivals etc. There is difficulty in classifying these dances as social, religious and martial. Many of these dances are performed by men alone, some exclusively by women. There are also dances in which men and women perform together. Most of the folk dances are performed to the accompaniment of songs which are sung by the dancers themselves or occasionally by a group of musicians. Some dances are performed to the accompaniment of musical instruments only. In several dances the performers form a circle and clap as they dance. Sometimes, instead of clapping they strike small sticks which they hold in their hands. The customs and ornaments are peculiar to the places to which they belong. The eloquent, effortless ease with which the dances are executed and the overwhelming buoyancy of spirit are wonderful. In these folk dances there is no difference between the performers and the audience. Almost all of these folk dances are simple but beneath this simplicity is a profundity of conception and a directness of expression which are of a high artistic order.

There are more than fifty well-known folk dances in Kerala. Of them the Kaliyattom, Mudiettu, Kolam Thullal, Kolkli, Poorakkali, Velakali, Kamapadavukali, Kanniyarkali, Parichmuttukali, Thappukali, Kuravarkali and Thiruvathirakali are the most popular.

Tribal Dances

The primitive inhabitants of Kerala, are only about two hundred thousand now and they are scattered in the jungles and hills of the state prominants.

There are about 35 different types of the tribals, among them being the Kurichiyar, Nayadi, Mullakurumbar, Uralikurumbar, Paniya, Mudaga, Irula, Ernadar, Kadar, Muthuvan, Kanikkar, Uralees, Paliyan, Malavedan, Vettuvar, Eravallan, Veda and Malayan.

They are unique examples of communities in isolated existence, still preserving their life, customs and manners almost untarnished by the advancing waves of urban civilization.Though adapted to different dialects and customs, their artistic expression evidently reflects the distinct, secluded and primitive social structure and nature of the people and it still survives as virile a state as ever in the tribal hamlets of the hilly tracts. Each of these aboriginal tribes has its own distinct dance tradition and invariably all of them are interwoven with the life of the people who dance it, so much so that it seems that some of their daily tasks are given to rhythmic pattern. In the background of mystery shrouded nature, tribal celebrations originate and the dances work up intoxicating excitement physical expressions of their joys and griefs, hopes and fears.

Some tribes have songs to accompany their dances. Either the dancers themselves sing or the on-lookers sing and thus participate. Special musical instruments are sometimes used, but the drum is almost an indispensable feature. The costumes of the dancers vary from approximate nudity to full attire and ornaments which are extremely colourful.

Like all tribal arts, Kerala's tribal dances are spontaneous. It is the most direct expression of the inner most spirit of a people and the instinct of rhythm is as natural and basic as human nature.

Some of the more known tribal dances of Kerala are Elelakkaradi, Kadarkali, Kurumbarkali, Paniyarkali, Edayarkali, Mudiyattom and Vedarkali.

Classical Dances

Classical dances are based fully or partly on the principles and techniques embodied in the ancient Hindu scriptures and technical texts on dance and allied arts. The earliest of these known scripts is Bharatha's Natya Shastra believed to have been written around the second century B.C. Most of the prevailing systems of classical dancing governed by elaborate techniques with a high degree of refinement have had their origin in the dances of the common people.The difference between classical dancing and folk dancing is mainly that there is a deliberate attempt at artistry in the former. Sophistication along the norms of the scriptures of advance theories on dance and dramaturgy are strictly adhered to. The concept of portraying emotion, the grace of the individual dances and the virtuosity of the isolated poses are all important in classical dances. Emphasis has been given to different aspects of the dance, namely pure bodily movement, aids to dance like theme, song, instrumental music, the expression of emotions, moods and sentiments, the dress, ornaments, makeup and the stage. Kuthu, Kudiyattom, Patakom, Ashtapadiyattom, Krishnattom, Thullal, Mohiniyattom and Kathakali are the most important classical dances.

Neo-Classical Dances

The neo-classical dances of Kerala represent a delicate fusion of the folk and classical traditions of Kerala's dances. But the fusion is not artistically complete to the extent that homogenous blending of the two dance forms has not been achieved to perfection. The neo-classical dances surfaced at some intermediate stage between the process of evolution from the folk tradition to the classical tradition.

The neo-classical dance thus retain not only the essential flavours of the folk and classical traditions but project distinctive individuality of their own.

Meenakshinatakom

Meenakshinatakom and Kamsanatakom are two crude dance dramas which are still in vague in some parts of Palakkad district. Meenakshinatakom and Kamasanatakom have the confluence of the characteristics of Mohiniyattom and Kathakali. The lasya of Mohiniyattom and the thandava of Kathakali are well mixed in the dance sequence of Meenakshinatakom. Even in the Elakiattom of Kathakali, male characters have to be done by Meenakshi in Meenakshinatakom. The songs are all a mixture of Tamil and Malayalam. The make-up and customs bear considerable resemblance to that in Kathakali. The characters are all allowed to speak.

Chavittunatakom

The Portuguese influence in Kerala helped the spread of Christianity along the south-west coast. As a result, a new type of community was slowly brought into existence, which being cut off from its original setup, had to look upon the Westerner for cultural sustenance. Out of this situation was born a new art form with songs, dialogues and dances, similar to the miracle plays of the West. They are known as Chavittunatakom. The stage settings, introduction of curtains costumes, masks, etc., show the influence of the West.

Genoa, Caralman Charitram, Nepoleon Charitram etc., are some of the important plays.

Modern Dances

Contributing to the already rich heritage of Kerala's dance art is the modern dance composition. Although they have no real roots in any of the above mentioned dance traditions they mime the characteristics of tribal, folk and classical type of dances. They manifest the growth and development of Kerala dances. Here efforts are made to combine choreography with classicism and fit traditional dance partners into new moulds. It has revealed a world of charm in its creation bringing a refreshing originality, a delightful native and a winsome simplicity. The Western type of dance forms called opera and ballet have come to be produced in purely local dance techniques.

Opera is a joint work of art produced by the union of poetry, drama, music and all subsidiary arts of the theatre.

Since singing and acting are to be done by the same person, the histrionic element is relegated more to the background. In opera, singers are often preferred to actors. The opera incorporates dances but the dance rhythm is not a continuous matrix in which the drama unfolds.

Ballet has this continuous rhythm, using expressive postures and movements involving the whole body. The mature gestural language of the Kathakali tradition is also mixed sometimes. The ballet relies mainly on instrumental music.

Cinema

Cinema is the popular art form which has been a good entertainer and a strong means of mass communication in Kerala from the previous century itself. It has the elements of different art forms including architecture and sculpture in it.

Moreover Malayalam films have their own existence in Kerala and is the most popular form of art enjoyed by the mass. Hence Cinema has its own influence on their culture.

The viewers in Kerala enjoy the films comprehending the reality in it. They possess high insight in distinguishing reality from fiction in the themes of experimentalism. Malayalam Cinema has contributed much to the creative and critical analysis sectors of Malayalam literature.

Kerala has a very rich art and cultural background. Its films are unique in several aspects. Unlike the other linguistic films which have started off taking themes from the Puranas, Malayalam films have taken relevant social issues as its theme from the beginning.

The all time geniuses like Aravindan, Adoor Gopalakrishnan, John Abraham, Ramu Karriat, P A Bakkar, K.G. George, M.T. Vasudevan Nair, Padmarajan, Bharathan, T.V. Chandran, P.N. Menon, Shaji. N. Karun, K. P. Kumaran, K.R. Mohanan, Jayaraj... are the contributors of Malayalam to the world Cinema.

The first silent movie in Malayalam "Vigatha Kumaran" was screened in 1930, when movies abroad has already begun to 'talk' and by 1931 sound films were also made in India.

Language and Literature

Malayalam is the official language of Kerala and the mother tongue of the Keralites. A Dravidian language originated as an offshoot of Tamil and nurtured with the aid of Sanskrit, Malayalam, is one among the major languages of India. Malayalam is a palindrome, and the composite form (mala + alam) literally refers to the mountainous habitat of the people. This phrase, which once elucidated the geographical location of the region, was later replaced by Kerala.

Malayalam is probably the most Sanskritised of all the languages, with an influence of the Dravidian forum. Although only 10% of Sanskrit words are used in the verbal language, the written language imbibes more than 40% of them, including direct borrowals and derivatives. Besides Sanskrit, one can also find many paronyms from Portuguese, Dutch, English, Arabic, Marathi and Persian absorbed which points to their influence on the culture. However, English is widely spoken and understood throughout the state and even in the remotest of villages one can find bill boards and hoardings in English.

Both the language and its writing system are closely related to Tamil, although Malayalam has a significantly larger phoneme inventory. Malayalam has a script of its own. Malayalam literature reflects the spirit of accommodation and has over the centuries developed a tradition, which, even while rooted in the locality, is truly universal in taste. It is remarkably free from the provincialism and parochial prejudices that have bedeviled the literature of certain other areas.

Malayalam literature reflects the spirit of accommodation and has over the centuries developed a tradition, which, even while rooted in the locality, is truly universal in taste. It is remarkably free from the provincialism and parochial prejudices. To its basic Dravidian stock have been added elements borrowed or adopted from non-Dravidian literature such as Sanskrit, Arabic, French, Portuguese and English. The earliest of these associations was inevitably with Tamil. Sanskrit, however, accounts for the largest of the "foreign" influences, followed closely in recent times by English. This broad based cosmopolitanism has indeed become a distinctive feature of Malayalam literature.

The history of Malayalam literature dates to the 13th century. Indigenous ballads and folk songs belong to the earliest times. Later literature was long influenced by Sanskrit, the language of scholarship, and by Tamil, the language of administration.

Thunchath Ramanujan Ezhuthassan, is considered as the father of Malayalam literature. Thunchan Parambu is highly venerated and its sand is believed to be sacred. Ezhuthachan's work is a fine expression in Malayalam, of the Bhakti tradition. His version of the Ramayana, is read aloud in hundreds of Hindu homes in Kerala. The influence of the west began with the arrival of the Portuguese. In the second half of the 18th century, Clement Patiri published the Samkshepa Vedartham, the first printed book in Malayalam. Herman Gundert, the renowned German missionary and Malayalam scholar par excellence, is best remembered for his Malayalam-English dictionary, published in 1872.

Poetry

The 19th century saw the flowering of Malayalam poetry, in the courts of Swati Thirunal. The period also produced the grammar works of 'Kerala Panini' A. R. Raja Raja Varma. His popular poem, Malayala Vilasam, marks the beginning of the modern era of Malayalam poetry, according to scholars. But the Golden Age undoubtedly, revolves around the famous trinity of Kumaran Asan, Ulloor S. Parameshwar Iyer and Vallathol Narayana Menon. Several other poets followed - Nalappat Narayana Menon and Balamani Amma, to name a few.

Contemporary Malayalam poetry is diverse and prolific, though critics say, it has lost the vibrancy and eclectic passion of the 70's, when progressive radicalism swept in influences from Soviet socialist realism to Latin American voices. But Malayalam poetry is alive and kicking. Contemporary poets include O. N. V. Kurup, Ayyappa Panikkar, Kadamanitta Ramakrishnan, Madhavikutty, Sugatha Kumari, Kavalam Narayana Panikkar and Sachidananthan.

Prose

The earliest Malayalam novel was Kundalata, by T. M. Appu Nedungadi, published in 1887. The historical novels of C. V. Raman Pillai, Chengalathu

Kunhirama Menon and Sardar K. M. Panikkar chronicle events in Kerala's growth as a state. Malayalam literature did not take long to address the issues of the masses. Thakazhi Sivasankaran Pillai, P. Kesavdev, Vaikom Mohammed Basheer, S. K. Pottekkat and P. C. KuttiKrishnan spearheaded the break with traditionalism. The current generation of Malayalam writers contain brilliant talents like O. V. Vijayan, M. T. Vasudevan Nair, M. Mukundan, C. V. Sriraman and Zachariah, Sara Joseph to name a few. In addition to this, Kamala Das, and Arundhati Roy, writers from Kerala, have carved a niche for themselves in the English literary scene.

Handicrafts

Industrial arts and handicrafts form an invaluable part of the Cultural heritage of Kerala. Metal crafts have the pride of place among the traditional arts. Bell-metal casting is an old time industrial art. Images or idols of deities made out of copper, 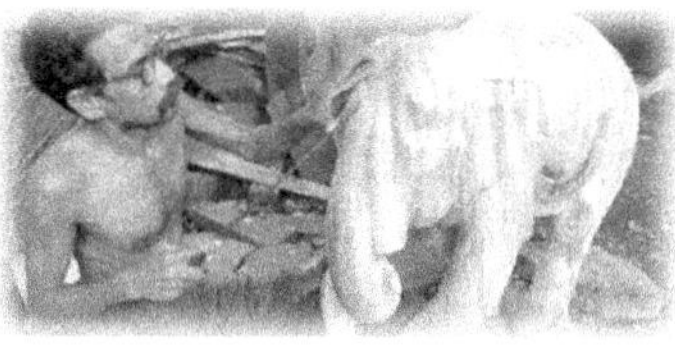 bronze and brass are used for consecration in temples and other religious purposes. Huge Varpus (shallow basins of hemispherical shape), multi-layered lamps and household utensils are all made of these metals. These products are noted for their high degree of perfection.

Lamps of the most artistic beauty are also made by Kerala craftsmen. The Greek lamp (Changalavatta), the Archana lamp, the Arati Dipa etc., deserve mention in this context. The Koftagari work, one of the popular metal crafts of India, is also being practised by a few artisans in Trivandrum. Figures of deities, landscapes, floral designs and fancy articles of a wide variety are produced in Koftagari.

Wood craft is one of the ancient arts of Kerala as is testified to by the temples and churches of the State which abound in wood carvings. Items of furniture like chairs, tables settees, sofas, almirahs, cots, radio castings etc., and models of animals and deities, toys and Kathakali accessories produced by Kerala craftsmen are very much in demand. The models of caparisoned elephants and the carvings of Kathakali dance-dolls are items of popular demand.

The craftsmen of Kerala have also developed a variety of handicrafts using the rich wealth of flora in the State. Screw pine mat weaving is one of such handicrafts. Such articles as pillow covers, cushions, vanity bags, purses, hats etc., are also made of screw pine. Coir carpets and mattings produced in many attractive designs and colours find a ready market in India and abroad.

Lace and embroidery work of high quality is being done by women in several parts of Kerala. The Talangara village of Kasargode taluk is famous for the textile cap making industry. The cotton caps manufactured here find a ready market in the African and Gulf countries.

Ivory carving is another traditional art of Kerala. The art was given an impetus by Swathi Thirunal Maharaja. An ivory throne made by Swathi Thirunal is still preserved as a show piece. The craftsmen engaged in this art at present produce a variety of models of mythological characters, animals, birds, cigarette cases etc.

Architecture

Kerala has made its notable contributions to the science of architecture, both secular and religious. The Tantrasamuchaya, Vastuvidya, Manushyalaya-Chandrika and Silparatna are well-known treatises on the subject. The Manushyalaya Chandrika is a work devoted to domestic architecture.

The Kerala temple has a distinct architectural style which has been acquired as a result of a long process of evolution. The rock-cut temples are among the earliest known of the temples of Kerala and they are assigned to the period prior to 800 AD. They come mainly under two groups, the southern Vizhinjam, Madavurppara, Kottukal and Kaviyur and the latter of those of Trikkur, Irunilacode and Bhrandanpara. The Saivite cult dominated the architectural style of the temples of both these groups. Those of southern group are of Pandya origin and of the northern group of Pallava origin. In addition to these two groups of rock-cut temples, there is also the rock-cut temple of Kallil near Perumbavur which is at present a Bhagavati temple, but was formerly a Jain Shrine.

The structural temple of Kerala had its origin during the 9th century A.D. The Krishna temple at Trikkulasekharapuram near Tiruvanchikulam and the Kizhthali Siva temple nearby are dated to this period on the basis of inscription and stylistic evidences. The origin of the Kandiyur Siva temple is ascribed to 823 AD on the basis of clear inscriptional evidence. In the course of centuries Kerala evolved its distinctive types of temple architecture each of which is associated with some area or other in the State. The Kerala temples have been built on square, rectangular, circular, apsidal and elliptical ground plans. The dominance of the circular shrine is a unique feature of temple architecture in Kerala. The southern half of the

State has a preponderance of circular shrines. The apsidal temples lay scattered all over the west coast up to Thiruvananthapuram but there is a concentration of this type in central Kerala. The rectangular and elliptical ground plans can be seen only in a few temples in Kerala. As the rectangular plan was more suited for enshrining Vishnu as Anantasayanam, the Sree Padmanabha Swami temple, Thiruvananthapuram, follows this type. The Siva temple at Vaikom is built on the elliptical plan. It may also be noted that majority of the Kerala temples have walls made of laterite blocks, but some made entirely of granite except the superstructure may also be in wood carvings, representing Puranic stories. The slopping roof and the lavish use of wood have also invested the Kerala temples with a distinct style of their own.

Sculpture

The stone and wood carvings of Kerala show the high level of sculptural excellence attained by Kerala artists. The earliest specimen of stone carvings in Kerala may be seen in the Edakkal Caves in Sultan's Battery in Wayanad. They depict human and animal  figures and objects of human use and symbols. It has not been possible to fix the date of these stone carvings with any degree of accuracy. In the rock-cut temples of the post-Sangam period are found some of the specimens of early sculptural art. While the sculptures in the southern group show traces of Pandyan influence, those in the northern group are reminiscent of Pallavan influence.

The stone images of the Buddha sittings in the yogasana posture discovered from such places as Karumadi, Mavelikkara, Bharanikkavu, Maruthurkulangara and Pallikkal are also among the finest examples of early Kerala stone sculpture. They are believed to show traces of the influence of the Buddhist art of Sri Lanka. The Jain images of Parswanatha, Mahavira and other Tirthankaras obtained from such places as Kallil, Chitaral, Sultan's Battery, Pallikunnu etc., also form an invaluable part of the sculptural heritage of Kerala.

Paintings

Kerala has a tradition in the field of painting as is evidenced by the murals in temples, palaces and churches. The murals of Tirunandikkara (now in Kanyakumari district) and Tiruvanchikulam are reckoned as the earliest specimens of Kerala painting. These have been assigned to the period from the 9th to the 12th century A.D. Most of the murals now seen in Kerala temples belong to the period from 15th century onwards.

The murals in the Sree Padmanabha Swami temple, Trivandrum, depicting Puranic themes are noted for their remarkable finish and grace and they belong to the period from the middle of the 17th to the 18th century when the pictorial art enjoyed full State patronage. The Vishnu temple at Trikodithanam, the Siva temples at Ettumanur and Vaikom, the Subramonia temple, Udayanapuram, the Vadakkunathan temple, Trichur, the Krishna temple, Triprangode are among the many temples of Kerala which contain exquisite mural paintings.

The churches of Kerala contain paintings which depict characters and scenes from Christian mythology. The paintings of Virgin Mary in the churches at Edappalli and Vechur are of deep religious significance to the devotees. The Orthodox Syrian churches at Cheppad at Mulanthuruthi contain interesting murals. The outer walls of the Kanjur church have a huge mural which depicts the scene of a battle fought between the armies of Tipu Sultan on the one side and those of the English East India Company, aided by the bare-footed local militia, on the other.

Swathi Thirunal, the great ruler of Travancore, extended generous patronage to the art of painting. Alagiri Naidu, a distinguished painter from Madurai adorned his Court. He gave training in the art of painting to Raja Raja Varma of the Kilimanur royal family and the latter in his turn trained up his talented nephew Raja Ravi Varma. The well-known European oil painter, Theodore Jenson, also initiated Raja Ravi Varma into the technique of European oil painting and helped him to achieve international renown. The innumerable pictures of Gods and Goddesses painted by Raja Ravi Varma which adorn most of the Hindu homes all over India are even today objects of mass worship. Raja Ravi Varma's own sister, Mangalabhai Tampuratti, specialised herself in painting pictures of women and children which won universal appreciation from connoisseurs of art.

In modern times, Kerala produced two outstanding painters, viz., K. Madhava Menon and K.C.S. Panikar. The former excelled in the portrayal of plant and animal life. A refreshingly original style of his own is Panikar's legacy in the field.

Cultural Organisations

Kerala Sangeetha Nataka Academy

The Academy is the nucleus of all amateur arts clubs and training institutions in the State and it always stands for the betterment of art forms. The Academy is affiliating all cultural institutions in the State. The Academy conducts festivals, competitions and seminars for promoting dance, drama and music. The Academy conducted the 'International Drama Festival 2011' during the year. Dance festival, Swathi Sangeetha Festival , State professional drama competition and other cultural events were organized during the year.

Kerala Lalithakala Academy

The Academy promotes the talents of painters and sculptures through camps, demonstrations and exhibitions. The academy organizes many national and State level camps and exhibitions on drawing, sculpture, photography etc. in which renowned artists took part.

As an attempt to search the roots of the pictorial art of Kerala, Academy has organized the 16-day Kalamezhuthu Programme.

Kerala Folklore Academy

The Kerala Folklore Academy is an autonomous institution closely associated with folklore subjects. The objectives of the Academy are promotion of traditional folk arts of Kerala, dissemination of folk performing arts, welfare of the folk artists and scientific documentation of these arts and their classification and publication of books, journals promoting culture and traditional art forms.

State Institute of Children's Literature

The Institute was established with the ultimate aim of all-round literary and cultural prospects of the children of the state. With a view to promote the creative and cultural growth of the children belonging to the different strata of the society, the Institute organizes programmes, literary competitions and publishes children's books and periodicals. The Institute provides good quality reading material for children in Kerala.

The children's monthly magazine "Thaliru" has been brought out in new form since June 2007. The Institute organizes 'Thaliru vayana matsaram', possibly the largest reading promotion campaign in the country. One of the main objectives of the Institute was the publication of an Encyclopaedia in eight volumes.

Centre for Heritage Studies (CHS, Thrippunithura)

Centre for Heritage Studies was incepted in the year 2000 as an autonomous academic and research centre for promoting heritage and cultural studies. The centre conducts P.G. diploma in three subjects viz. Archaeology and Museology, Archival Studies and Conservation. PG diploma course in Heritage Ship Technology was also started during the year. It is also a training centre for teachers and demonstrators in theoretical and practical subjects like primitive, ancient, medieval and modern art.

The centre has conducted work shop on Muziris Heritage Project, one day seminar on 'Accessibility to the Museums' and Hortus Malabaricus Project Awareness programme during the year. The CHS has set up a conservation laboratory for the Muziris Heritage Project at North Paravur.

Margi

Margi is a cultural centre for promoting 'Kathakali' and 'Kudiyattam'. Kudiyattam has been proclaimed as a World Heritage art by UNESCO in 2001. Margi has a permanent group of forty traditionally trained senior artists of which 28 are for Kathakali and 12 for Kudiyattam.

Part time training in Kathakali is given to school students without fees to promote interest in youngsters in traditional arts. Special training is given with stipends in Kudiyattam under a special programme of the Kendra Sangeetha Nataka Academy, New Delhi.

Kerala Kalamandalam

Kerala Kalamandalam is an institution for training and research in classical art forms such as Kathakali, Mohiniyattom, Chakyarkuthu, Thullal and Kalari arts. Kalamandalam gained the status of a Deemed University in 2007. Kalamandalam has initiated several measures for upgrading the institution to the standard of a Deemed University. The institution has introduced PG and research courses, initiated infrastructural developmental activities, enhanced the library referral unit etc. by adhering to UGC norms.

Mohiniyattom was staged in the commonwealth games inauguration ceremony. 50 students from Kalamandalam participated in the prestigious ceremony.

Vasthuvidya Gurukulam

Vasthuvidya Gurukulam in Aranmula is a unique institution under the Department of Culture to promote and preserve the traditional architecture, mural painting and other related subjects. In the absence of a statutory council for Vasthu Sasthra, Human Resource Department, Ministry of India declared Vasthuvidya Gurukulam as a nodal agency for Vasthu and other related subjects. University recognized Vasthuvidya course is being conducted by Vasthuvidya Gurukulam. Consultancy service in Vasthu principles is rendered for constructing houses and other buildings. Gurukulam has so far completed the renovation work at Sree Padmanabha Swami temple and Aranmula Parthasaradhi temple and renovation work at Tali temple is going on. Vasthuvidya Gurukulam is conducting four academic courses in Vasthuvidya and mural painting based on the basic texts of Vasthuvidya. Gurukulam is also documenting important Traditional architectural structures in Kerala.

Guru Gopinath Natana Gramam

Guru Gopinath Natana Gramam is a cultural institution for imparting training in classical dance and music with special focus on popularising "Kerala Natanam" which is a combination of Kathakali and Kudiyattam. The institution provides necessary facilities for imparting art education to children and training to talented youths.

Natana Gramam conducts regular and vacation classes in dance, music and other performing arts. The construction of National Museum is in progress. Documentation works of "Kerala Natanam" was completed during this period.

Kumaranasan National Institute of Culture

Kumaranasan National Institute of Culture is the first memorial constituted by the Govt. of Kerala in the name of the great poet Sri Kumaranasan. It started functioning in the year 1966 with the main mission of spreading Kumaranasan's works and his messages among the public. In order to achieve this objective Kumaranasan National Institute has promulgated a Comprehensive Development Project of Construction of an International Convention Centre, International Library, National Heritage Museum, Institute for Research and Development, Eco Garden, Cultural Tourism etc. The land now available with the Institute is not sufficient to construct all the above projects and hence procedure for acquiring 1.1 hectares of land is nearing completion. For this purpose the institute has remitted ₹1.80 crores to the Revenue Department.

During the year 2010 the Institute has published complete works of Kumaranasan containing 4000 pages in four volumes. The construction of the four statues by the noted sculpturer Sri Kanayikunhiraman is going on. The present research institute being recognized by the Kerala University has been advantageous to the students with new books and new research and study materials. In addition the functioning of the medicinal garden has been expanded with more rare medicinal plants and high quality seeds. Arrangements have also been made to start the works of construction of the projects.

Multipurpose Cultural Complex Society (Vyloppilly Samskrithi Bhavan), Thiruvananthapuram

Vyloppilly Samskrithi Bhavan is an institution built with the support of Government of India to function as a research, documentation and performance centre of traditional and classical cultural traditions. It is one of the few institutions of its kind in India and is a UNESCO approved centre for cultural heritage preservation. The Mudra Fest is an important annual programme of Samskrithi Bhavan. It is conceived as a forum to study and appreciate the value of classical dances from the great masters of the country. Classical dances and lecture demonstrations were conducted in which renowned artist's performed.

Jawahar Balabhavan

Balabhavan imparts training in arts and crafts for children between the age of four and sixteen. Classes are held after school hours and during vacations. Training is imparted in all forms of creative arts and crafts, general knowledge, yoga, electronics, spoken English, personality development, aero modeling, kalaripayattu etc. Nearly 1994 children attended the vacation classes in Thiruvananthapuram.

Kerala State Film Development Corporation, Thiruvananthapuram

KSFDC (a public limited company) has been providing support facilities for the production of theatre films and documentaries since 1975. The Corporation owns ten theatres and the Chitranjali Studio. KSFDC has successfully launched several modernizing works and evolved new programmes for raising its revenue during the year. Chitranjali Studio has been modernized by equipping it with modern lights, track, trolley and other latest film equipments.

Kerala State Chalachitra Academy

The Kerala State Chalachitra Academy is the only Academy for motion pictures in India. The Academy organizes many programmes for promoting film and TV media. The Academy organized 15th International film festival in December 2010. About 220 movies were screened in the festival. The Academy also conducted Documentary-Shot Film Festival, National Film Festival of Kerala, Touring Talkies programmed Visual Appreciation Camps for Children etc., during the year.

KNOW THE FACTS

☞ *Kathakali is the most famous art form of Kerala.*

☞ *'Margam Kali' is a traditional art form prevelent among the Christians of Kerala.*

☞ *Chemmin was the first Malayalam film to get National Award (1965). It was directed by Ramukaryat.*

☞ *First Malayalam film Vigathakumaran was released in 1928. J.C. Daniel was its Producer, Director and Cameraman. J.C. Daniel Award is given for around contributions given to Malayalam film.*

☞ *First Malayalam talkie film was 'Balan'.*

☞ *Udaya Studio (1948) is the first Cinema studio in Kerala.*

☞ *Padayani is the traditional art of Pathanamthitta.*

☞ *'Sixth sense' is an English film directed by Manoj Night Shyamalan. His films were nominated for Oscar award.*

TEST YOUR SELF

1. Irayimman Thampi of Kerala was famous ....
   A. Composer
   B. Singer
   C. Dancer
   D. Painter

2. Which among the following is not included in Panchavadyam?
   A. Maddalam
   B. Idakka
   C. Kombu
   D. Chenda

3. Church which depicts the scene of a battle fought between the armies of Tipu Sultan and East India Company?
   A. Kanjur Church
   B. Edappalli Church
   C. Vechur Church
   D. Cheppad Church

4. Madhava Menon is related to which of the following art form?
   A. Dancing
   B. Singing
   C. Painting
   D. None of these

5. Edakked caves which are famous for its earliest specimen of stone carvings in Kerala located in ....
   A. Kannur
   B. Wayanad
   C. Idukki
   D. Kollam

6. The stone images of Buddha sitting in the yogasana posture discovered from ....
   A. Kallil
   B. Chitaral
   C. Pallikkal
   D. Sultan's Battery

7. Silparatna is a work devoted to ....
   A. music
   B. dance
   C. singing
   D. architecture

8. The famous Padmanabha Swami Temple is located at ....
   A. Kottayam
   B. Alappuzhoa
   C. Kasargode
   D. Thiruvananthapuram

9. The Mappila Pattukal are the folk songs of ....
   A. Hindus
   B. Muslims
   C. Buddists
   D. Christians

10. Kerala Kalamandalam gained the status of a deemed university in ....
   A. 2007
   B. 2005
   C. 2001
   D. 2009

ANSWERS

1	2	3	4	5	6	7	8	9	10
A	D	A	C	B	C	D	D	B	A

□□□

21

TOURISM

Kerala is a green strip of land, in the south west corner of Indian peninsula. Its unique feature, culture and traditions, coupled with its varied demography has made Kerala one of the most popular tourist destinations in the world. This Tropical paradise with its spectacular and diverse natural attractions has greatly attracted holiday makers from across the world. Kerala is one among the longest-lived, healthiest, most gender equitable and most literate regions makes it distinct from other states. Realising the importance of tourism in stimulating the economic development of the state, the Government of Kerala declared tourism as an industry in 1986. Today, tourism is Kerala's booming industry and one of the fastest growing, high income and employment generating sector. Constant efforts are on to promote Kerala abroad and marketing strategies are being evolved along with new and exciting tourism products. The state department of tourism along with private entrepreneurs is taking steps to improve the facilities and infrastructure at places with tourism potential.

Kerala, promoted as "God's Own Country" is blessed by nature with varied geographical features like beaches, hill stations, backwaters, national parks and wild life sanctuaries. The centuries-old holistic medicine of Ayurveda, the unique boat races that is the largest team sport in the world, the ride through the winding waterways in a cosy houseboat or the colourful and exotic festivals, Kerala offers a multitude of experience to the tourist. Popular attractions in the state include the beaches such as Kovalam, Varkala, Marari, Bekal and Kannur. Kerala's most popular backwater destinations are Kumarakom, Alappuzha, Kollam, Kochi and Kozhikode, and its best known hill stations are Ponmudi, Munnar, Wayanad and Wagamon. Kerala has a number of well-known wildlife reserves, including the Periyar Wildlife Sanctuary, Eravikulam National Park, Thattekkad Bird Sanctuary and Parambikulam Wildlife Sanctuary.

Eco-Tourism

Eco-tourism means management of tourism and conservation of nature in a way so as to maintain a fine balance between the requirements of tourism and ecology on one hand and the needs of the local communities for jobs, new skills, income generation and a better status for women on the other. The World Tourism Organisation has defined Eco-tourism as 'Tourism that involves travelling to relatively undisturbed natural areas with the specified objects of studying, admiring, and enjoying nature and its wild plants and animals, as well as existing cultural aspects found in these areas'. In total, the definitions focus on three significant aspects—nature, tourism and local communities. It differs in the meaningful ways from mass tourism that aims at consuming nature and leaving it depleted on more than one front. Eco-tourism aims at promoting environmental values and ethics and preserving nature in its uninterrupted forms. It thus benefits wildlife and nature by contributing towards ecological integrity. The tourist have a first hand encounter with nature and learn to admire it than to ravage it. Since the essence of eco-tourism lies in admiration of nature and out door recreation, it encompasses a wide range of activities such as trekking, hiking, mountaineering, bird watching, boating, rafting, biological explorations and visiting wildlife sanctuaries.

The key elements of eco-tourism are
1. A well preserved eco-tourism site to attract tourists
2. Cultural and adventure activities
3. Active involvement of local people who are able to provide authentic information about nature, culture and their ethnic traditions to the visitors.
4. Empowering the local communities to manage eco-tourism so that they ensure conservation through alternate livelihood opportunities.

India has a wide potential for eco-tourism that needs to be tapped for economic benefits and for the conservation and preservation of nature.

The State Govt. of Kerala has declared sixteen eco-tourism hotspots in Kerala. They are Thenmala, Periyar, Parambikulam, Eravikulam, Aralam, Neyyar, Peppara, Arippa, Shenduruney, Gavi, Rhodovalley, Chimmini, Mankayam, Palaruvy, Konny and Thommankuthu.

Thenmala Eco-tourism Destination

Thenmala in Kerala is India's first planned eco-tourism destination. Thenmala is situated in Kollam district of Kerala and is about 72 kms from Thiruvananthapuram, the state capital of Kerala. The Thenmala eco-tourism shares its resources with the famous Shenduruney Wildlife Sanctuary at the foothills of the Western Ghats. The word Thenmala in the local language Malayalam means 'Honey Hill'. It is believed that the honey collected from this region is of very good quality owing to its unique biological settings. Divided into different zones with a particular theme, the project area currently has three major zones viz. Culture Zone, Leisure Zone and Adventure Zone.

In Kerala there are a large number of wildlife parks and sanctuaries. Kerala is considered to be a green paradise on earth. The dense green forests with a wide variety of animals such as elephants, tigers, deers, leopards etc and water birds provide a great opportunity to the tourists to sight these different creatures.

Bird Sanctuaries

Kerala is becoming a favourite hot spot among bird lovers and nature lovers from across the world. A visit to Kerala bird sanctuaries will give the pleasure to meet a variety of migratory birds that cluster in thousands, some from the Himalayas, and some even from Siberia. In Kerala, one can enjoy the priceless show of avian acrobats, pulsating on the beats of nature. During the rains, some of India's most spectacular avians gather in their finest haunts to court their mates and nest in huge colonies in the trees lining the paths of the sanctuaries.

Kadalundi Bird Sanctuary

The Kadalundi Bird Sanctuary is a Heaven for migratory birds. Terns, Gulls, Herons, Sand pipers, Whimbrels and other such migratory birds flock from the month of November and returns only by the end of April.

Over a hundred species of native birds have been recorded in the sanctuary, including about 60 species of migratory birds which visit seasonally; these include terns, gulls, herons, sandpipers and cormorants. Notable species are Whimbrels and Brahminy Kites. The sanctuary is well known for a wide variety of fish, mussels and crabs. This is one of the important Bird-Sanctuaries of Kerala.

Kumarakom Bird Sanctuary

Kumarakom Bird Sanctuary, Kottayam is one of the best destinations of wild life sanctuaries in Kerala. It is located on the banks of Vembanad Lake. A cruise along the Vembanad Lake is the best way to experience the sanctuary.

The main attractions are local birds like the waterfowl, cuckoo, owl, egret, heron, cormorant, moorhen, darter, Brahminy kite and the duck, as well as the migratory Siberian crane. Parrot, teal, lark, flycatcher and other birds are seen here during their respective migratory seasons. Some of the migratory birds come from the Himalayas, and a few from far away Siberia. The best time for bird watching in Kumarakom Bird Sanctuary is between June and August. This is the breeding season of resident wetland birds like Siberian stork, cormorants, darter, white ibis, egret, heron and teal. In the case of migratory birds like pintailed duck, garganey teal, spot billed duck, osprey, marsh harrier, steppey eagle etc. November to May is the breeding season.

Thattekad Bird Sanctuary

This is one of the famous Bird-Sanctuaries of Kerala. Established in the Ernakulam District in the year 1983. The Thattekkad Bird Sanctuary was the first bird sanctuary of Kerala. It has dense tropical evergreen forest and a population of over 500 species of exotic birds. This world famous bird sanctuary owes much of its fame to Dr. Salim Ali, the internationally renowned ornithologist. The sanctuary covers an area of 25 sq. km. stretching between the branches of river Periyar. There is also a rich variety of butterflies here.

Several species of birds, both forest birds as well as the water birds, visit the sanctuaries, and the important ones include the following: The Indian Pitta, which visits the sanctuary during winter and spends almost six months here. Ground Thrush, an orange-headed bird, Large-billed Leaf-warbler, Jerdon's Nightjar, Indian Cuckoo, Darters, Cormorants, Whiskered Terns, Collared Scops Owl, Frogmouths, which are nocturnal birds, Pompadour Green Pigeon, Yellow-browed Bulbuls. The Edamalayar forest is located about 15 kms from Thattekad Bird Sanctuary. This is also an evergreen forest located above the Edamalayar River. The Mountain Hawk Eagles are found in this forest. Other birds in this forest include Dark-fronted Babbler, Brown-cheeked Fulvetta, Brown-backed and White-rumped Needletails, and Emerald Green Pigeons.

Zoological Parks

Zoo is one of the places which attract the tourists. Not only tourists but also the local people like to spend their holiday by visiting the zoo. It is liked by the people of all ages. There are two main zoos in Kerala one at Thiruvananthapuram and another at Thrissur. Both these zoo have museums, botanical and zoological garden in the zoo premises. The wildlife includes tigers, lions, deers, hippopotamus, monkeys, crocodiles etc. Besides these, there are birds and snakes as well. The main aim of the zoo is conservation of animals as most of the animals at present fall under the category of endangered species. So it is necessary to conserve them before they become totally extinct.

Thiruvananthapuram Zoo

The Thiruvananthapuram Zoo is located at the centre of the city of Thiruvananthapuram, the capital of Kerala. Set among woodland, lakes and lawns this zoo is one of the well designed zoos in Asia. It is one of the oldest zoos in the country which was established by Travancore King in the year 1857 as an annex to the Napier Museum. And it covers a total area of 55 acres (22 hectares). There are a variety of plants and trees in the premise that beautifies the zoo.

The sole purpose of the zoo was recreational but gradually the purpose of the zoo changed from recreation to conservation. Sprawling over an area of 55 acres of land the zoo offers rare opportunity for picturesque surroundings besides a rich collection of wild life. The Zoo has 82 different species of animals from all over India and abroad. It has several species of animals and birds from Ethiopian and Australian Zoo geographic regions. The Lion tailed Macaque, Nilgiri Langur, Nilgiri Tahr, One Horned Great Indian Rhino, Asiatic Lion, Royal Bengal Tiger are prominent among the indigenous endangered fauna whereas, Giraffe, Hippo, Zebra, Cape Buffalo are the guests from African region. It will usher in a new era with the completion of the ongoing modernization works in the Zoo. Thrilling encounters with the animals out in their open air landscapes are order of the day now. As aviary and reptile house with various poisonous and non-poisonous snakes, which is located within the zoo premises. There is also a Botanical Garden within the zoo premises which has various species of tropical plants and trees.

Thrissur Zoo

Thrissur zoo was established in the year 1885 in Chembukavu in Thrissur district. It covers a total area of 13.5 (5.5 hectares) acres of land. It is at a walking distance from the famous "Thrissur round" (one of the longest inner ring roads in India) and the famous Vadakkunnathan temple. Thrissur zoo is small, but the Museum houses a large number of historic items such as swords, jewellery, rocks, stuffed butterflies etc. There is also a small snake park inside the zoo.

The main aim of this zoo is conservation of animals and it has taken measures for breeding of animals. Research is also being conducted from here. It is one of the oldest zoos in the country, and is home to the wide variety of animals, reptiles, and birds. The zoo compound includes a natural history museum and an art museum that showcase the socio-cultural heritage of the region. The zoo includes a Zoological Garden, Botanical Garden, Art Museum, and Natural History Museum in its compound. Wildlife at the Thrissur zoo includes tigers, lions, deers, sloth bears, monkeys, hippopotamus, camels, cobras, kraits, vipers, rat snakes, pink flamingos, mithun of the north-eastern hills, and lion-tailed macaques and an assortment of many other species in myriad hues. There is also a special building which houses snakes. The public zoo of Thrissur is all through adorned by landscaped gardens. A natural history museum and an art museum are also enclosed within the same premises showcasing the socio-cultural heritage of the region.

Hill Stations in Kerala

Ilaveezhapoonchira

This is a picnic spot located in the midst of the beautiful hillocks near (55 kms from Kottayam, 20 kms from Thodupuzha) Kanjar. It is easily accessible from Palai in Kottayam district. Surrounded by three enchanting hillocks - Mankunnu, Kodayathoormala and Thonippara - that makes this place ideal for trekking.

Ponmudy

Located within a short driving distance of Thiruvananthapuram, Ponmudi is an enchanting hill resort with narrow winding pathways and cool green environs. Along with a beautiful array of mountain flowers, exotic butterflies and small rivulets, Ponmudi offers excellent opportunities for trekking. With its tea estates and mist covered valleys Ponmudi is a fast developing hill resort with cottages and dormitory accommodation facilities.

Agasthyakoodam

It is 70 km from Thiruvananthapuram. The Agasthya forest is believed to have been the abode of sage Agasthya, a character from mythology. Trekking trails and thick forests around here. Agasthyakoodam, the spectacular peak in the Western Ghats rises to a majestic 1890 m in the form of a sharp cone. A haven for rare herbs and medicinal plants, its slopes are a breathtaking sight when they transform into colourful glades of the 'Neelakurinji', a flower which blooms only once in twelve years.

Maniyamkunnu

The majestic mountains here that slope down to meet the beautiful valleys below are truly spellbinding.

Charalkunnu

This picturesque hill station offers a panoramic view of the nearby valleys. A camp house on the hill provides comfortable lodging.

Nelliyampahy

From the town of Nenmara in Palakkad district, the cloud-caressed peaks of the majestic Nelliyampathy hill ranges are a sight to behold. The height of the hills ranges from 467 m to 1572 m. To reach Nelliyampathy, one has to take the road starting from Nenmara that proceeds to the Pothundy Dam.

The Pothundy Dam is a picturesque locale with facilities for boating and is a nice option as a picnic place. As the Ghat road winds its way up to Nelliyampathy, at certain places there are viewpoints from where the vast stretches of Palakkad district are visible with its extensive paddy fields forming a verdant carpet. It also offers a splendid view of the Palakkad Gap, which is a geographical phenomenon in the Western Ghats formation in this region, bringing into view, parts of the adjoining State of Tamil Nadu. The hills of Nelliyampathy are also well known for its orange cultivation.

The bio-farms located here are a major landmark as one proceeds up before reaching the topmost point at Palagapandi estate. Not far away from Palagapandy is Seethakundu where one can have a fantastic valley view, and a 100 m high waterfall providing an added attraction. From Palagapandy, one can trek or go by jeep to reach Mampara; another breathtaking vantage point at Nelliyampathy. The area in and around Palagapandy estate has tea, cardamom and coffee plantations with adjoining hills allowing one to catch a glimpse of the wildlife in the form of Indian gaur, elephants, leopards, giant squirrel etc. and is also a paradise for birdwatchers.

Munnar

It is one of the attractions that contributed to Kerala's popularity as a travel destination among domestic and foreign travellers. Situated at the confluence of three mountain streams-Muthirapuzha, Nallathanni and Kundala, and perched about 1600 m above sea level, the hill station of Munnar once used to be the summer resort of the erstwhile British administration in south India.

This hill station is marked by vast expanses of tea plantations, colonial bungalows, rivulets, waterfalls and cool weather. It is also an ideal destination for trekking and mountain biking. The phenomenon of once in twelve years occurring on the fabled hills of Munnar is attributed to the blooming of Neelakurinji flowers.

One of the main attractions in and around Munnar is the Eravikulam National Park. Located about 15 kms from Munnar, this park is famous for its endangered inhabitant - the Nilgiri Tahr. Spread over an area of 97 sq. km., this park is also home to several species of rare butterflies, animals and birds. A great place for trekking, the park offers a magnificent view of the tea plantations and also the rolling hills caressed by blankets of mists. The park becomes a hot destination when the hill slopes here get covered in a carpet of blue, resulting from the flowering of Neelakurinji. It is a plant endemic to this part of the Western Ghats which blooms once in twelve years. The last time it bloomed was in 2006.

Anamudi Peak

Located inside the Eravikulam National Park is the Anamudi Peak. This is the highest peak in south India standing at a height of over 2700 m. Treks to the peak are allowed with permission from Forest and Wildlife authorities at Eravikulam.

Mattupetty

Another place of interest, located about 13 kms from Munnar Town, is Mattupetty. Lying at a height of 1700 m above sea level, Mattupetty is known for its storage masonry dam and the beautiful lake, which offers pleasurable boat rides, enabling one to enjoy the surrounding hills and landscape. Mattupetty's fame is also attributed to the dairy farm run by the Indo-Swiss Livestock Project, where one would come across different high yielding breeds of cows. Mattupetty with its lush green tea plantations, rolling grasslands and the Shola forests is also ideal for trekking and is home to a variety of birds.

Pallivasal

Pallivasal, located at about 3 kms from Chithirapuram in Munnar is the venue of the first Hydro-electric project in Kerala. It is a place of immense scenic beauty and is often favoured by visitors as a picnic spot.

Chinnakanal

Near the town of Munnar is Chinnakanal and the waterfalls here, popularly known as Power House Waterfalls, cascade down a steep rock 2000 m above sea level. The spot is enriched with the scenic view of the Western Ghat ranges.

Anayirangal

At about seven kilometers from Chinnakanal, is Anayirangal. Anayirangal is 22 kms from Munnar, is a lush green carpet of tea plants. A trip on the splendid reservoir is an unforgettable experience. The Anayirangal dam is surrounded by tea plantations and evergreen forests.

Top Station

Top Station, which is about 3 kms from Munnar is at a height of 1700 m above sea level. It is the highest point on the Munnar-Kodaikanal road. Travellers to Munnar make it a point to visit Top Station to enjoy the panoramic view it offers of the neighbouring state of Tamil Nadu. It is one of the spots in Munnar to enjoy the Neelakurunji flowers blooming over a vast area.

Tea Museum

Munnar has a legacy of its own when it comes to the origins and evolution of tea plantations. Taking account of this legacy and to preserve and showcase some of the exquisite and interesting aspects on the genesis and growth of tea plantations in Kerala's high ranges, a museum exclusively for tea was opened some years ago by Tata Tea in Munnar. This Tea Museum houses curios, photographs and machineries; all of which have a story to tell on the origins and growth of tea plantation in Munnar. The museum is located at the Nallathanni Estate of Tata Tea in Munnar and is worth a visit.

Pullumedu

The winding journey to this hill along the Periyar River, offers a stunning view of hills draped in lush greenery. Velvet lawns and rare flora and fauna add to the beauty of Pullumedu. The famous Sree Ayyappa Temple at Sabarimala and the Makara Jyothi illuminations at the shrine are visible from here.

Dhoni

15 km from Palakkad, It takes a three hour trek from the base of the Dhoni hills to reach this reserve forest area with its small, beautiful waterfall.

Ramakkalmedu

Located in Idukki district of Kerala, Ramakalmedu is about 40 kms from Thekkady, which is one of the popular wildlife destinations in Kerala. Traveling on the Thekkady-Munnar road, one can reach the captivating hills of Ramakalmedu in the Western Ghats, which is about 16 kms from Nedumkandam.

Peermede

Peermede is a lovely hill station at 915 m above sea level. It is an ideal retreat in the Western Ghats and a choice break for tourists *en route* to the Periyar Tiger Reserve. Sprawling gardens of tea, coffee, cardamom, rubber and eucalyptus lying side by side with natural grasslands, pine forests and waterfalls make this an ideal summer resort. The summer palace of Rajas of erstwhile Travancore is today an important monument here. Peermede and its surroundings are suitable for trekking, cycling and horse riding. Kuttikanam a place for adventure tourism and trekking is just 3 km from Peermede.

Another attraction here is Thrissanku Hills, about 4 kms away. The rolling hills, the lovely landscape and the gentle breeze make this a choice spot for long walks. The hills offer a breathtaking view of the sunrise and sunset.

Rajamala

About 15 kms from Munnar, the famous hill station of Kerala, is the beautiful Rajamala. The natural habitat of the Nilgiri Tahr *(Hemitragas hylocres)*, the Eravikulam-Rajamala region is now home to half the world Tahr population. But the Tahr is only one of the reasons to make a visit to Rajamala. The picturesque beauty of this mountain makes one want to tent here forever!

Mattupetti

Cradled by the undulating plantation hills of Munnar, and not far away from the Anamudi peak is Mattupetty. Situated in the famous hill town of Munnar, Mattupetty located 13 kms from Munnar is situated at a height of 1700 m, and is a delight for nature lovers.

Mattupetty offers many fascinating sights to relish. Besides the lush green tea plantations, and the rolling grasslands, the Shola forests in and around Mattupetty are ideal for trekking and are habitat to a variety of birds. Rivulets and cascades crisscross the terrain here, which again adds more attraction to the place.

One of the main attractions in Mattupetty is the beautiful lake, and the Mattupetty Dam, which are ideal picnic spots. The District Tourism Promotion Council (DTPC), Idukki provides boating facilities in the Mattupetty Dam. Speed launch, slow speedboat and motorboats are available on hire. Other nearby places of interest include the picturesque Kundala tea plantations and the Kundala Lake.

Of all the main attractions at Mattupetty is the dairy farm, run by the Indo-Swiss Livestock Project. The dairy farm is a unique one of its kind with several varieties of high-yielding cattle being reared.

Vilangankunnu

This (7 kms from Thrissur) is a beautiful hill which is a good picnic spot.

Pattumala

This silken hill, in Peermede in exhilarating Idukki, has charms like no other. The lofty peaks, the little streams and the green expanse of the tea plantations give the hills an ethereal beauty. An early morning walk through all this breathtaking loveliness might make one want to repeat the immortal lines, Bliss was it that dawn to be alive! At the top of a hill is the Velankanni Matha Church, a famous pilgrim center, which is built entirely of granite. Pattumala is also home to two of the biggest names in the tea production sector.

Vagamon

Vagamon Hill is one of the most beautiful hill stations in Kerala is engulfed by three hills. It is from here one can see the green grass covering the hills and the smooth lawns like silk carpets with the fresh mountain air—make Vagamon Hill the most sought after tourist destination. Beautiful flowers, bluish brown hills, cotton mist, meadows, breathtaking view all of it can be enjoyed in the enchanting land of Vagamon Hill. Adventure enthusiasts can enjoy trekking on the mountains, para gliding and rock climbing. Have fun on the boat ride on the lakes or one can sit on the banks or hours and watch the sun go down. If lucky the tourists may spot wild animals like the elephants, wild buffalos and deer.

Vattavada

Located about 45 kms east of Munnar is the serene village of Vattavada. At Vattavada, in comparison to other regions in Munnar, instead of tea plantations, it is the predominance of vegetables that occupy the terraced slopes and valleys of Vattavada.

The scenic hilly tract of Vattavada is at an altitude of 6500 feet above sea level, and is a refreshing experience, which is yet to come under the constant gaze and the footprints of visitors. The place receives plenty of sunshine and the winter temperatures never dip below unbearable levels. Besides the slopes of vegetable fields, one could also find forest patches, interspersed with eucalyptus and conifers. The area also teems with bird life and also other winged beauties like butterflies in various colour, size and shape. Vattavada could be taken for a place significant for trekking.

Thrisanku Hills

The rolling hills (4 kms from Peermede, 1/2 km from Kuttikanam), the lovely landscape and the gentle breeze make this an ideal spot for long walks. The hills offer a breathtaking view of the sunrise and sunset.

Nilambur

It is located 40 kms from Malappuram town, Malappuram district, north Kerala. Nilambur is renowned for the oldest teak plantation in the world, the Conolly's Plot, just 2 kms from town. The place is also noted for its tribal settlements, the world's first Teak Museum, vast rain forests, waterfalls and ancient kovilakoms—residences of maharajas. Heavy restrictions are imposed in a measure to save the existing forest land. A half hour journey from here, through the dense forests, by jeep takes one to Mancheri, the home of the Cholai Naikars, a primitive tribe.

Ranipuram

Situated 750 m above sea level, Ranipuram is famous for its trekking trails and varied vegetation—evergreen shola woods, monsoon forests and grasslands. This area was formerly known as Madathumala. The extensive forests of Madathumala merge with the forests of Karnataka. Ranipuram in its natural beauty is comparable to Ooty. Wild elephants can be seen wandering on the top of the mountains.

Wayanad

A bio-diverse region spread across 2,132 square kilometre on the lofty Western Ghats, Wayanad is one of the view districts in Kerala that has been able to retain its pristine nature. Hidden away in the hills of this land are some of the oldest tribes, as yet untouched by civilization. And the very first prehistoric engravings in Kerala discovered in the foothills of Edakkal and around Ambukuthimala bear testimony to a prehistoric culture dating back to the Mesolithic Age. Strikingly scenic, it is known for its sub-tropical savannahs, picturesque hill stations, sprawling spice plantations, luxuriant forests and rich Cultural traditions. A holistic confluence of wilderness, history and culture, Wayanad is located on the southern tip of the magnificent Deccan plateau.

Vellari Mala

Verdant, rolling landscape, with numerous brooks, cascades and breathtaking waterfalls, Vellari Mala offers a true abode for you to unwind and to immerse in the whiff of its limitless fresh air. River Kanjirapuzha, a tributary of the River Chaliyar, meanders through the rocky terrain, creating cascades and breathtaking waterfalls at many points. The land's beauty and topography is truly a trekker's paradise and is also an ideal picnic spot for people of all age group to have a good time.

Iringal

The famous son of Iringal, Kunjali Marakkar went on to become the trusted admiral and commanded the Zamorin's fleet and thwarted the efforts of Portuguese vessels trying their best to make a landing on the Kerala coast. The birthplace of this valiant admiral of the Zamorin is situated on the southern bank of the Mooradi River. Today, Keralites remember his valour and selfless service rendered for his motherland with lot of reverence.

Beaches of Kerala

Kovalam

16 kms south of Trivandrum, this internationally renowned destination comprises three adjacent crescent-shaped beaches, of which the southernmost known as the Lighthouse Beach, is the most popular. Kovalam offers a variety of activities including snorkelling, catamaran rides etc.

Shankhumugham

8 km from centre of Trivandrum, this beach has an indoor recreation club, the matsya kanyaka (a gigantic 35 m long sculpture of a mermaid) and a restaurant shaped like a starfish.

Chowara

8 kms south of Kovalam: Pristine and serene, this fishing hamlet is an unending stretch of white, sandy beaches.

Poovar

12 kms south of Kovalam: An isolated but spectacular beach, Poovar is situated close to the Neyyar River estuary.

Varkala

45 kms north of Trivandrum: A beach destination, it is also an important Hindu pilgrimage centre. The Papanasham Beach fringed by red laterite cliffs, cool mineral springs, serene backwaters, the 2000- year-old Sree Janardhana Swamy Temple, a century old tunnel and a Nature Cure centre are the key attractions.

Kappil

A confluence of the sea, river and the backwaters, this secluded spot near Varkala (53 kms north of Trivandrum and 16 kms south of Kollam) is worth visiting.

Thirumullavaram

This secluded beach (6 kms north of Kollam) is a beautiful picnic spot.

Alappuzha Beach

3.5 kms from Alappuzha town: A 137-year-old pier which extends into the sea and an old lighthouse add to the attractions of the beach.

Fort Kochi Beach

At Fort Kochi: Overlooking the Arabian Sea, with its legendary Chinese fishing nets dotting the foreground, Fort Kochi Beach offers views of spectacular sunsets. Waterfront stalls serving fresh catch prepared according to taste are the main attractions here.

Cherai

21 kms from Ernakulam: This lovely beach bordering Vypeen Island is ideal for swimming. Dolphins are occasionally spotted here. A typical Kerala village nearby, with paddy fields and coconut groves is an added attraction.

Nattika Beach

24 kms from Thrissur: Fringed by palm trees, this picturesque beach is hot spot of picnickers.

Padinjarekkara

5 kms from Chemravattom, Ponnani: Famous for bird watching, the beach also offers a breathtaking view of the confluence of the Bharathapuzha, the Tirur Puzha and the Arabian Sea.

Vallikunnu

40 kms from Malappuram: A beach resort set in the midst of a coconut grove is the main attraction here.

Kozhikode Beach

1/2 km from Calicut city: This beach is a favourite haunt of sunset viewers. Adding to its natural beauty is the old-world charm retained by the ancient lighthouse and the two crumbling piers, each more than a hundred years old.

Beypore

10 kms south of Calicut: One of the prominent ports and a maritime trading centre of ancient Kerala. Beypore is famous for its boat building yard where the Uru (Arabian trading vessel) is constructed.

Kappad

16 kms north of Calicut: This is the historic beach where Vasco da Gama landed on the 27th of May 1498, with 170 men in three vessels. The rock-studded beach is locally known as Kappakadavu.

Payyoli

38 kms north of Calicut: The shallow waters of this beautiful beach are ideal for swimming. During November-December, hordes of the endangered Olive Ridley turtle come in to lay eggs.

Sand Banks

52 kms north of Calicut: This beach at Vdakara where the Kottakal River merges into the sea is stunningly beautiful and is a favourite spot for locals and tourists.

Payyambalam

2 kms from Kannur town: This beach is famous for its flat laterite cliffs that just out into the sea. The well-laid gardens and the massive landscaped sculpture of Mother and Child make it extremely captivating. The nearby Baby Beach is delightfully quiet.

Kizhunna Ezhara Beach

11 kms south of Kannur: This beautiful stretch of sand is one of the most secluded beaches in Kerala.

Meenkunnu

12 kms north of Kannur: Uncrowded, the beach is a tourist paradise, with golden sand and surf.

Muzhappilangad

15 kms south of Kannur: A swimmers paradise, this is Kerala's only drive-in beach. Adventure sports like paragliding and parasailing are possible here.

Pallikere

1 km from Bekal Fort: Also known as the Bekal Fort Beach, this shallow beach offers a spectacular view of the fort and has ample facilities for recreation.

Kappil Beach

2 kms from Bekal Fort: Remote and secluded, this beach is fast becoming

a major tourist spot. The nearby Kodi Cliff offers a panoramic view of the Arabian Sea.

Kanwatheertha

3 kms from Manjeswaram: A large swimming pool-like formation of the sea on the vast beach is the main attraction here.

Waterfalls in Kerala

Adyanpara Falls

Nestled in the land of perennial springs and lush green mountains, Adyanpara falls is a cascading waterfall set in the Kurmbalangod village of Nilambur Taluk in Kerala. Adyanpara waterfalls from a height of 300 feet. Adyanpara is famous for its waterfalls and the splendor of its lush jungles. Kurmbalangod village is rich in wildlife and it attracts numerous variety of birds including the migratory birds. It is a charming and picturesque picnic spot.

Alakapuri Falls

An Alakapuri waterfall is located in the Kanjirakkolly in the Kannur district, which contains 3 phases. First phase is known as Elappara waterfalls; second phase is the famous one and is also known as Alakapuri waterfalls and the third phase contains the biggest waterfall in the monsoon season. The water falls located between the foot hills of Western Ghats, bordering the Coorg area of Karnataka Evergreen Forests. The second stage of the waterfalls contains seven stages of shelves of rock. On the both sides of the waterfall, hard Rocks look like Salamanders of the forest. The surrounding area of the falls filled with "Kurinji" and which blossomed it in every 8 years of the era. In October 2002 and then in November 2010, the plant produced blue flowers and which looks like a blue bed in that large area. The water here is starting in the area under Karnataka and then flowing through the Kerala region.

Aruvikkuzhi Falls

Aruvikkuzhi is a beautiful picnic spot with a waterfall cascading down the mountains from a height of 100 ft that make irregular noise and is mainly connected with various streams. It is located in Kumarakom, a few km away from Kottayam town. It is a very beautiful picnic location. This waterfall is surrounded by large rubber plantations that provide shade to travellers. There are several small streams that make noise as it flows. Near to this lie another waterfall called as the Maramala waterfall which also attracts some tourists.

Athirappally Falls

Athirappally waterfalls is located 78 kms from Kochi (Cochin), located at the entrance to Sholayar ranges, this waterfall is a popular picnic spot. Affording to the onlookers, one of the most bewitching sights, Athirappally falls is about 80 feet high and located in the forest area. The magnificent Athirappally falls start calmly from the mountains, crash through gorges overhung with trees and finally plummet over 80 ft to join the Chalakkudy River in its course. Its cool misty waters surrounded by thick tropical rain forests provide a serene haven away from the hustle and bustle of everyday life.

Aripara Falls

Aripara waterfalls is a tourist spot in Thiruvambadi panchayat in Kozhikode district, Kerala. It is located on the Thiruvambadi-Anakkampoyil route, 15 kms from Thiruvambadi. The waterfall is a tributary of Iruvanjippuzha.

Attukad Falls

A landscape of falling water and hills, Attukad, situated between Munnar and Pallivasal. This waterfall drops from a height of 100 feet. Numerous people come here to enjoy a picnic. Several streams come out of this fall and head to the rubber plantations nearby. The place is also ideal for long trekking and hiking but assumes a cascading and roaring beauty during the monsoons.

Chellarkovil Falls

Chellarkovil is a small village in Idukki district. Here, there are many plains and waterfalls which are very beautiful. This village is border to the coconut groves of Cumbum in Tamil Nadu. A specialty of this waterfall is that it starts to fall from Kerala and touches the land in Tamil Nadu. The view of the green valleys, beautiful mountains and brooks are really breathtaking.

Cheeyappara Falls

Cheeyappara waterfalls is located between Neriamangalam and Adimali on the Kochi-Madurai highway in Idukki district. The Cheeyappara Falls cascades down in seven steps. It is a real feast for the eyes. This is also a great place for trekking. Cheeyappara Waterfalls is considered as one of the best waterfalls in Kerala. Not only tourist the locals are also visits this venue regularly. As it is situated away from the city, it gives an opportunity to everyone to make pleasure trip. Sometimes the Great Hornbill known locally as 'Malamuzhakki Vezhambal' is often found here. It is one of the significant excursion points lying in the region surrounding Cochin.

Chethalayam Falls

Chethalayam falls is situated at 12 kilometres distance from Sulthan Bathery, Wayanad district. It is located near Wayanad Wildlife Sanctuary. The environment of the Chethalayam falls and its surroundings are breathtakingly beautiful. Its surroundings offer a number of vantage points for bird-watching. It is also popular with trekking enthusiasts.

Kaalakkayam Falls

Kaalakkayam waterfall located in the forests near Idinjaar in Thiruvananthapuram district. The waterfall is part of the Mankayam stream that originates in the Agasthyavanam forest. A pool formed at the base of the waterfall is indeed worth a dip and the cool water simply enlivens your body. The forest nearby the waterfall is also a great spot to watch birds and also other species of fauna and flora. A trail along the stream to explore the sights on either side is yet another option for those who would love to walk around a bit.

Kanthapara Falls

The Kanthapara Waterfalls is situated south-east of the town of Kalpetta, which is around 8 kms from Meppadi, Wayanad. This waterfall drops from a height of more than 30 metres. It is a comfortable hiking place, located close to the main road connecting Kalpetta.

Keezharkuth Falls

Rainbow waterfall is situated about 25 kms from Thodupuzha in Idukki district. It is also called as Keezharkuth waterfalls. It falls at a height of 1500 m. It is surrounded by forest which is believed to be rich in various medicinal plants. Tourists come here to enjoy the beauty of the waterfalls and also become engaged in activities such as rock climbing, mountaineering, trekking etc. The Rainbow waterfalls, which cascades down a rock from a height of about 1500 m is a wonderful attraction of this spot. It can be seen throughout the year in full swing.

Madatharuvi Falls

Madatharuvi is a stream that joins the Pamba River in Ranni. It consists of a series of waterfalls and rapids that pass through pristine tropical forests. Untouched by industries the water is pure and fresh with a few species of fresh water fish.

Mankayam Falls

Close to Kerala's Capital City of Thiruvananthapuram is Mankayam, situated near Palode in Nedumangad Taluk. Rising from the hill ranges of

Chemunchi, the river Chittar, flowing down through the forests of Brymore creates a tributary in the form of Mankayam river. The Mankayam river in its course further down, produces two spectacular waterfalls. One is at Kalakayam, which is one of the biggest waterfalls in the area and the other at Kurissadi. With rich forest setting, the area in and around the waterfalls are overwhelmingly green. Shrubs to gigantic and lofty trees of evergreen and semi-evergreen grasslands are found here.

Meenmutty Falls

Meenmutty falls is located 29 kms from Kalpetta in Wayanad district, Kerala. It is a three-tiered waterfall with a height of 300 metres. Meenmutty falls, the largest and most spectacular waterfalls in the Wayanad district, is a 2 kms ride through the jungle from the main Ooty road. It is Kerala's second largest waterfalls and the one most unspoiled in its natural setting. Each of its three tiers requires a separate hike through a moist, deciduous forest. The path is quiet dangerous and tiresome, but the waterfalls are worth it.

Meenvallam Falls

Meenvallam waterfall is situated in Palakkad district and it originates from Tripunithura river. The waterfalls from a height of around 25 ft and the depth of the water is 20 ft. This waterfall has 10 steps and the 8 steps lies in dense forest. Each of these steps has a height that ranges from 5 to 40 m. All these steps within the forests are not accessible.

Mulamkuzhi Falls

Mulamkuzhi waterfall is situated in Mulamkuzhi village in Malayattoor in Ernakulam district. This waterfall originates from Mulamkuzhi river and flows through the hill ranges. This water is considered to be medicated and is clear and sweet. The village Mulamkuzhi lies at the juncture of the rivers Periyar and Perumthode. This is a tiny village nearly 15 kms from Malayattur. The crystal clear medicated water of the River Mulamkuzhi and the waterfalls of Venanbravady near Malayattur is an enchanting sight. There is also a confluence of the rivers Periyar and Perumthode. It is a picturesque location and a very famous tourist site.

Nyayamkad Falls

Nyayamkad waterfall is situated in Idukki district. It lies between Munnar and Rajamala. This beautiful waterfall flows from a hill at a height of 1600 m. This is an ideal place for trekking and as a picnic spot. Some of the nearby attractions include the Pallyvasal Hydel Power Project and tea estates. It is an important tourist destination and one can enjoy the beautiful picturesque from here. Nyayamkad Waterfalls is 10 kms from Munnar.

Palaruvi Falls

The Palaruvi waterfall is located in Kollam, Kerala. It is the 40th highest waterfall in India. It is a single drop, horsetail type waterfall with a total height of 91 metres (299 ft). The Palaruvi Falls is across the Kallada river. The waters of Palaruvi falls apparently have ayurvedic healing properties as the stream flows through some natural herbal groves further upstream.

New Initiatives in Tourism sector

- 'Wake up to Malabar'—Comprehensive plan to promote North Kerala
- 'Grand Kerala Shopping Festival'—A bold initiative to make Kerala, the shopping hub in the country- steady increase in participation – 13 lakhs coupons were distributed during the second edition compared to that of 6 lakhs in the 1st edition.
- 'Utsavam'—Year-long festival of traditional arts spread through out the state—23 venues – 805 programmes – with more than 1000 artists
- 'Dream Season' campaign launched to tackle seasonality
- Monsoon Tourism—offering many packages by travel and tourism industry
- 'Vazhiyoram' – a unique scheme for development of way side facilities through private participation.

Threats to the Tourism Industry in Kerala

- Global Warming and changing weather patterns
- Differing monsoon pattern
- Global Economic Recession
- Opening of Sri Lanka as a safe destination.

KNOW THE FACTS

☞ *Munnar is known as Kashmir of South India.*

☞ *Malampuzha gardens is known as the 'Vrindavan of Kerala'.*

☞ *Kerala's most important coastal tourism destination is Kovalam.*

☞ *Silent Valley National Park is in Palakkad district.*

☞ *Kuntipuzha flows through Silent Valley.*

☞ *Nehru Trophy Boat Race is known as the king among water festivals.*

☞ *Kerala Government proclaimed tourism as an industry in 1986.*
☞ *Wayanad district is most suited for adventure tourism in Kerala.*
☞ *Kerala was the first Indian state to accept tourism, as an industry.*

TEST YOUR SELF

1. In which district of Kerala Wellington Island is situated?
   A. Ernakulam
   B. Thiruvananthapuram
   C. Thrissur
   D. Kollam

2. Eravikulam Wildlife Sanctuary is situated in which district?
   A. Idukki   B. Alappuzha   C. Kozhikode   D. Kollam

3. Which among the following places is not included under Kerala 'Special Tourism Zone'?
   A. Kovalam
   B. Munnar
   C. Thiruvananthapuram
   D. Kumarakon

4. Temple of Sabarimala is dedicated to which of the following God?
   A. Lord Agasthya
   B. Lord Ayyappa
   C. Lord Sastha
   D. Lord Savathy

5. Kalady in Kochi is situated on the banks of which river?
   A. Cheranppuzha
   B. Periyar
   C. Mahi
   D. Chalakkudy

6. Which district of Kerala is also known as 'Gateway of Kerala'?
   A. Thrissur   B. Palakkad   C. Kochi   D. Wayanad

7. In which district of Kerala Vembanand lake is situated?
   A. Alappuzha   B. Kochi   C. Kottayam   D. Kollam

8. Which district of Kerala is known as 'Land of Forts and Beaches'?
   A. Kasargode   B. Kozhikode   C. Kannur   D. Kochi

9. Which among the following is the eco-tourism destination in Kerala?
   A. Aralam   B. Chinnar   C. Peppara   D. Thenmala

10. Which Bird Sanctuary owes much of its fame to Dr. Salim Ali?
    A. Thattekad Bird Sanctuary
    B. Kadalundi Bird Sanctuary
    C. Kumarakon Bird Sanctuary
    D. None of these

ANSWERS

1	2	3	4	5	6	7	8	9	10
A	A	C	B	B	B	C	C	D	A

❑❑❑

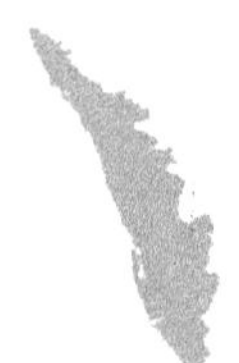

22

TRANSPORT & COMMUNICATION

Transport sector plays a pivotal role in the overall development of the country which enables social and culture and trade development between countries. Transport infrastructure consists of fixed installations necessary for transport, such as roads, railways, airways, waterways, canals, pipelines, and terminals. Terminals may be used both for interchange of passengers and cargo and for maintenance. Kerala holds a good transport system.

Roads in Kerala

An efficient road infrastructure is an essential requirement for sustained growth of the economy and to ensure cost effective movement of people and goods. The major road network of Kerala, though well connected, faces severe constraints due to the urban sprawl and the haphazard ribbon development all along the routes. The existing traffic levels at most stretches are excessive and beyond the road capacity. The traffic on roads is steadily increasing at a rate of 10 to 11 per cent a year. Capacity augmentation of existing roads is beset with problems relating to limited right of way and land acquisition.

The most important challenge in the road sector involves building all weather roads connecting each and every village. Even though Kerala is comparatively better placed than most other States as regards road length, the condition of many of these roads is very poor. Therefore, the main emphasis under road development in Kerala has been on improvement and up gradation of existing roads rather than construction of new roads. This requires institutional strengthening, adoption of standards applicable to the Indian Road Congress (IRC)/Ministry of Road Transport and Highways (MORTH) specifications, strict quality control and adoption of self-financing revenue models suited to the State. The investment need in the road sector is of high magnitudes that are beyond the resources available with the

Government. Therefore, there is an imperative need to motivate private and other non-governmental agencies/corporate sectors to participate in road construction and up gradation of selected highways.

Total road length in Kerala during 2015-16 is 205545.616 km. This includes classified and non classified roads as stipulated by Indian Road Congress. Road density in the State is 528.8 km/100 sq.km and it is far ahead of the national average of 387 km/100 sq.km

Agency-wise Distribution of State Roads in Kerala during 2015-16

Sl.No.	Name of Department	Length (Km)	Percentage
1.	Panchayats (LSGDs)	139380.410	67.81
2.	PWD (R&B)	31812.096	15.48
3.	Municipalities	18411.870	8.96
4.	Corporations	6644.000	3.23
5.	Forest	4575.770	2.23
6.	Irrigation	2611.900	1.27
7.	PWD (NH)	1781.570	0.87
8.	Others (Railways, KSEB)	328.000	0.16
	Total	**205545.616**	**100**

Source: Various Departments

National Highways

The National Highway Wing of State PWD is responsible for the upkeep and development of National Highways in the State mainly with the funds allocated by the GoI. There are Eleven National Highways together constituting 1781.57 km length in the State, of which 1,339 km (76.6 per cent) are under various development stages by the National Highways Authority of India (NHAI). Development of the remaining 408 km, which is under the control of the State PWD, is the responsibility of the State Government.

Research and Development in Road Sector

Research and Development activities play a crucial role in meeting the challenges of modernizing road system, technology upgradation, road safety, traffic control and finding cost effective solution to infrastructure problems in general. NATPAC, KHRI and DRIQ Board are the agencies engaged in Research and Development of the Road Sector.

National Transportation Planning and Research Centre (NATPAC)

The broad area of activities of NATPAC includes Rural/Regional Transportation, Transportation Planning and Road Safety, Highway Engineering, Traffic Engineering and Management, Project Planning, Training and Extension Programmes.

Kerala Highway Research Institute (KHRI)

KHRI, Kariavattom, Thiruvananthapuram is the only Research Institute under Kerala PWD. The major objectives and functions of the Institutes are:

- to impart quality control in PWD by carrying out laboratory and field tests of all types of building materials;
- undertake applied research works (R&D works)
- to function as a regular training institute

Design, Research, Investigation and Quality Control Board (DRIQ Board)

Designing and Construction of Bridges, Research and Project Preparation, Quality Control and Computerisation are the major activities of DRIQ Board. The major achievements during 2010-11 are given below.

- The wing had completed 41 structural design and 20 nos of partially completed work which cost about ₹210 crores and is expected to complete structural design of 80 works for an amount of ₹400 crores.
- Structural design of 50 bridges (Total cost ₹300 crores) were completed during the review year.
- DPR preparation of widening of 6/4 lane from Karamana to Kaliyikkavila of NH 47-Phase I from Karamana to Vazhimukku alignment plan submitted and approved.
- The preliminary report along with alignment plans of Vizhinjam International Container Terminal 2 KM road connectivity forwarded to VISI.

Kerala State Transport Project (KSTP)

Kerala State Transport Project (KSTP) is a World Bank assisted project and Bank has approved a cost of ₹ 2,403 crore (US$ 445 ml). The loan agreement with Bank was signed on June 19, 2013 and the effective date is September 2013. The loan closure date is April 2019. The disbursement ratio is 56 per cent by World Bank and 44 per cent by GoK for the eligible items (except land acquisition and operation cost). The State Government had accorded sanction for the project for an amount of ₹ 2,500 crore.

The KSTP is implementing the Kerala State Transport Project -Phase II. The objective of the project is to improve the riding quality in 363 km road section with enhanced road safety provisions. The project has three components—(1) Upgradation of 363 km of road, (2) Road Safety Management and (3) Institutional Strengthening.

Railways in Kerala

Railways are essentially the cause for Industrial upsurge in the nation and it still remained the largest employment provider for the huge population of the country. The total length of track used by Indian Railways is about 1,13,994 Kms and the total route length is 67,312 kms. The State total Railway route has a length of 1588 Kms and covers 13 Railway routes. The Railway Divisions at Thiruvananthapuram, Palakkad and Madurai jointly carry out Railway Operations in Kerala.

Kochi Metro

Kochi Metro Rail Project (KMRP) is the flagship project of the Government of Kerala designed to address the transportation woes of Kochi City. The project is implemented through the Kochi Metro Rail Ltd (KMRL) which is a Special Purpose Vehicle jointly owned by the Government of Kerala and Government of India with equity participation. The Union Government gave sanction for the project in July 2012 at a total cost of ₹ 5,181.79 crore. KMRL has signed an agreement with GoI and Delhi Metro Rail Corporation Ltd (DMRC) for executing the project and as per the tripartite agreement signed between Govt. of India, Govt. of Kerala and KMRL, the project is expected to be completed by June 2017.

Rail Coach Factory, Palakkad

A Rail Coach Factory would be set up at Palakkad in the state of Kerala. RITES has conducted a detailed study on this project.

Air Transport

Kerala has three Air Ports at Thiruvananthapuram, Kochi and Kozhicode handling both International and Domestic flights. Thiruvananthapuram and Kozhicode Air Ports are owned by Government of India and Kochi Air Port is owned by Cochin International Air Port Ltd (CIAL), a company set up by Government of Kerala with Public Private Participation.

Kannur Air port

The State's prestigious greenfield airport project named 'Kannur International Airport' will be coming up close to Mattannur in Kannur district of Kerala State. It is only 20 kms away from Kannur city, and 2 kms from Mattannur on Kannur – Mattannur – Mysore road. The Airport will have a runway length of 3400 metres. The orientation of the runway is 07/25, which permits obstacle free approach. The airport is expected to have an annual traffic of more than 1 million international passengers and above 0.3 million domestic passengers as per 2009-2010 estimate.

Cargo Traffic

Kerala State Industrial Enterprises Ltd, a PSU under the industries department is the management of the two Air Cargo Complexes at Thiruvananthapuram and Calicut Airport. The Company is the custodian of these two Air Cargo Complexes as appointed by the respective commissioners of customs. KSIE provides necessary infrastructural facilities for the promotion of exports through these Air Cargo Complexes.

Water Transport

The Kerala state lies in the south west corner of the Indian peninsula. It has a coastal length of 585 kms and the state has an average width of about 60 kms with one major port at Cochin and 17 non major ports. The non major ports are under the administration of Government of Kerala. Government of Kerala intends to provide a boost to coastal shipping with the development of ports. Kerala state has got the Ghats in the east and the Arabian Sea on the west. The forest area in the east and coastal area in the west are environmentally very sensitive areas. The midland and coastal lowland are thickly populated. The physical and geographical features of Kerala and shortage of land causes main hardships for port development and industrialization in Kerala. The geographical location of Kerala is very close to international shipping route. There are seventeen minor ports in Kerala, out of which three are considered as intermediate ports based on berthing, cargo handling and storage facilities available in them. These have contributed much to the development of industry, trade, commerce and agriculture in the country.

Presently cargo operations take place only in three ports – *i.e.* in Vizhinjam, Beypore and Azhikkal ports. Vizhinjam handles about 1000 tonnes. Beypore 50,000 tonnes and Azhikkal about 5000 tonnes annually. The remaining minor ports in Kerala are now defunct due to various reasons. As stated above the intermediate and minor ports are to be developed and modernized to meet the expected increase in traffic and also to tap the potential available. These developmental activities have to be taken up and completed in the Eleventh Plan.

Cochin Port

Cochin Port is the only major port in Kerala. It spreads over 827 hectares. It has a water frontage of 7.5 Kms. The port has connectivity to hinterland through NH 47, NH 17 and NH 49. Rail links to the Konkan and Southern Railway also give key rail access to its hinterland. An inland waterway connecting Kollam and Kottappuram on either side is being developed by the Inland Waterways Authority of India.

Vallarpadam International Container Transshipment Terminal

The Prime Minister of India laid the foundation stone for Vallarpadam International Container Transshipment Terminal in 1995. Completion of this prestigious project would make the Cochin port a major hub port in the Indian Ocean region. At present containers from the Indian sub continent are being transshipped to Colombo. With the development of Vallarpadam Mother Vessels will come to Kochi and consolidate and carry the containers from other ports of India to the outside world.

Vizhinjam Deep Water International Container Transshipment Terminal

Vizhinjam International Deep Water multipurpose Seaport is a flagship project of Government of Kerala being developed on a landlord port model. Vizhinjam Intermational Deep Water multipurpose Seaport Limited (VISL) is a special purpose government company (fully owned by government of Kerala) that would act as a implementing agency for the development of a Greenfield port.

Vizhinjam is a natural port, which is located close to the international ship route. So it is expected that at least 50% of the (nearly 20,000) ships that pass through the Suez canal (per annum) will anchor at Vizhinjam Port. It is expected that with the functioning of Vizhinjam port in its full swing, the ports of Colombo, Singapore and Dubai might face serious competition from India. This will boost the trade and commercial activities not only in Kerala but also to entire India. It is estimated that India could save more than a 100 million U.S. dollars per year in terms of foreign exchange.

Inland Water Transport

The State of Kerala, with numerous backwaters, is one of the State in India, where waterways are successfully used for commercial Inland Water Transport. The transportation is mainly done with country craft and passenger vessels. There are 41 navigable rivers in Kerala. The total length of the Inland Waterways in the State is 1687 Kms.

The Government agencies engaged in the development of Inland Water Transport in the State are Coastal Shipping and Inland Navigation Department (CSIND), State Water Transport Department (SWTD) and Kerala Shipping and Inland Navigation Corporation Ltd. (KSINC).

State Water Transport Department

State Water Transport Department formed during 1968 with the objectives to provide transport facilities to the people residing in the water logged areas at cheaper rates and Cargo transportation. Construction of roads, bridges and speedy transportation-roadways shortened the operation of the Department to passenger transport only-in the backwaters and ferries. But in the world of speed and hurry the advantage of this pollution free, accident free and cheaper transport system beckons least preferences.

Kerala Shipping and Inland Navigation Corporation Ltd.

The Corporation was formed in 1989 by the statutory amalgamation of Kerala Inland Navigation Corporation Ltd. (KINCO) and Kerala Shipping Corporation Limited (KSC) the two Government of Kerala Companies. The main objective of the company is to develop passenger and cargo transportation through Inland Waterways of Kerala, docking and repair of marine vessels, construction of boats, conducting navigation training programmes, conducting tourist cruises, providing navigational aids and maintenance in National Waterway-III.

Postal Network

Kerala Postal circle includes the entire State of Kerala, the Union Territory of Lakshadweep and Mahe under the Union Territory of Puducherry. Kerala is the only postal circle where every village has at least one post office. As on September 30, 2016, there are 5,066 post offices in the circle, of which 1,457 are Departmental post offices and 3, 558 Extra Departmental post offices. On an average each post office in the State serves an area of 7.69 sq.km and a population of 6,609 as against the national average of 21.21 sq.km and a population of 7,175 people. In total, 83 per cent of the post offices are located in rural areas.

Kerala State Information Technology Mission (KSITM)

Kerala State IT Mission is a society registered under the Travancore Cochin Literary Scientific & Charitable Societies Registration Act. It is an autonomous nodal IT implementation agency of the Department of Information Technology, Government of Kerala which provides managerial and technical support to various initiatives of the Department.

The major objectives of KSITM are interfacing between the Government and the industry, interacting with potential investors, strengthening the IT/ITeS industry base, holding promotional campaigns in the State, ICT dissemination to bridge the digital divide, e-governance, developing human resources for IT and ITeS and advising the Government on policy matters. As a result of these proactive policies and projects, Kerala achieved major progress in the transformational journey towards "Digital State".

KNOW THE FACTS

☞ *The name "Anchal" was given to the early postal system of Kerala by Col. Munro.*

☞ *Indian Postal Department issued stamp bearing the figure of Sri Narayana Guru in on August 21, 1967.*

☞ *First Post Office in Travancore was started in 1857 in Alappuzha during the period of Uthram Thirunal Marthanda Varma.*

☞ *Telegraph System was started in Travancoree in 1863.*

☞ *Malaylam Telegraph was started in 1994.*

☞ *Kerala Postal Circle came into existence in 1961.*

☞ *Telephone service was started in Thiruvananthapuram in 1931.*

☞ *Malayalam Radio Broadcasting was started for the first time from Chennai in 1939.*

☞ *Sir. C.P. Ramaswami Ayyer took initiative to start Radio Broadcasting in Travancore.*

☞ *Television Broadcasting was started for the first time in Kerala by Keltron (1982).*

☞ *Doordarshan started broadcasting in Kerala in November 1982 Malayalam programmes began to be broadcasted from Thiruvananthapuram on January 1, 1985.*

☞ *First satellite television channel in Malayalam is Asianet. It is also the first private television channel in Kerala. It began in 1992.*

☞ *First Speed Post Centre in Kerala was started in Ernakulam (November 1986).*

☞ *Kerala is the first Indian state to have telephone facilities in all Panchayats.*

TEST YOUR SELF

1. National Waterway in Kerala connects Kottapuram with
   A. Kannur
   B. Kozhikode
   C. Kasargode
   D. Kollam

2. During which year Kerala State Transport Project was launched in the state?
   A. 2000
   B. 2001
   C. 2002
   D. 2003

3. Number of National Highways in Kerala are
   A. 8
   B. 11
   C. 10
   D. 9

4. The longest distance covering train 'The Kerala Express' connects Thiruvananthapuram to which Metropolitan city in India?
   A. New Delhi
   B. Mumbai
   C. Kolkata
   D. Hyderabad

5. NH-47 connects Valayar to ....
   A. Edappaly
   B. Kaliyikkavia
   C. Kundannur
   D. Vallarpadam

6. Kerala Highway Research Institute is located at ....
A. Thiruvananthapuram (Kariavattom)
B. Wayanad
C. Thrissur
D. Kannur

7. The High Speed Rail Corridor in Kerala will connect Thiruvananthapuram to ....
A. Wayanad
B. Kannur
C. Idukki
D. Kasargode

8. Kerala has a coastal length of ....
A. 558 kms
B. 570 kms
C. 585 kms
D. 620 kms

9. Which among the following is the major port in Kerala?
A. Cochin
B. Vizhinjam
C. Beypore
D. Azhikkal

10. Kerala Shipping and Inland Navigation Corporation Ltd. was formed in ....
A. 1970
B. 1972
C. 1989
D. 1983

ANSWERS

1	2	3	4	5	6	7	8	9	10
D	C	B	A	B	A	D	C	A	C

23

IMPORTANT PERSONALITIES

Justice K.G. Balakrishnan

He was the Chief Justice of the Supreme Court from 2007-2010. He was the 37th Chief Justice of India. He was the first Chief Justice of India belonging to a scheduled caste. He was also the Chairman of National Human Rights Commission.

Asan, Kumaran

He belongs to the famous "trio" in the Malayalam poetry. The others being Ulloor, and Vallathol. He was a renowned social worker. He died in a boat capsize.

Shivsankar Menon

He is a senior Indian foreign service official, had been appointed as the Foreign Secretary of India. Mr. Menon has held important posts of High Commissioner to Pakistan, High Commissioner to Sri Lanka, Ambassador to Israel and Ambassador to China.

M. Krishnan Nair

Eminent oncologist, Dr. Krishnan Nair was appointed member of the World Health Organisation's (WHO) Cancer Control Advisory Committee.

Vijay Nambiar

Vijay Nambiar, a senior Indian diplomat and former envoy to the United Nations, who was a member of U.N. Secretary General Kofi Annan's team of top advisors.

Capt. Krishnan Nair

Leela Group Chairman Capt. Krishnan Nair was elected by the United Nations as the South Asia Chairman of the World Committee on Tourism Ethics (WCTE). The Leela group headed by Mr. Nair has contributed a lot to the Tourism industry in India.

Justice K. Narayana Kurup
He was nominated by the New York based World Trade Centre's Association as its "Global Ambassador of Peace". He was the former acting Chief Justice of the Madras High Court.

Joseph Edamaruk
He was a well known rationalist and former president of Indian Rationalist Association. He died in 2006. He had worked very hard to eradicate superstitions and other irrational beliefs in the society.

Appukuttan
An Indian-American pioneer in digital education has won the 2006 Champions Digital Literacy Inspiration Award for his contribution globally to bridging the digital divide.

Prof. Ayyappa Panicker
Poet, critic and teacher who made a bold and meaningful intervention in the literary, cultural and intellectual realms in India. Almost all the noted literary related awards and honours had come his way. Padmashree in 2004, Saraswathi Samman in 2006 etc.

Sardar K.M. Panikkar
Eminent historian, writer and diplomat. He was one of the member in the first Indian team to the United Nations. He was Ambassador to China, Egypt and France. He was the first president of the Kerala Sahitya Academy.

E.V. Krishna Pillai
Prominent Satirist, playwright, actor, lawyer; a versatile genius. He was editor to a Malayalam daily and Manorama cartoon Weekly. His works evoked laughter and thoughts to ponder. Seetha Lakshmi, Chiriyum Chinthayum, Kavitha Case were some of his works.

Chithira Tirunal Balarama Varma
He was the last of the Maharajas of Travancore. He did a lot for the uplift of the people of the state. Sree Moolam Assembly, Sri Chitra State Council, was formed in his tenure. He was the one who proclaimed the famous Temple Entry proclamation in 1935. He became Raj Pramukh in 1943, when Thiru-Kochi State was formed.

Sree Narayana Guru
He was a popular social reformer. He founded the Sree Narayana Dharma Paripalana Yogam in 1903. Tagore, Gandhiji were some of the dignitaries who visited him. "One caste, one religion, one God" was his motto. He is considered as the father of modern renaissance in Kerala.

Vallathol

He was one of the modern poet trios. He was an eminent writer, poet and journalist. He edited Keralodayam and Atmaposhini. Received Padma Bhushan in 1955. He was poet laureate of Kerala.

O.N.V. Kurup

Poet, lyricist and teacher. He was the Chairman to Kerala Kalamandalam. He had carved himself a place in the contemporary Malayalam literature. He had won Kerala Sahitya Academie, Soviet Land Nehru Awards, Vayalar Award etc. Mattuvin Chattangale, Aganisalabhangal, Bhumikku oru Charama Geetham were some of his works. He died in 2016.

V.S. Achuthanandan

Former Chief Minister of Kerala (2006-2011). He had proved himself as an integral part of the political field in Kerala. As a leader par excellence, he always stood for social issues and every major events in the state.

O.V. Vijayan

Ottupulakkal Velukutty Vijayan was a novelist, short story writer, journalist and a popular cartoonist. The Legend of Khazak, The Saga of Dharmapuri, Gurusagaram were some of his works. Every literary awards came to him, some of them were Ezhuthachan Puraskaram, Vayalar Award, Mathrubhumi, Sahitya Puraskaram etc.

V.T. Induchoodan

Real name is K.K. Neelakantan. He was a renowned ornithologist and writer. He was the founder president of the Kerala Natural History Society. He proved his eminency in positions as vice president of Nature Protection Committee, State Committee member to World Wild Life Fund for Nature, State Wild Life Protection Board etc.

A.K. Antony

Former Defence Minister of India, was also a former Chief Minister to the State of Kerala, and was Cabinet Minister once. He is a prominent leader of the Indian National Congress. As Chief Minister, he introduced "Unemployment allowance", festival allowance for the employees and implemented prohibition of Liquor in the state.

M.T. Vasudevan Nair

Novelist, short story writer, director, and editor. He was one of the leaders of renaissance in the short story genre in Malayalam. He scripted and directed five Malayalam films. Winner of the Jnanpith 1995. Vallathol Award 2005, and won national awards for Screenplay. Olavum Theeravum,

Kuttyedathi, Panchagni were some of his screenplays and Vanaprastham, Randamoozham, Manju were some of his works.

G. Sankarakuruppu

He was the first Malayali to win the Jnanpith Award 1965. He was a great poet, teacher, translator and a member of Rajyasabha. Odakkuzhal Award is instituted in his name. In varied genre of literature he had written about 50 books.

Joseph Mundasseri

Popular writer, journalist, educationist and statesman. He was the minister of education in the first Kerala Ministry. He was the first vice chancellor to the Cochin University founded in 1972. He was editor to the monthlies Kairali and Navajeevan.

E.M.S. Namboothiripad

First Chief Minister of the State of Kerala. He was one of the founding leaders of the communist party of India. Wrote under the pen-name P.S. Surendran.

C. Achutha Menon

Former Chief Minister of Kerala. He was the first CM to complete the tenure of 5 years continuously (1969-70, 1970-77). He implemented Land Reform Act and Dias-Non.

Ayyenkali

A prominent leader of the oppressed classes. Born in 1863, he successfully organised educational and other rights for people of the lowest strata of society.

Ayyappan (Sahodaran Ayyappan)

A noted leader of the oppressed classes. He started the paper Sahodaran in 1921 and hence the name Sahodaran Ayyappan. He was a noted member of the ministries of Kochi from 1946 onwards till 1949. Died in 1968. The main arterial road from East into Kochi is today named after him.

Aromal Chekavar

Legendary figure of 12th century AD. Hero in many Vadakkan Pattu or local chronicles. Reputedly man of great chivalry and bravery. His memory is revered in many parts of Kerala to this day.

Ezhuthachan

Ezhuthachan is considered as the 'Father of Modern Malayalam'. He has written a number of books. His 'Adhyatma Ramayanam' and 'Mahabharatham, are the most important. These are independent translations from Sanskrit originals. Ezhuthachan is supposed to have lived some 550 years ago. He was born at Thunchan Parampu in Thrikkandiyoor in Malappuram district. His exact name is not known.

Gubernador, Paremackel

A priest from a small parish of Ramapuram, he undertook a journey to Rome in 1778. Thereafter he wrote the first ever Travelogue in Malayalam.

Kunjali Marakkar

Kunjali Marakkar was the commander of the navy of the Zamorin of Calicut. The Portuguese came to India in 1498. They first established trade in Calicut. Even before this the Arabs were carrying on trade with Calicut. When the Portuguese attacked on Arab ship coming to Calicut the Zamorin was angry with them. The Zamorin decided to attack the Portuguese. Kunjali fought and defeated them in several battles. Kunjali was a great patriot.

Kelappan

A Gandhian who fought ceaselessly against all form of subjugation and oppression. Closely identified with the Vaikom Satyagraha (temple entry for all castes).

Kunjan Nambiar

A great Malayalam poet in the court of Marthanda Varma. Ottan Thullal is a very popular art form of Kerala. Kunjan Nambiar is the founder of this art form. Nambiar was a learned man and a born poet. He was born at Killikkurrisimangalam near the Lakkidi railway station in Malabar. Later on he went to Ambalapuzha and lived in the court of the Raja there. It was here that Nambiar wrote his first Thullal Kadha. He used to play 'Mizhavu' for Chkkyar Koothu in the temple.

Marthanda Varma

The founder of the unified state of Thiruvithamkur in the 18th century. He conquered all the medium sized principalities upto Kochi and laid the foundations of a modern state. He employed people with known capabilities in the military, administration and education.

Panampilly Govinda Menon

An eminent political figure of Kochi. He was the Chief Minister of Kochi in 1947 and 1955. He was also member of the Union Cabinet.

Pazhassi Raja

The Pazhassi Raja led an insurrection against British rule in Malabar in 1797. The British took casualities in the beginning, but asserted themselves as the campaign wore on. By 1804 Pazhassi's revolt was all but suppressed. In 1805 he was killed in the forests of Wayanad. He is to this day revered as one of the greatest patriots of Kerala.

Sir C. P. Ramaswamy Iyengar

Powerful Dewan of Thiruvithamkur state at Independence. It must be said that Sir CP (as he was popularly known) nursed ambitions of making Thiruvithamkur an independent country. However, a violent personal attack on him demoralised him and he went to self exile.

Sakthan Thampuran

Sakthan Thampuran was the Raja of Cochin some 200 years ago. He become king when he was very young. He was a brave and able ruler. His real name was Rama Varma. He punished criminals and wrong doers mercilessly. Such people were afraid of him. He meted out justice without any mercy. So people called him Sakthan Thampuran.

Sree Sankara

Sree Sankara was one of the most illustrious son of Kerala. He was born in a poor Brahmin family at Kalady. His father was Sivaguru and mother Arya Devi. Sankara lost his father when he was very young. So he was brought up by his mother. When he was a boy, Sankara wanted to become a Sanyasin. But his mother would not allow him. One day while bathing in the Periyar a crocodile caught hold of his leg and began dragging him into the deep waters. His mother began to cry. Sankara said that the crocodile would let him go if he was allowed to become Sanyasin. So his mother gave him permission. So Sankara left home and travelled all over India. Even when a boy he had learned all the 'Sastras'. He accepted Govindacharya as his spiritual Guru. He became the greatest scholar of his time. He originated the 'Adwaidasiddhantha'. He had large number of disciples. He set up monasteries at Badrinath, Dwaraka and Sringeri. He died at the age of 32.

Swathi Thirunal

Swathi Thirunal was the king of Travancore from 1829 to 1848. He was heir to the throne even in his mother's womb. So he was known as 'Garbasreeman'. His mother ruled the country till he attained maturity. He learned many languages and become a scholar. He learned music and was a good musician. He was also a great composer of music. He was a great lover of arts and patronised artists. He was also a great administrator. It was he who began English Education in Travancore. It was during his time that law courts were first established in Travancore. The reign of Swathi Thirunal is often called the 'Golden age of Kerala Music'.

Thacholi Othenan

Another legendary warrior from North Kerala at the end of the 16th century. Highly stylised songs and stories of his valour and chivalry abound. He was born in the family of 'Manikothy' in Thacholi near Badakara. He was a brave warrior, merciless to enemies, but a friend of the helpless. Even the Zamorin of Calicut respected him. He defeated Mathiloor Gurukkal and killed him. But one of the Gurukkal's disciple cheated and killed Othenan. His real name was Udayanakurup. He died at the young age of 32. He is praised about in Vadakkanpattu.

Unniarcha

Legendary warrior figure , sister of Aromal Chekavar, mother of Aromalunny. The songs and chronicles have to this day kept the legend alive. She was born in the 'Puthooram Veedu' family. The famous warriors 'Aromal Chevakar' and 'Unnikannan' were her brothers. Like her brothers Unniyarcha was also trained in the arts of war. She is praised in Vadakkanpattu. She is considered as a heroine and symbol of female ability.

Velu Thampi Dalawa

Velu Thampi led what is perhaps the most courageous rebellion against the British which started as a direct fall out of the British Resident Macauly's humiliating interference in the affairs of the Thiruvithamkur. The revolt started in 1808. The Kundara Proclamation of 1809 was an open call to arms and thousands flocked to his banner. Initially, he was helped in his cause by the Dewan of Kochi, Paliath Achan, but in the later stages he fought a lonely campaign against the British. He was no match for the military might of the British Army and finally fled the state and reportedly committed suicide in March 1809. Most of Velu Thampi's followers were either hanged or imprisoned after the termination of hostilities. There would not be any insurrection on this scale for the rest of the British presence in Kerala.

Lakshmi Sehgal

She was a Captain of Rani of Jhansi Regiment under the command of the INA.

Amritanandamayi

A well-known spiritualist from Kerala whose charisma has won followers throughout the world.

Swamy Atmananda

Advaita philosopher. He was a master of the house. He retired as police chief. There were a number of disciples from all over the world.

Arundhati Roy

Writer awarded by the Booker Prize in 1997 for The God of Small Things. Born in Kerala.

Balamani Amma

Poet, won one of the highest literary awards in India, the Saraswathi Samman.

Kamala Das

English poet and feminist, also wrote in Malayalam under the pen-name Madhavikkutty. The first Indian woman to write openly about sexuality of woman. Adopted Islam and the name Kamala Suraiyya in 1999. Won Asian Poetry Prize, 1964, Kent Award, 1965.

Kesari Balakrishna Pillai

Social thinker, literary critic who influenced a generation of writers and other intellectuals in Kerala during the first half of the 20th century. The name of one of his books "Navalokam" (New World) is the symbolic representative of his intellectual contribution.

Shashi Tharoor

Novelist, Commonwealth Writers Prize, 1991, Assistant Secretary-General (Communication and Public Information) of the United Nations.

Anju George

The only Indian to win a medal at the World Athletics Championships.

I M Vijayan

Football player who played for the national team and football clubs leading Indian as Mohan Bagan. He was a forward and scored many goals.

PT Usha

One of the greatest athletes of India, which just missed a bronze medal in 0.01 seconds in the event of 400 metres hurdles at the 1984 Olympics in Los Angeles.

Mammootty

One of the best actors of India. Winner of National Best Actor 3 times.

Mohanlal

Considered one of the best actors in India and winner of national award for best actor in 1992 (Bharatham) and 2000 (Vaanaprastham).

KJ Yesudas

Great classical musician and singer.

Adoor Gopalakrishnan

Internationally recognised instructor. Films include Elipathayam (Mousetrap) and Mathilukal (walls).

G. Aravindan

Director and noted designer. Films include Kanchana Seeta, Kummatty (bogey) and Chidambaram. His cartoon series "Lokavum Cheriya Manushyarum" was very popular.

Padma Lakshmi

Padma Lakshmi is a New York-based American-Indian model, actress and award-winning cookbook author.

Padma Kutty

Padma Kutty is a Carnatic music teacher in southern California, and many people under his direction, performed their Arangetram (first performance by an interpreter for an invited audience) with flying colours.

Shobana

Actress and dancer of Bharatanatyam. Two times national award winner.

G. Madhavan Nair

Former chairman of ISRO. He is a native of Kanyakumari district of Tamil Nadu.

Prof. MGK Menon

Known cosmic ray physicist, was director of the Tata Institute of Fundamental Research. Later, the EU ministers for Science and Technology.

Dr. MS Swaminathan

A well-known agricultural scientist, was the president, Indian Council of Agricultural Research.

Mrinalini Sarabhai

Famous dancer. She was the wife of the late Indian physicist, Dr. Vikram Sarabhai, Mallika Sarabhai's mother and sister of Captain Lakshmi.

VP Menon

The right hand of Sardar Patel in the unification of princely states during the formation of the Indian Union.

KNOW THE FACTS

☞ *Justice K.G. Balakrishnan is the first Chief Justice of India belonging to a scheduled caste.*

☞ *Sardar K.M. Panikkar was the first president of the Kerala Sahitya Academy and one of the member in the first Indian team to the United Nations.*

☞ *Chithira Tirunal Balarama Varma was the last of the Maharajas of Travancore and the one who proclaimed the famous Temple Entry proclamation in 1935.*

☞ *Sree Narayana Guru founded the Sree Narayana Dharma Paripalana Yogam in 1903 and is considered as the father of modern renaissance in Kerala.*

☞ *V.T. Induchoodan was a renowned ornithologist and writer and was the founder president of the Kerala Natural History Society.*

☞ *G. Sankarakuruppu was the first Malayali to win the Jnanpith Award 1965.*

☞ *Joseph Mundasseri was the minister of education in the first Kerala Ministry. He was the first☞Vice chancellor to the Cochin University founded in 1972.*

☞ *E.M.S. Namboothiripad was the First Chief Minister of the State of Kerala.*

☞ *C. Achutha Menon was the first CM to complete the tenure of 5 years continuously (1969-70, 1970-77).*

☞ *Ezhuthachan is considered as the 'Father of Modern Malayalam'.*

☞ *Gubernador, Paremackel wrote the first ever Travelogue in Malayalam.*

☞ *Marthanda Varma was the founder of the unified state of Thiruvithamkur in the 18th century.*

☞ *Panampilly Govinda Menon was the Chief Minister of Kochi in 1947 and 1955.*

☞ *Pazhassi Raja was revered as one of the greatest patriots of Kerala who led an insurrection against British rule in Malabar in 1797.*

☞ *Sree Sankara originated the 'Adwaidasiddhantha' and set up monasteries at Badrinath, Dwaraka and Sringeri.*

☞ *Swathi Thirunal was the king of Travancore from 1829 to 1848 and began English Education in Travancore. The reign of Swathi Thirunal is often called the 'Golden age of Kerala Music'.*

☞ *Lakshmi Sehgal was a Captain of Rani of Jhansi Regiment under the command of the INA.*

☞ *Amritanandamayi is a well-known spiritualist from Kerala whose charisma has won followers throughout the world.*

TEST YOUR SELF

1. Which among the following is an eminent oncologist, who appointed member of the World Health Organisation's Cancer Control Advisory Committee?
   A. Vijay Nambiar
   B. Shivsankar Menon
   C. M. Krishnan Nair
   D. K. Narayan Kurup

2. Who among the following was an eminent historian, writer and diplomat?
   A. K. M. Panikkar
   B. E. V. Krishna Pillai
   C. O. V. Vijayan
   D. M. T. Vasudevan Nair

3. Who founded the Sree Narayama Dharma Paripalana Yogam?
   A. Vallathol
   B. Sree Narayana Guru
   C. Appukuttam
   D. V.S. Achuthanandan

4. The Legand of Khazak is a famous cartoon work of ....
   A. V.T. Induchoodan
   B. O.V. Vijayan
   C. M.T. Vasudevan Nair
   D. G. Sankarakaruppu

5. Name the great poet and a member of Rajyasabha, who won the Jnanpith Award 1965.
   A. G. Sankarakuruppu
   B. O.V. Vijyam
   C. Joseph Mundasseri
   D. None of these

6. Who is the first chief minister of Kerala to complete the tenure of 5 years?
A. A.K. Antony
B. C. Achutha Menon
C. V.S. Achuthanandan
D. None of these

7. Who among the following is considered as the Father of Modern Malayalam?
A. Ezhuttachan
B. Kunjali Marakkar
C. Kelappan
D. Kunjan Nambiar

8. The Pazhassi Raja led an insurrection against British rule in ....
A. Cochin
B. Malabar
C. Thrissur
D. Wayanad

9. Kalappan was associated with ....
A. Salt Satyagraha
B. Vaikom Satyagraha
C. Malabar Revolt
D. None of these

10. Name the novelist who is also the winner of Commonwealth Writers Prize.
A. Shashi Tharoor
B. Balakrishna Pillai
C. Anju George
D. Unniarcha

ANSWERS

1	2	3	4	5	6	7	8	9	10
C	A	B	B	A	B	A	B	B	A

❑❑❑

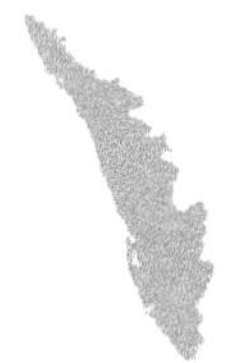

24

ADMINISTRATION & GOVERNANCE

According to the Constitution of India, Kerala has a parliamentary system of representative democracy for its governance; universal suffrage is granted to state residents. The government structure is organised into the three branches:

KERALA LEGISLATURE

The unicameral legislature, the Kerala Legislative Assembly, comprises elected members and special office bearers; the Speaker and Deputy Speaker elected by the members from among themselves. Assembly meetings are presided over by the Speaker and in the Speaker's absence, by the Deputy Speaker. The state has 140 assembly constituencies. The state elects 20 and nine members for representation in the Lok Sabha and the Rajya Sabha respectively.

A glimpse into the evolution of the Legislative Assembly of Kerala indicates different phases of development, matching the social, political and economic changes over the years. The evolutionary cycle ranges from the parallel but heterogeneous courses of development in the erstwhile Princely States of Travancore and Cochin and British Malabar, to the uniform progress in the integrated State of Kerala.

The Princely States of Travancore and Cochin were unified and the Part B State of Travancore -Cochin was formed on July 1, 1949. The State of Travancore -Cochin and the Malabar district of the State of Madras, excluding certain areas constituted the State of Kerala as per the States reorganization on 1st November 1956.

The starting point of the formation of a legislative body in Travancore, can be traced to January 1888 when the Dewan T. Rama Rao proposed to the Maharaja, the organisation of a Legislative Council so that "the Dewan would gain the benefit of discussing with and taking the opinion of responsible officers associated with him in matters of legislation, one of the most important functions of Government". This proposal was readily approved by Sri Mulam Thirunal Maharaja and a regulation was passed on 30th March, 1888, creating a Legislative Council, of three year tenure, and composed of 8 members of whom 6 were to be officials and 2 non-officials nominated by the Maharaja. The Dewan was to preside over the meetings.

In order to widen the opportunities for increased association of the people with administration, on the 1st of October 1904, one more representative body, namely the Sri Mulam Popular Assembly of Travancore was formed. This Assembly "of the representatives of the landholders and merchants", aimed at giving "the people an opportunity of bringing to the notice of Government their requirements, wishes or grievances on the one hand, and on the other, to make the policy and measures of Government better known to the people so that all possible grounds of misconception may be removed". The Members were to be selected by the Division Peishcars (the District Heads). Two representatives were to be chosen for each taluk, from among the landholders who pay on their own account an annual land revenue of not less than Rs. 100, and landholders or traders whose net annual income was Rs. 6000 or above. On October 22, 1904, the Victoria Jubilee Town Hall of Trivandrum became the venue of the first Meeting of the Sri Mulam Popular Assembly.

A novel mark appeared on May 1, 1905, when a regulation was issued to grant to the people the privilege of electing members to the Assembly. Of the 100 members, 77 were to be elected and 23 nominated, for a tenure of 1 year. The right to vote was given to persons who paid on their account an annual land revenue of not less than Rs. 50 or whose net income was not less than Rs. 2000 and to Graduates of a recognized University, with not less than 10 years standing and having their residence in the taluk. There were General as well as Special Constituencies.

In 1907, the Assembly was conferred the right to select 4 members to the Legislative Council. The year also saw the formation of a legislative committee to look into the system of inheritance and Marumakkathayam. The Sixth to the Eleventh Councils were held during the period from 1904 to 1919. In 1919, a major structural shift occurred by a regulation aimed at broad basing the administration and the powers of the Council. The strength of the Legislative Council was raised to a maximum of 25, with a bare official majority. Provision was made for election to 8 out of the 11 non-official seats. Besides, the members were given the rights to discuss the annual budget and to ask interpellations.

A parallel development emerged in Cochin, where the Cochin Legislative Council Regulation Act, 1923 provided for a Legislative Council.

The First Council (1925-28), with 45 members (30 elected and 15 nominated), was constituted in April 1925, under the Presidentship of Sri T. S. Narayana Aiyar. The franchise was based on property and allied qualifications. There were General and Special Constituencies. The Council was allowed to introduce Bills, ask questions, move resolutions and discuss and vote on Budget Demands.

Malabar, which was a district of Madras Province under the British rule, had representatives in Madras Legislative Assembly from 1920's.

On October 28, 1932, a momentous structural addition was made by the Travancore Legislative Regulation. Bicameralism took a new shape, with the creation of a Lower House, the Sri Mulam Assembly, the Upper House, the Sri Chitra State Council. The earlier bodies were abolished. In the new Assembly, there were to be 72 members, of whom 62 were to be non-officials. Of the 72 members, 43 seats were reserved for minority communities. The Sri Chitra State Council had 37 members, of whom 27 were non-officials (16 from General Constituencies, 6 from Special Constitutencies and 5 nominated). This bicameral setup was established on January 1, 1933.

Power was given to the Assembly to vote on the Demands for Grants and to reduce or omit any item of the demand. In 1932, a Joint Committee of both the chambers was created. The year witnessed the constitution of the Public Accounts Committee, heralding a tradition of executive accountability.

On 12th December 1933, the Viceroy Lord Wellington laid the foundation stone for a new Assembly building at the Northern side of the Secretariat. The new building was opened by Sir C. P. Ramaswamy Aiyar, on 8th February, 1939. On the very next day, (9th February, 1939), the Second Sri Mulam Assembly (1937-44), in its 4th Session met in the new Chamber. A Proclamation dated 18th March 1939, stated that all regulations till then and future enactments were to be styled as Acts.

The waves created by the birth of independent India had stirring repercussions in native States. On September 4, 1947, the Maharaja of Travancore announced the move to establish a responsible Government. A new Assembly, called the Representative Body was to function as the Constituent Assembly. 120 members were elected on the basis of adult franchise. The Assembly (1948-49) held its first sitting on March 20, 1948 under the Presidentship of Sri A.J. John. Sri G. Chandrasekhara Pillai was the Deputy President. Altogether, there were 36 sittings, in which 20 bills were passed. Considering the desire of the Assembly to be granted the powers and functions of a Legislative Assembly and to have a Ministry responsible to it, the Travancore Interim Constitution Act was promulgated on March 24, 1948, providing for a Council of Ministers headed by a Prime Minister and responsible to the Assembly. The Maharaja was to be the Constitutional Head.

A Council of Ministers, under the Prime Ministership of Sri Pattom A Thanu Pillai began to serve from March 24, 1948. In October 1948, Sri T.K. Narayana Pillai succeeded as the Prime Minister.

The merger of Travancore and Cochin was realized on July 1, 1949. The Maharaja of Travancore became the Rajapramukh of the new Travancore-Cochin State. The First Legislative Assembly (1949-51) was composed of 178 members of the Legislative bodies of Travancore and Cochin. Sri T.K.Narayana Pillai, the Chief Minister of Travancore became the Chief Minister of the new State.The Ministry headed by Sri T.K.Narayana Pillai resigned on March 1,1951 and a Ministry headed by Sri C.Kesavan came to power on 3rd March 1951 which continued till 12th March 1952. The Speaker was Sri T.M. Varghese.

In the Travancore-Cochin State, elections were held in January 1954 to the 118 member Assembly. Sri V. Gangadharan was elected as the Speaker on 22nd March 1954. Sri Pattom A Thanu Pillai, of the Praja Socialist Party, formed a Ministry with the support of the Congress. This Ministry, which fell in 1955, was succeeded by the Ministry of Sri Panampilly Govinda Menon, who had to end the term on March 23, 1956, due to the resignation of 6 members. On the advice of the Rajapramukh, President's rule was imposed in the State for the first time and the Assembly was dissolved.

Kerala Legislature—Duration of Each Assembly

No. of the Assembly	Date of Constitution	Date of Dissolution
I. Kerala Legislative Assembly	1-4-1957	31-7-1959
II. Kerala Legislative Assembly	22-2-1960	10-9-1964
III. Kerala Legislative Assembly	3-3-1967	26-6-1970
IV. Kerala Legislative Assembly	4-10-1970	22-3-1977
V. Kerala Legislative Assembly	22-3-1977	30-11-1979
VI. Kerala Legislative Assembly	25-1-1980	17-3-1982
VII. Kerala Legislative Assembly	24-5-1982	25-3-1987
VIII. Kerala Legislative Assembly	25-3-1987	5-4-1991
IX. Kerala Legislative Assembly	21-6-1991	14-5-1996
X. Kerala Legislative Assembly	14-5-1996	16-5-2001
XI. Kerala Legislative Assembly	16-5-2001	12-5-2006
XII. Kerala Legislative Assembly	13-5-2006	14-5-2011
XIII. Kerala Legislative Assembly	14-5-2011	20-05-2016
XIV. Kerala Legislative Assembly	20-05-2016	till date

Kerala Executive

The Governor of Kerala is the constitutional head of state, and is appointed by the President of India. The executive authority is headed by the Chief Minister of Kerala, who is the *de facto* head of state and is vested with extensive executive powers; the head of the party attaining majority in the Legislative Assembly is appointed to the post by the Governor. The Council of Ministers, has its members appointed by the Governor, taking the advice of the Chief Minister. Auxiliary authorities known as *panchayats,* for which local body elections are regularly held, govern local affairs.

Chief Secretaries of State

	Name	Period
1.	Sri V. Krishnamoorthy	8-12-1949 — 21-9-1959
2.	Sri D. Thirumalai Iyengar	22-9-1949 — 1-8-1964
3.	Sri L. Dharmaraja Iyer	2-8-1964 — 3-8-1967
4.	Sri V. P. Neelakantan Namboothiri	4-8-1967 — 5-11-1969
5.	Sri R. Prasannan	6-11-1969 — 27-4-1984
6.	Sri K. P. Padmanabhan	28-4-1984 — 8-5-1987
7.	Sri K. Balagopalan (in-charge)	9-5-1987 — 31-3-1989
8.	Sri R. Rajendra Babu	1-4-1989 — 29-2-1992
9.	Sri Jacob Kurian (in-charge)	29-2-1992 — 31-5-1992
10.	Sri J. M. James	1-6-1992 — 4-7-1996
11.	Sri S. Krishnamoorthy (in-charge)	4-7-1996 — 16-10-1997
12.	Sri R. Rajendra Babu	17-10-1997 — 6-3-1999
13.	Sri K. Gopalakrishnan Unnithan (in-charge)	6-3-1999 — 30-6-2000
14.	Sri N. K. Jayakumar	1-7-2000 — 14-6-2001
15.	Sri S. Rajachandra Babu (in-charge)	15-6-2001 — 1-7-2001
16.	Sri K. R. Udayabhanu	2-7-2001 — 27-10-2004
17.	Sri K. Retnakumari (in-charge)	27-10-2004 — 21-11-2004
18.	Sri M. C. Valson	22-11-2004 — 21-11-2006
19.	Sri Marimma Varghese (in-charge)	21-11-2006 — 30-11-2006
20.	Dr. N. K. Jayakumar	1-12-2006 — 31-12-2008
21.	Sri R. Prassanna Kumari (in-charge)	1-1-2009 — 14-1-2009
22.	Sri P. D. Rajan	15-1-2009 — 13-1-2012
23.	Sri P. K. Muraleedharan (in-charge)	13-1-2012 — 30-11-2012
24.	Sri P. D. Sarangadharan	30-11-2012 — 18-5-2016
25.	Sri K. Mohandas (in-charge)	18-5-2016 — 31-5-2016
26.	Sri S.M. Vijayanand	01-06-2016 — 01-04-2017
27.	Nalini Netto	01-04-2017 — ....

Districts

For administrative purposes the State is divided into 14 revenue districts: Thiruvananthapuram, Kollam, Alappuzha, Pathanamthitta, Kottayam, Idukki, Ernakulam, Thrissur, Palakkad, Malappuram, Kozhikode, Wayanad, Kannur and Kasargode.

A district is governed by a District Collector, who is an officer from Indian Administrative Service (IAS) of Kerala cadre and is appointed by the State Government of Kerala. Functionally the district administration is carried on through the various Departments of the State Government each of which has an office of its own in the district level. The District Collector is the executive leader of the district administration and the District Officers of various Departments in the district render technical advice to him in the discharge of his duties.

The District Collector is a key functionary of Government having immence powers and responsibilities. He/She has a dual role to both as the agent of the Government of the state and also as the representative of the people in the district. He/She is also responsible for the maintenance of the law and order of the district.

Palakkad

Palakkad is rightfully known as the Gateway of Kerala, giving the rest of India access to the State. For quite sometime the district was also called by its anglicised name Palghat. It's known to be rich in flora and fauna.

It commands Palghat Gap, on its eastern border, a pass or natural depression through the Western Ghats ranges that run parallel to the west coast of India, and connects Kerala to the plains of the state of Tamil Nadu to the east. The Silent Valley National Park that abruptly rises to the Nilgiris is an everlasting marvel to the tourists.

Palakkad is the repository of a rich folk culture and folk art forms like Kanniyar Kali and Porattu Natakam. It is also home to well-known percussion artists. The district is perhaps the foremost in fostering Carnatic music. Great musicians like Chembai Vaidyanatha Bhagavathar, Palakkad Mani Iyer, M D Ramanathan and K V Naryanaswami who have enriched Carnatic music by their contributions, hailed from this district.

Palakkad witnessed invasions of historical importance that have left indelible impressions on the history of Kerala. Bharathappuzha, the longest river in Kerala, originates from the highlands and flows through the entire district. The district is one of the main granaries of Kerala and its economy is primarily agricultural.

Kozhikode

The History of the district is inevitably intertwined with the history of the city of Kozhikode. Calicut is the anglicized form of Kalikooth, the name used by Arabs to refer to Kozhikode. According to the historian K.V. Krishnan Iyer, the word Kozhikode is derived from Koyil (Palace) Kodu (fortified), meaning 'Fortified Palace'.

The ports of the Malabar Coast had participated in the Indian Ocean trade of spices, silk, and other goods for over two millennia. Kozhikode emerged as the centre of an independent kingdom in the 14th century, whose ruler was known as the Zamorin.

During the Yong Le era of the Ming Dynasty of China, Admiral Zheng He and his treasure fleet visited Kozhikode. Their visits were documented by on-board Arab language translators Ma Huan, Fei Xin and Gong Zheng.

Trade with several kingdoms of Asia, Africa and the middle- east made Kozhikode a popular trading centre. Vasco da Gama landed at Kappad (18 kilometres north of Kozhikode) in May 1498, as the leader of a trade mission from Portugal and was received by the Zamorin himself. During the 16th century the Portuguese set up trading posts to the north in Kannur and to the south in Kochi. However, the Zamorin resisted the establishment of a permanent Portuguese presence in the city.

The history of Kozhikode district as an administrative unit begins from January 1957. When the states of the Indian Union were reorganised on linguistic basis on 1st November, 1956, the erstwhile Malabar district was separated from Madras state (Tamil Nadu) and added to the new unilingual state of Kerala.

Kottayam

The town of Kottayam is located in central Kerala and it is also the administrative capital of Kottayam district. Bordered by the lofty and mighty Western Ghats on the east and the Vembanad Lake and paddy fields of Kuttanad on the west, Kottayam is a land of unique characteristics. Panoramic backwater stretches, lush paddy fields, highlands, hills and hillocks, extensive rubber plantations, places associated with many legends and a totally literate people have given Kottayam District the enviable title: The land of letters, legends, latex and lakes. The city is an important trading centre of spices and commercial crops, especially rubber. Most of India's natural rubber originates from the acres of well-kept plantations of Kottayam, also home to the Rubber Board. Kottayam is also called as "Akshara Nagari" which means the "city of letters" considering its contribution to print media and literature.

Kottayam is the first town in India selected by the Ministry of Environment and Forests, Government of India to be transformed as an Eco City. The Sri K R Narayanan, the former President of India hails from Kottayam District. Kottayam is the ideal take off point for visits to Peermade, Munnar, Thekkady, Ernakulam and the temple city, Madurai. It is also a gateway to the pilgrim centres of Sabarimala, Mannanam, Vaikom, Ettumanoor, Bharananganam, Erumeli, Manarcaud, and so on.

Malappuram

Malappuram district is Kerala's Cultural Crucible.The classic medieval center of Vedic learning and politics, Thirunavaya, home of the traditional Ayurveda medicine, Kottakkal and the oldest centre of education of Islam, Ponnani are situated in Malappuram District along with economically booming towns like Manjeri (former capital of the Cholanaikkans), Perinthalmanna, Chemmad, Edappal, and Kottakkal. In 1921, present day Malappuram district witnessed a devastating revolts and massacres known as the Moplah rebellions, followed by decades of frozen economical, social, and political development. In the early years of the Communist rule in Kerala, Malappuram now part of the newly formed Kerala state, saw large land reforms under the Land Reform Ordinance.

Malappuram is one of two Muslim majority districts or Union Territories in south India other being Lakshadweep. The Hindu temples and Moplah mosques of the region are known for their colorful festivals. It is the most populous district in Kerala. The populations include Muslims, Hindus, Christians, various tribal religion believers, Buddhists, Sikhs, Jains and others.

Pathanamthitta

It is the pilgrim centre of Kerala, renowned for the shrine of Lord Ayappa in the Sabari Hills, drawing millions of devotees from near and far off places. The story of life of Lord Ayyappa which has the imprint of the cultural and spiritual aspiration of the people of Pampa Valley is itself an epitome of the inter religious brotherhood. The Ayyappa pilgrimage creates an ethos not only for Kerala but the whole country.

The district is also known as a centre for experiencing and learning some of the cultural as well as traditional practices of Kerala. Today Pathanamthitta district has emerged as an important hub of professional education in the State. Kollam, Kottayam and Alappuzha form the adjoining districts of Pathanamthitta.The district is frequented by visitors from India and abroad often for its water fiestas, religious shrines and the cultural training centre.

Kollam

Kollam district is located on the southwest coast of India, bordering Arabian Sea in the west, the state of Tamil Nadu in the east, Kerala district of Alappuzha in the north, Pathanamthitta in the northeast and Thiruvananthapuram in the south. It covers 2,492 square kilometres (962 sq mi).

Kollam, called Quilon by the Europeans, was an ancient port on the west coast. It flourished as a trading centre even in pre-christian centuries as can be surmised from the numismatic evidences left by ancient Phoenicians and Romans. The present Kollam district was notable for economic activity from time immemorial. Kollam is thus the timeless city of Kerala. Ibn Batuta visited Kollam in the 14th century and he recorded that Kollam was one of the five important ports he visited during his travel of twenty four years. A prosperous Chinese trading community settlement flourished in Kollam till the advent of Europeans. Probably traders of ancient nations rubbed shoulders for trade on the shores of Kollam.

Kollam was the original capital of Venad rulers and it developed into the most important port in South India over several centuries. The glory of Venad rulers of Kollam reached its height during the reign if Sangramadheera Ravi Varma Kulasekhara who crowned himself emperor of South India at Madurai and later Thanjavur after conquering the Pandya and Chola kingdoms in the first decade of 14th century. In 15th century Venad split into two branches – one at Padmanabhapuram and the other at Kollam. Even after independence Kollam has remained a major trade centre with considerable export of marine products and cashew kernels. Neendakara, lying adjacent to Kollam is the largest fishing harbour on the west coast.

Ernakulam

Ernakulam district is situated almost at the middle of Kerala State and on the coast of the Arabian Sea. It has the credit of being the economic nerve centre of the State. It is also the most industrially advanced and flourishing District of Kerala compared to the other districts.

This district was formed in 1958 by carving out regions from Thrissur and Kottayam district. The district is named after the erstwhile Ernakulam town, the name of which in turn is said to have been derived from the word Rishinagakulam, a tank in the famous Siva Temple in the town.

The District comprises areas of the erstwhile Travancore, Cochin and Malabar states. The headquarters is at Kakkanad.

Alappuzha

The name Alappuzha is derived from the geographical position and physical features of the place. It means the land between the sea and network of rivers flowing into it. The district is bounded on the north by Kochi and Kanayannur taluks of Ernakulam district, on the east by Vaikom, Kottayam and Changanassery taluks of Kottayam district and Thiruvalla, Kozhencherry and Adoor taluks of Pathanamthitta district, on the South by Kunnathur and Karunagappally taluks of Kollam district and on the west by Lakshadweep sea.

Alappuzha, came into being as a district, in the political map of Kerala on the 27th of August, 1957. Before the formation of the district, a major part of this area was of Kollam district and the rest, of Kottayam district. Though Alappuzha, with its past glory has a historic tradition of its own, with its abundant trade activity. Alappuzha is famous for the first labour upsurge against autocratic regime which is known as Punnapra-Vayalar agitation.

Alappuzha town has earned for itself the fame of being styled as the Venice of the East. The port at this place owes its origin to the ingenuity and imagination of a great administrator of the erstwhile Travancore, Raja Kesavadas, the Dewan of His Highness the Maharaja Rama Varma. He constructed the two main canals, running parallel to each other through the heart of the town, linking the backwaters with the seashore. He brought here the Gujaratis, Kutchimemons and Parsis to start trade in hill-produce, copra and coconut oil. The port was open for foreign trade in 1792 and it remained the commercial metropolis of Travancore for over a century. Kuttanad, the rice bowl of Kerala is in Alappuzha district and this is the only region in the state, lying below the sea level. Alappuzha is the most important centre in the State for coir industry.

Idukki

Idukki district was formed on 26 January 1972. The district consists of Devikulam, Udumbanchola and Peermedu taluks of the erstwhile Kottayam district and Thodupuzha taluk (excluding two villages Manjallore and Kalloorkadu) of the erstwhile Ernakulam district. At the time of formation the district headquarters started functioning at Kottayam and from there it was shifted to Painavu in Thodupuzha taluk in June 1976.

Idukki means a place with a deep gorge. River Periyar flowed through a canyon between two rocky mountains—Kurava and Kurathy. The legend told from generation of the ancient Adivasi Muthuvan tribe here is that Sita, during her forest sojourn with Rama, bathed in the canyon, and on seeing an Adivasi couple - Kuravan and Kurathy watching her naked beauty, she cursed them into two rocky mountains. Modern technology has bridged them at the gorge to form the marvel of Idukki arch dam, the first of its kind in Asia. When a new district was carved out, it shared the place name of the arch dam. This beautiful High range district of Kerala is geographically known for its mountainous hills and dense forests. For the people of Kerala, Idukki is always associated with power generation. About 66% of the State's Power needs come from the Hydroelectric Power Projects in Idukki. Idukki holds the key to solve the Kerala's energy problem. Incesant wind at Ramakalmedu and neighbouring places is estimated to yield above a 1000 MW, more than what the arch dam could yield. It is only waiting to be tapped.

Kasargode

Lying on the north western coast of the State, Kasargode was famous from time immemorial. Many Arab travellers, who came to Kerala between 9th and 14th centuries A.D., visited Kasargode as it was then an important trading centre. They called this area Harkwillia. Mr. Barbose, the Portuguese traveller, who visited Kumbla near Kasargode in 1514, had recorded that rice was exported to Male Island whence coir was imported. Kasargode was part of the Kumbala Kingdom in which there were 64 Tulu and Malayalam villages. When Vijayanagar empire attacked Kasargode, it was ruled by the Kolathiri king who had Nileswar as his headquarters. It is said that the characters appearing in Theyyam, the ritualistic folk dance of northern Kerala, represent those who had helped king Kolathiri fight against the attack of the Vijayanagar empire.

During the decline of that empire in the 14th century, the administration of this area was vested with the Ikkeri Naikans. They continued to be the rulers till the fall of the Vijayanagar empire in 16th century.

In 1763 Hyder Ali of Mysore conquered Bednoor and his intention was to capture entire Kerala. But when his attempt to conquer Thalassery Fort was foiled, Hyder Ali returned to Mysore and died there in 1782. His son, Tipu Sultan, continued the attack and conquered Malabar. As per the Sreerangapattanam treaty of 1792, Tipu surrendered Malabar except Tulunadu (Canara) to the British.

The British got Canara only after the death of Tipu Sultan in 1799. Kasargode was part of Bekal taluk in the South Canara district of Bombay presidency. Kasargode taluk came into being when Bekal taluk was included in the Madras presidency on April 16, 1882.

Kasargode became part of Kerala following the reorganisation of states and formation of Kerala in November 1,1956.

Thiruvananthapuram

Thiruvananthapuram district is considered as the most salubrious segment of Kerala, the 'Gods Own Country'. Proximity of the high mountains on the east and the ocean and lakes on the west has blessed the district with a temperate climate. This gift from nature is augmented by illustrious human activity in history, culture and social reformation. Historically, the 'Aye' kingdom flourished here and it lost prominence after its defeat in a naval battle with the navy of Raj Raja Chola, near Vizhinjam, its capital, in the early centuries of the Christian era. Later the powerful Venad Kingdom arose here with the decline of the Chera dynasty at Kondungalloor. Venad left great imprints like the Padmanabhapuram Palace, Padmanabhaswami Temple, Kuthiramalika etc.

Thiruvananthapuram was the cradle of the great ideas of social revival and renaissance heralded by great stalwarts like Sree Narayana Guru, Ayyankali, Dr. Palpu et al. In recent times Thiruvananthapuram has become the springboard of India's leap in the field of Space Science and Technology with the headquarters of ISRO here.

Thiruvananthapuram is the first tourism hotspot of Kerala with the opening of the internationally famous Kovalam beach resort, followed up later by the equally fascinating beaches like Varkala – Papanasam, Poovar and Chowara. Sree Padmanabha Swami Temple, conjectured as the richest temple in the world with enormous repositories of gold, precious gems and rare artifacts is at the centre of the city like the acropolis in Athens.

Thrissur

From ancient times, Thrissur district has played a significant part in the political history of south India. The early political history of the district is interlinked with that of the Cheras of the Sangam age, who ruled over vast portions of Kerala with their capital at Vanchi. The whole of the present Thrissur district was included in the early Chera empire.

The history of Thrissur district from the 9th to the 12th centuries is the history of Kulasekharas of Mahodayapuram and the history since 12th century is the history of the rise and growth of Perumpadappu Swarupam. In the course of its long and chequered history, the Perumpadappu Swarupam had its capital at different places.

The Perumpadappu Swarupam had its headquarters at Mahodayapuyram and had a number of Naduvazhies in southern Kerala. Central Kerala recognised the supremacy of the Perumpadappu Moopil and he is even referred to as the 'Kerala Chakravarthi' in the 'Sivavilasam' and some other works.

One of the landmarks in the history of the Perumpadappu Swarupam is the foundation of a new era called Pudu Vaipu era. The Pudu Vaipu era is traditionally believed to have commenced from the date on which the island of Vypeen was thrown from the sea.

The district can claim to have played a significant part in fostering the trade relations between Kerala and the outside world in the ancient and medieval period. It can also claim to have played an important part in fostering cultural relations and in laying the foundation of a cosmopolitan and composite culture in this part of the country. Kodungalloor which had the unique distinction of being the 'Premium Emporium India', also belongs to the signal honour or having first given shelter to all the three communities which have contributed to the prosperity of Malabar'. These three communities are the Christians, the Jews and the Muslims.

Wayanad

Wayanad district stands on the southern top of the Deccan plateau and its chief glory is the majestic Western ghats with lofty ridges interspersed with dense forest, tangled jungles and deep valleys, the terrain is rugged.

Comprising an area of 2,132 sq. kilometres, Wayanad has a powerful history. Historians are of the view that organised human life existed in these parts, at least ten centuries before Christ. Countles evidences about New Stone Age civilisation can be seen on the hills of Wayanad. The two caves of Ampukuthimala located between Sulthan Bathery and Ambalavayal, with pictures on their walls and pictorial writings, speak volumes of the bygone era and civilisation. Recorded history of this district is available from the 18th century. In ancient times, this land was ruled by the Rajas of the Veda tribe. In later days, Wayanad came under the rule of the Pazhassi Rajas of Kottayam royal dynasty. When Hyder Ali becomes the ruler of Mysore, he invaded Wayanad and brought it under his sway. In the days of Tipu, Wayanad was restored to the Kottayam royal dynasty. But Tipu handed over the entire Malabar region to the British, after the Sreerangapattanam truce, he made with them. This was followed by fierce and internecine encounters between the British and Kerala Varma Pazhassi Raja of Kottayam. When the Raja was driven to the wilderness of Wayanad, he organised the war-like Kurichiya tribals into a sort of people's militia and engaged the British in several guerrilla type encounters. In the end, the British could get only the dead body of the Raja, who killed himself somewhere in the interior of the forest. Thus, Wayanad fell into the hands of the British and with it came a new turn in the Home of this area. The British authorities opened up the plateau for cultivation of tea and other cash crops. Roads were laid across the dangerous slopes of Wayanad, from Kozhikode and Thalassery.

Kannur

The district is bound by the Western Ghats in the East (Coorg district of Karnataka State), Kozhikode and Wayanad districts, in the South, Lakshadeep sea in the West and Kasargode, the northern most district of Kerala, in the North. The district can be divided into three geographical regions—highlands, midlands and lowlands. The highland region comprises mainly of mountains.

The Thaliparamba-Kannur-Thalassery area abounds in rock-cut caves, dolments, burial stone circles and menhirs, all of megalithic burial order. It can be assumed that the first batch of Aryan immigrants into the State entered the district through the Tuluva region. Early in the 9th century A.D., the Cheras re-established their political supremacy in Kerala under Kulasekhara Varman. This second line of Chera emperors ruled till 1102 A.D. with their capital at Mahodayapuram. The bulk of the area, comprising of the present Kannur district, seems to have been included in this empire. A separate line of rulers known as the Mooshaka kings held sway over Chirakkal and Kasargode areas (Kolathunad) with their capital near Mount Eli.

The Kolathiris were a power to reckon with at the time of the arrival of the portuguese towards the end of the 15th century. They were political and commercial rivals of the Zamorins of Kozhikode.

Though Vasco da Gamma, the famous portuguese navigator, did not visit Kannur on his way to Kozhikode in May 1498, he established contacts with the Kolathiri ruler. Francisco de Almeida was sent from Portugal with specific instructions to erect forts at strategic points. He started constructing the Kannur Fort in 1505 and it was named St. Angelo.

The English East India Company got its first foothold in the district towards the closing years of the 17th century, when it acquired a site at Thalassery for the erection of a fort and a factory.

A branch of the All India Home Rule League, founded by Dr. Annie Beasant, functioned in Thalassery during this period and among its active workers was V.K. Krishna Menon. The All India Conference of Kisan Sabha, held at Kannur in 1953, resolved to initiate struggles for new tenancy legislations. The movement for Aikya Kerala (united Kerala) also got momentum during this period and all sections of the society rallied under the movement.

Local Self Government

The local self-government bodies; Panchayat, Municipalities and Corporations existed in Kerala since 1959, however, the major initiative to decentralise the governance was started in 1993, conforming to the constitutional amendments of central government in this direction. With the enactment of Kerala Panchayati Raj Act and Kerala Municipality Act in the year 1994, the state implemented various reforms in the local self-governance. Kerala Panchayati Raj Act envisages a 3-tier system of local-government with Gram panchayat, Block panchayat and District panchayat forming a hierarchy. The acts ensure clear demarcation of power among these institutions. However, Kerala Municipality Act envisages a single-tier system for urban areas, with the institution of municipality designed at par with Gram panchayat of the former system. Substantial administrative, legal and financial powers are delegated to these bodies to ensure efficient decentralisation. As per the present norms, the state government devolves about 40 per cent of the state plan outlay to the local government.

Municipalities

A total of 87 municipalities are in Kerala. Karunagapally (Kollam), Maradu, Thikkakara, Eloor (Ernakulam), Kottakkal, Nilambur (Malappuram) and Nileshwaram (Kasargode) are the newly added municipalities. The important municipalities in each district are given below:

Thiruvananthapuram

1. Attingal
2. Neyyattinkara
3. Nedumangad
4. Varkala

Kollam

1. Karunagapally
2. Paravoor (South)
3. Punalur

Alappuzha

1. Alappuzha
2. Chengannur
3. Cherthala
4. Kayamkulam
5. Mavelikkara

Pathanamthitta

1. Adoor
2. Pathanamthitta
3. Thiruvalla

Idukki

1. Thodupuzha

Kottayam

1. Kottayam
2. Palai
3. Vaikom
4. Changanancherry

Ernakulam

1. Aluva
2. Angamaly
3. Kalamassery
4. Kothamangalam
5. Muvattupuzha
6. North Paravoor
7. Maradu
8. Perumbavoor
9. Thrikkakara
10. Thripunithura
11. Eloor

Thrissur

1. Chalakkudy
2. Chavakkad
3. Guruvayoor
4. Irinjalakuda
5. Kodungallur
6. Kunnamkulam

Palakkad

1. Ottappalam
2. Palakkad
3. Shornur
4. Chittur–Tattamangalam

Malappuram

1. Malappuram
2. Manjeri
3. Kottakkal
4. Nilambur
5. Perinthalmanna
6. Ponnani
7. Tirur

Kozhikode

1. Koyilandy
2. Vadakara

Wayanad

1. Kalpetta

Kannur

1. Kannur
2. Koothuparamba
3. Mattannur
4. Payyannur
5. Thalassery
6. Thaliparamba

Kasargode

1. Kasargode
2. Kanhangad
3. Nileshwaram

There are Six Municipal Corporations in Kerala

1. Thiruvananthapuram Corporation
2. Kollam Corporation
3. Cochin Corporation
4. Thrissur Corporation
5. Kozhikode Corporation

Kerala Judiciary

The judiciary consists of the Kerala High Court and a system of lower courts. The High Court, located at Kochi, has a Chief Justice along with 23 permanent and seven additional *pro tempore* justices as of 2012. The high court also hears cases from the Union Territory of Lakshadweep.

High Court

High Court of Kerala came into being from 1st November 1956, with its seat at (Kochi) Ernakulam. Its roots go back to the Rulers of Travancore-

Cochin, to Colonel Munro—the British Resident and Diwan in the Travancore State and the political agent in Cochin State—the architect of the well regulated judicial system in both these native states, to the High Court of Madras with its tradition of a hundred years and over, to the Travancore High Court, to the Cochin High Court and to the Travancore Cochin High Court.

Till the time of Colonel Munro, who was the British Resident and Diwan of Travancore, there was no provision for the administration of justice in the form of independent Tribunals. In order to reform the Judicial System he submitted a regulation to reorganise the courts to her Highness the Rani who insisted upon the preservation of the trial by ordeal and passed the Regulation in 1811.

In 1811, Zilla courts were established and in 1814, a Huzur Court (Court of Appeal) was also established. The Huzur Court was the final court of appeal. The Sadar Court replaced this court of appeal (Huzur Court) in 1861. The Sadar Court practically possessed all the powers now exercised by the High Court, it functioned from 1861 to 1881. The High Court of Travancore was established in 1887 with five Judges, one of whom was the Chief Justice with a Pandit to advise the judges on points of Hindu Law, by the illustrious sovereign Sri Visakham Thirunal of revered memory. The first Chief Justice of Travancore High Court was Mr. Ramachandra Iyer a young man of 35 then.

It was during the Diwanship of Col. Munro in 1812 A.D. that graded law courts came to be established for the first time in Cochin State. Prior to that Desavazhis and Naduvazhis settled disputes according to custom. More serious disputes were sometimes taken to the king himself. Col. Munro established two Sub Courts one at Trichur and other at Tripunithura. A Huzur court of final appeal with three judges was also established in Ernakulam. This system continued till 1835. The Huzur Court was reconstituted as the Raja's Court of Appeal and the Sub Courts were reconstituted as the Zila Court. The Zilla Courts were given unlimited jurisdiction, but subject to confirmation by the Raja's court of appeal. It was in 1900 that the Raja's Court of appeal was reconstituted as the Chief Court of Cochin with three permanent Judges with Mr. S. Locke, Bar at Law as the first Chief Judge. Thereafter, during the Diwanship of Sri Shanmukham Chettiyar, the Chief Court became the High Court.

On the integration of Travancore-Cochin State after independence on 1st July 1949, it was on the 7th of July 1949 that the High Court of Travancore-Cochin was inaugurated with its seat at Ernakulam. The last Chief Justice of Travancore High Court was Sri Puthupally Krishna Pillai.

Under the state re-organisation Act, 1956 Travancore-Cochin State and Malabar were integrated to form the State of Kerala, on 1st November 1956. High Court of Kerala was thus established on that day. It inherited 3409 main cases from Travancore-Cochin High Court and 1504 cases from the High Court of Madras.

Article 230 enables the Indian Parliament, by law to extend the jurisdiction of a High Court to any Union Territory. By virtue of this the High Court of Kerala is also the High Court having jurisdiction over the Union Territory of Lakshadweep.

The High Court is a Constitutional Court in terms of Article 215. It is a court of record and has all the powers of such court including the power to punish for contempt of itself. Every High Court shall consist of a Chief Justice and such other judges as the President of India from time to time deem it necessary. At present, the sanctioned Judge strength of the High Court of Kerala is 27 Permanent Judges including the Chief Justice and 11 Additional Judges. Every judge including the Chief Justice shall be appointed by the President of India by warrant under his hand and seal. Every permanent judge will continue in office until he attains the age of 62 years. The Additional Judges are appointed for a period not exceeding two years taking into account the temporary increase in the business of the High Court. Such judge shall also not hold office after attaining the age of 62.

In terms of Article 226 of the Constitution of India, the High Court shall have power in relation to its territorial jurisdiction to issue Directions, Orders and Writs including the Writs in the nature of Habeas Corpus, Mandamus, Prohibition, Quowarranto and Certiorari for enforcement of fundamental rights guaranteed to the citizens under Part III of the Constitution or for any other purpose. The High Court shall also have superintendence over all Courts and Tribunals throughout the territory in relation to which it exercises jurisdiction, as provided in Article 227 of the Constitution.

The business and exercise of the powers of the High Court of Kerala are regulated by the provisions contained in the Kerala High Court Act, 1958 and the Rules of the High Court of Kerala, 1971 prescribed thereunder. The High Court has Original, Appellate as well as Revisional jurisdiction in both civil as well as criminal matters apart from the power to answer reference under certain statutes. The High Court transacts its business, judges sitting single, in division and in specifically referred matters in Full Bench.

KNOW THE FACTS

☞ *On the 1st of October 1904, Sri Mulam Popular Assembly of Travancore was formed.*

☞ *The Cochin Legislative Council Regulation Act, 1923 provided for a Legislative Council.*

☞ *The First Council (1925-28), with 45 members (30 elected and 15 nominated), was constituted in April 1925, under the Presidentship of Sri T. S. Narayana Aiyar.*

☞ *On September 4, 1947, the Maharaja of Travancore announced the move to establish a responsible Government.*

☞ *The merger of Travancore and Cochin was realized on July 1, 1949. The Maharaja of Travancore became the Rajapramukh of the new Travancore-Cochin State.*

☞ *The First Legislative Assembly (1949-51) was composed of 178 members of the Legislative bodies of Travancore and Cochin.*

☞ *In the Travancore-Cochin State, elections were held in January 1954 to the 118 member Assembly. Sri Pattom A Thanu Pillai, of the Praja Socialist Party, formed a Ministry with the support of the Congress.*

☞ *For administrative purposes the State is divided into 14 revenue districts.*

☞ *Kottayam is called as "Akshara Nagari" which means the "city of letters" considering its contribution to print media and literature.*

☞ *Kottayam is the first town in India to be transformed as an Eco City.*

☞ *Kuttanad, the rice bowl of Kerala is in Alappuzha district and this is the only region in the state, lying below the sea level.*

☞ *Kerala Panchayati Raj Act envisages a 3-tier system of local-government with Gram panchayat, Block panchayat and District panchayat.*

☞ *Kerala Municipality Act envisages a single-tier system for urban areas, with the institution of municipality designed at par with Gram panchayat of the former system.*

☞ *A total of 87 municipalities are in Kerala.*

☞ *High Court of Kerala came into being from 1st November 1956, with its seat at (Kochi) Ernakulam.*

☞ *In 1811, Zilla courts were established and in 1814, a Huzur Court (Court of Appeal) was also established.*

☞ *The High Court of Travancore was established in 1887.*

TEST YOUR SELF

1. During which year First Assembly Election took place in Kerala?
   A. 1956   B. 1957   C. 1958   D. 1959

2. Who laid the foundation of judicial system in Kerala?
   A. Colonel Thompson   B. Colonel Munro
   C. Colonel Sleiman   D. Colonel Mackenzie

3. Who was the first Chief Justice of High Court of Kerala?
   A. Justice K.T. Kosi   B. K. Sankaran
   C. M.S. Menon   D. T.C. Raghvan

4. The normal duration of Legislative Assembly can be extended upto how much period during emergency?
A. 3 months
B. 6 months
C. 1 year
D. indefinite period

5. During which year for the first time President Rule was imposed in Kerala.
A. 1963
B. 1964
C. 1965
D. 1966

6. Who among the following became the CM of Kerala for maximum times?
A. K. Karunakaran
B. E.K. Nayanar
C. A.K. Antony
D. C. Achuta Menon

7. In Kerala Niyamasabha refers to
A. Kerala Executive
B. Kerala Judiciary
C. Kerala Legislature
D. Kerala Police

8. Who was the Governor of Kerala when it came under President Rule for the first time?
A. Ajith Prasad
B. Dr. B. Amakrisna Rao
C. V.V. Giri
D. Bhagwan Sahay

9. The first Legislative Council was formed in which year in Kerala before independence?
A. 1935
B. 1930
C. 1925
D. 1924

10. Who was the first speaker of Kerala Legislative Assembly?
A. C.H. Mohammed
B. Pattom Thanu Pillai
C. Seethi Sahib
D. R. Sankaranarayana

ANSWERS

1	2	3	4	5	6	7	8	9	10
B	B	A	C	B	A	C	A	C	D

R. Gupta's®
GENERAL KNOWLEDGE BOOKS

Book Name	Code	Price(₹)
● Quick General Knowledge 2020	R-1716	45
● General Knowledge for All 2020	R-1641	25
● R. Gupta's® GK & Current Affairs *including Latest Who's Who*	R-1	35
● General Knowledge Hand Book (Junior)	R-3	50
● General Knowledge & Current Affairs	R-5	65
● General Knowledge At a Glance	R-7	75
● Popular General Knowledge	R-9	170
● General Knowledge Encyclopaedia	R-11	270
● Delhi General Knowledge	R-464	70
● Objective General Knowledge	R-177	170
● Kerala General Knowledge	R-1588	95
● Comprehensive J&K GK, Current Affairs & Who's Who	R-564	95
● J&K General Knowledge (with latest Facts & Data)	R-1605	45
● J&K General Knowledge – At a Glance	R-1066	55
● Haryana General Knowledge	R-505	95
● Himachal Pradesh General Knowledge	R-415	110
● Uttarakhand General Knowledge	R-469	65
● Odisha General Knowledge	R-518	140
● West Bengal General Knowledge	R-1070	65
● Arunachal Pradesh General Knowledge	R-1067	70
● India At a Glance (with Description of All States/Union Territories)	R-489	75
● Manipur General Knowledge	R-1864	110
● Manipur GK Handbook *(with Multiple Choice Questions)*	R-954	50
● Maharashtra General Knowledge	R-1043	75

 **Ramesh Publishing House** 2002

12-H, New Daryaganj Road, Opp. Officers' Mess, Delhi-110002

For Online Shopping: www.rameshpublishinghouse.com